Quantitative Aptitude

Progressive Mathematics

he Common Core for UPSC, UGC , General Studies, Banking Recruitment , Rail and LIC

Chandan Sengupta

Mathematics DLP Series

Quantitative Aptitude and Proogressive Mathematics

he Common Core for UPSC, UGC , General Studies, Banking Recruitment , Rail and LIC

This workbook is designed for students of Class VII having aspiration of preparing for NTSE and IMO. Some of the basic content areas assigned in National Curriculum Framework are incorporated in this workbook.

This book cannot replace any textbook of the referred standard of National Curriculum. It will be an added content upon the prescribed ones for developing and strengthening the basic understanding of mathematical concepts that the fellow students want to aspire for. It will also confer the regular mathematical practice with which one should move for reducing any specific problems related to the understanding of mathematical concepts.

It is true that we cannot remember hundreds and thousands of different types of problems related to mathematics. We must try to equip ourselves differently for addressing all sorts of numerical and space related problems. Daily Practice Problem (DPP) series of publications deals with facilitation of fellow students and their associates. This workbook is suitable for students of class 3 of National Curriculum. It can be used by other fellow students of Primary section for improving their mathematical skills. It can be used by students who are willing to opt for IMO , NTSE and other similar examinations. It will also develop the basic understanding related to Mathematical Skills.

It will enhance the competency set up of those students and equip them differently so as to make them competent for addressing higher challenges. Focus is entirely made on the content areas which felt difficult for students under observation.

Contents

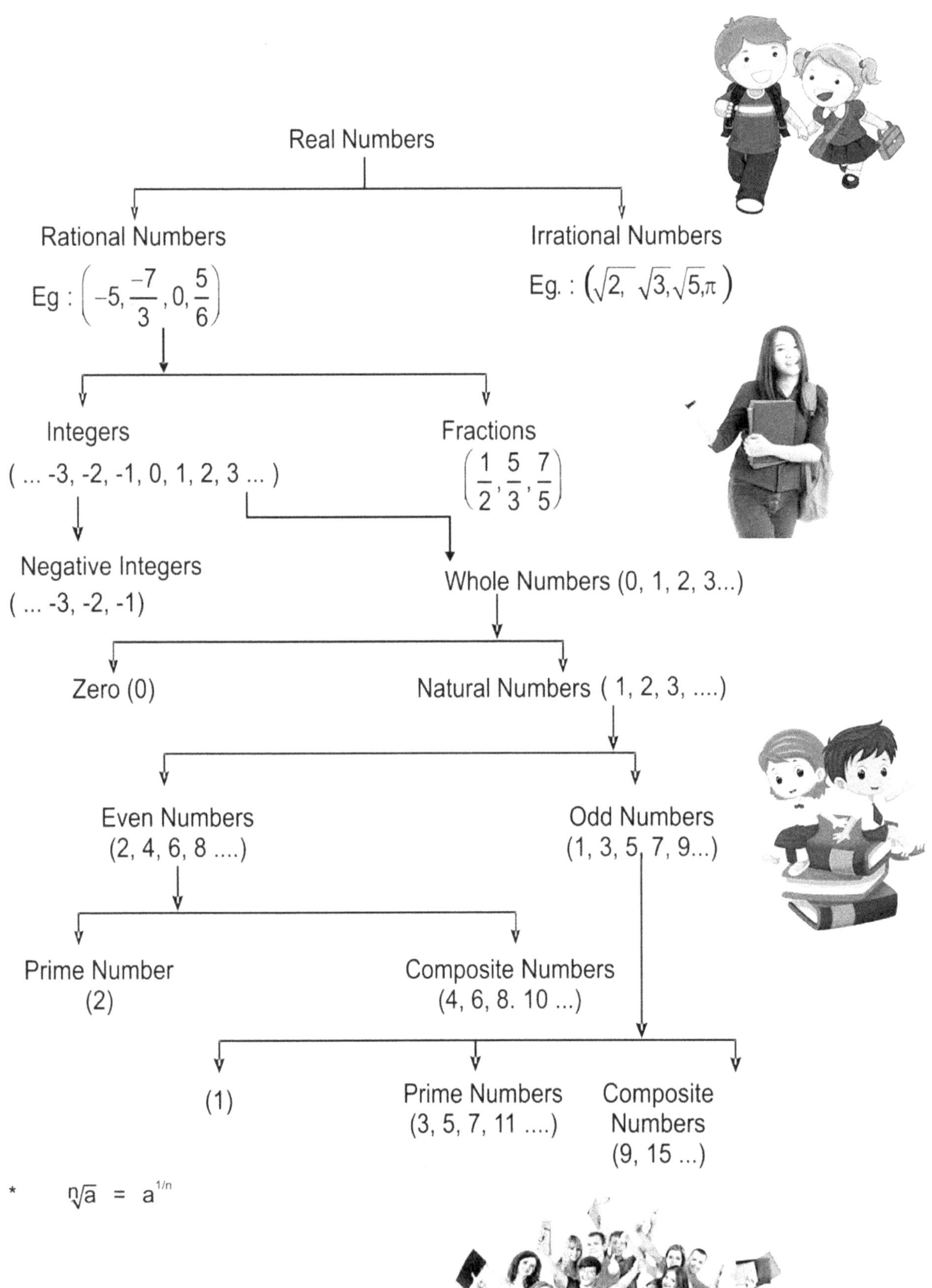
Real Numbers
Rational Numbers
Eg : $\left(-5, \frac{-7}{3}, 0, \frac{5}{6}\right)$
Irrational Numbers
Eg. : $(\sqrt{2}, \sqrt{3}, \sqrt{5}, \pi)$
Integers
(... -3, -2, -1, 0, 1, 2, 3 ...)
Fractions
$\left(\frac{1}{2}, \frac{5}{3}, \frac{7}{5}\right)$
Negative Integers
(... -3, -2, -1)
Whole Numbers (0, 1, 2, 3...)
Zero (0)
Natural Numbers (1, 2, 3, ...)
Even Numbers
(2, 4, 6, 8 ....)
Odd Numbers
(1, 3, 5, 7, 9...)
Prime Number
(2)
Composite Numbers
(4, 6, 8. 10 ...)
(1)
Prime Numbers
(3, 5, 7, 11 ....)
Composite
Numbers
(9, 15 ...)
* $\sqrt[n]{a} = a^{1/n}$

Revision Works

Revision Works 1

1: Write the following in decimal form.

a) 12/25 b) 1/8 c) one sixteenth of 125 d) $\left(\frac{1}{500}+\frac{1}{500}+\frac{1}{500}+\cdots\ldots 1{,}000\ times\right)X\frac{1}{16}$

2: You know that $\frac{1}{7} = 0.1\ddot{4}\ddot{2}857$. Predict what the decimal expansions of $\frac{2}{7},\frac{13}{7},\frac{4}{7},\frac{5}{7},\frac{6}{7},\frac{29}{7},\frac{55}{77},\frac{303}{707}$ are , without actually doing the long division.

3: What fraction of all the numbers starting from 1 to 1,000 are multiples of 125?

4: Express the following in the form of $\frac{p}{q}$.

a) $0.\overline{9}$ b) $0.\overline{901}$ c) $0.\overline{001}$ d) $0.\overline{47}$ e) $0.\overline{909}$ f) $0.\overline{201}$

5: If we start dividing 1 by 17 then after 16th digit of the result the remainder 1 is the same digit from which we started the division. $\therefore \frac{1}{17} = 0.\overline{0588235294117647}$, By using this division property Calculate the value of the following in decimal form.

a) $\frac{1000}{17}$ b) $\frac{1000}{17}$ c) $\frac{3901}{17}$ d) $1001\frac{2}{17}$ e) $4003\frac{11}{17}$

6: What least number should be subtracted from the greatest six digit number to obtain a six digit greatest multiple of 12?

7: Observe the following set of values and calculate the value of x.

√2 = 1.414213562 ……….. √3 = 1.732050808 ……. √5 = 2.23606797 …….

X = 15√(98) + 121√(243) + 1001√(125) - 2003√(32) + 1005√(27)

8: What percentage of all the natural numbers starting from 1 to 2,000 are multiples of 20?

9: $\frac{1}{16}\ X\ \left(\frac{1}{1{,}002}+\frac{1}{1002}+\cdots.+10{,}000\ times\right)X\ 2{,}004+0.125+\frac{1}{9}$ = …….

10. Complete the following number pattern:

1.1 X 1.1 = 1.21

1.11 X 1.11 = ………… X 10^{-4};

1.111 X 1.111 = …………….. X 10^{-6}

11: Third multiple of a number is 3 more than the six digit greatest number. Find fifth multiple of that number.

12: Two non-oeverlapping triangles can be drawn by using diagonal radiating out from one of the vertex of a quadrilateral. What is the minimum number of non-overlapping triangles which can be accommodated in a hexagon by using diagonals radiating out from any one of the vertex?

The Number System used in the field of School Mathematics is called Decimal Number System as it is designed on the basis of using ten different digits. We also use that system of numeration for performing different types of basic calculations.

Following numeration chart represents International system of Numeration. Complete this chart.

Numbers	Hundred Million	Ten Million	Million	Hundred Thousand	Ten Thousands	Thousands	Hundreds	Tens	Ones
450,090,802									
	3	5	6	0	8	0	9	7	2
21,594,606									
203,905,709									
	2	4	6	8	0	4	0	3	1
304,098,102									

There is another system of numeration which is called Indian-Arabic System of Numeration.

Numbers	....	....	....	Lakh	Ten Thousands	Thousands	Hundreds	Tens	Ones
21,34,35,546									
	3	5	6	0	8	0	9	7	2

Few of the lower terms of both the numerations are identical. Higher terms of numeration and number separator commas differ in both cases.

Try to place the following number in both system of numeration:

A) 43 thousands + 121 hundreds + 1032 hundreds + 10234 tens + 1232

B) 32 X 10,000 + 132 X 100,000 + 432 X 1,000 + 21,032 + 212,121

C) 102 X 20,000 + 204 X 3,000 + 305 X 200,200 + 109 X 20,004

D) 1.004 + 11.009 + 102.09001 + (2.1 + 2.1 + ... 1001 times)

Representation of decimal numbers:

Numbers	....	....	....	Tenths	Hundredths	Thousandths	Ten Thousandths	Hundred Thousandths	....
213.435546									
	3	5	6	0	8	0	9	7	2

2 tenths = 2 X $\frac{1}{10}$; 2 hundredths = 2 X $\frac{1}{100}$; 2 thousandths = 2 X $\frac{1}{1000}$; 2 ten thousandths = 2 X $\frac{1}{10000}$;

Write the following in standard form:

A: $\frac{1}{10}+\frac{11}{100}+\frac{111}{1000}+\frac{1101}{10000}+121=$ ....

B: $\frac{21}{10}+\frac{221}{100}+\frac{333}{1000}+\frac{4353}{10000}+2021=$...........

There are some numbers having mixed values taken up by adding whole numbers and decimal numbers. Before adding or subtracting such numbers we always convert such numbers in like decimals.

$0.63 \times 1000 = 630$	$0.63 \div 1000 = 0.00063$	$0.63 \div 3000 = 0.00021$
$0.63 \times 100 = 63$	$0.63 \div 100 = 0.0063$	$0.63 \div 300 = 0.0021$
$0.63 \times 10 = 6.3$	$0.63 \div 10 = 0.063$	$0.63 \div 30 = 0.021$
$0.63 \times 1 = 0.63$	$0.63 \div 1 = 0.63$	$0.63 \div 3 = 0.21$
$0.63 \times 0.1 = 0.063$	$0.63 \div 0.1 = 6.3$	$0.63 \div 0.3 = 2.1$
$0.63 \times 0.01 = 0.0063$	$0.63 \div 0.01 = 63$	$0.63 \div 0.03 = 21$
$0.63 \times 0.001 = 0.00063$	$0.63 \div 0.001 = 630$	$0.63 \div 0.003 = 210$

Find the value of each variable. Use the patterns in exercise 27 to help you.

a. $0.6 \times a = 0.006$ **b.** $44 \div m = 4400$ **c.** $7.6 \div c = 3800$

d. $5.42 \times t = 542$ **e.** $3.16 \div n = 0.316$ **f.** $2.05 \div w = 41$

g. $1.14 \times b = 0.00114$ **h.** $0.216 \times r = 0.00216$ **i.** $10.2 \div s = 0.34$

Simplify:

$\left(1+\frac{1}{2}\right)\left(1+\frac{1}{3}\right)\left(1+\frac{1}{4}\right) \ldots\ldots\ldots\ldots\ldots \left(1+\frac{1}{10,000}\right) X \left(1-\frac{1}{10,001}\right) X\ 1,250 = 5^p \text{ X } 10^q$; p = ...; q = ...;

32 tens + 132 hundreds + 20 thousands + 21 thousandths + 102 hundredths + 1001 tenths = ...

Revision Works 2

1. $\begin{array}{r} 3.12 \\ +9.94 \\ \hline \end{array}$

2. $\begin{array}{r} 0.51 \\ 0.0029 \\ +0.0018 \\ \hline \end{array}$

3. $\begin{array}{r} 0.008 \\ 0.11 \\ 0.5 \\ +0.993 \\ \hline \end{array}$

4. $\begin{array}{r} 497.386 \\ +556.22 \\ \hline \end{array}$

5. $\begin{array}{r} 390.809 \\ 905.5 \\ 8.87064 \\ +330.008 \\ \hline \end{array}$

Find the difference.

6. $\begin{array}{r} \$100 \\ -\ \$55.99 \\ \hline \end{array}$

7. $\begin{array}{r} 0.1 \\ -0.0001 \\ \hline \end{array}$

8. $\begin{array}{r} 412.009 \\ -228.4 \\ \hline \end{array}$

9. $\begin{array}{r} 1.2 \\ -0.772 \\ \hline \end{array}$

10. $\begin{array}{r} \$50 \\ -\ 23.75 \\ \hline \end{array}$

Align and add.

11. 0.67 + 39 + 7.5 + 58.22

12. 4,509.88 + 430.618 + 777.1

13. 0.49 + 0.006 + 0.213 + 0.1

14. 8.02029 + 28.98 + 617.7

15. 629.55 + 401.39201

16. 4,040 + 3,049.89 + 2057.52

Align and subtract.

17. 30 − 28.735

18. 9,002 − 4,887.56

19. 30.801 − 17.91

20. 497.1 − 437.805

21. 3,108.77 − 2,974.557

22. 1,001.1 − 802.22

Compare. Write <, =, or >.

23. 12 − 0.0009 _?_ 12 − 0.00009

24. 412.089 + 34.71 _?_ 498 − 52.075

25. 0.501 + 0.3 + 0.44993 _?_ 1.2593

26. 55.01 − 5.501 _?_ 50.001 − 0.99

26. What fraction of all the natural numbers starting from 1 to 1000 are multiples of 125?

27. Is there any pair of number having HCF 19 and LCM 12321?

28. If 125 X 8 = 1,000 and 25 X 40 = 1,000 ; then find the value of 121X 125 X 40 X 8 X 25

29. If 11 X 11 = 121 and 111 X 111 = 12321 then find the product of 1,111,111X 1,111,111

30. Cistern A can fill up a water tank in 40 minutes. Cistern B can fill it up in 60 minutes. Find the time taken by both the cisterns to fill up the water tank if they work jointly.

31. Mohanlal can paint a piece of poster in 6 days while working 2 hours a day. He preferred working 3 hours a day for finishing three such paintings. Find the number of days taken by Mohanlal to finish the work.

32. Mrs Jenna travelled half of the distance while moving back from the countryside by bus, half of the remaining distance was covered by her along with other friends in by car. She travelled half of the remaining distance by auto. She covered last portion of 1.5 km simply by walking. Find out the distance of her farm house in km.

Revision Works 3

Evaluate each expression when $a = {}^{+}5$, $b = {}^{-}4$, $c = {}^{-}2$, and $d = 0$.

1. $b \div c$
2. $a - b$
3. $a + b \cdot c$
4. $(b - d) \div c$
5. $\frac{ab}{2c}$
6. $a - \frac{b}{c}$
7. $cd - a$
8. $\frac{bd}{{}^{-}3c}$
9. $(a + b)^3 + c$
10. $bd - a^2$
11. $a^2 + bc$
12. $b \div (c \cdot d)$

Solve each equation. Use the replacement set $\{{}^{+}5, {}^{-}5, 0, {}^{+}25, {}^{-}25\}$.

13. $n - {}^{+}10 = {}^{-}15$
14. $n + {}^{+}10 = {}^{-}15$
15. $n + {}^{-}5 = {}^{+}20$
16. $n - {}^{+}5 = 0$
17. ${}^{+}25 = n + 0$
18. $n - {}^{-}25 = {}^{+}5$

Solve and check.

19. $b + {}^{-}4 = {}^{-}6$
20. $x - {}^{+}3 = {}^{+}11$
21. ${}^{+}5 + h = {}^{-}13$
22. ${}^{+}8t = {}^{-}104$
23. $\frac{y}{{}^{-}6} = {}^{+}9$
24. ${}^{+}15z = 0$
25. $\frac{d}{{}^{-}10} = 0$
26. ${}^{+}14 - g = {}^{-}1$
27. ${}^{-}9 + f = {}^{-}20$
28. ${}^{+}15 = \frac{v}{{}^{+}3}$
29. ${}^{-}33 = {}^{+}11r$
30. ${}^{-}243 = {}^{-}9p$

Write and solve an equation for the variable used.

31. A number z divided by 8 equals ${}^{-}20$.
32. ${}^{-}4$ less than a number y is ${}^{-}7$.
33. A number r increased by 15 equals ${}^{-}22$.
34. The product of a number d and ${}^{-}12$ is ${}^{+}60$.

35. Solve the following: ...

If $a > 0$, $b > 0$ and n is a positive rational number, then

1. $(\sqrt[n]{a})(\sqrt[n]{b}) = \sqrt[n]{ab}$
2. $\frac{\sqrt[n]{a}}{\sqrt[n]{b}} = \sqrt[n]{\frac{a}{b}}$
3. $\sqrt[m]{\sqrt[n]{a}} = \sqrt[mn]{a} = \sqrt[n]{\sqrt[m]{a}}$
4. $\sqrt[n]{a^p} = a^{p/n}$ and $\sqrt[n]{a^p} = \sqrt[n]{\sqrt[m]{(a^p)^m}}$

Express the following surds in their simplest form as multiples of smaller surds:

(a) $\sqrt[3]{1458}$ (b) $\sqrt[3]{144}$ (c) $\sqrt[4]{1024}$

solutions ...

(a) $\sqrt[3]{1458} = \sqrt[3]{2(9^3)} = 9\sqrt[3]{2}$.

(b) $\sqrt[3]{144} = \sqrt[3]{2^4(3^2)} = \sqrt[3]{2^3(2)(3^2)} = 2\sqrt[3]{18}$.

(c) $\sqrt[4]{1024} = \sqrt[4]{2^{10}} = \sqrt[4]{(2^8)(2^2)} = \sqrt[4]{2^8}\,\sqrt[4]{2^2} = 4\sqrt{2}$.

Revision Works 5

1: Observe the following diagram carefully and answer the questions as follows.

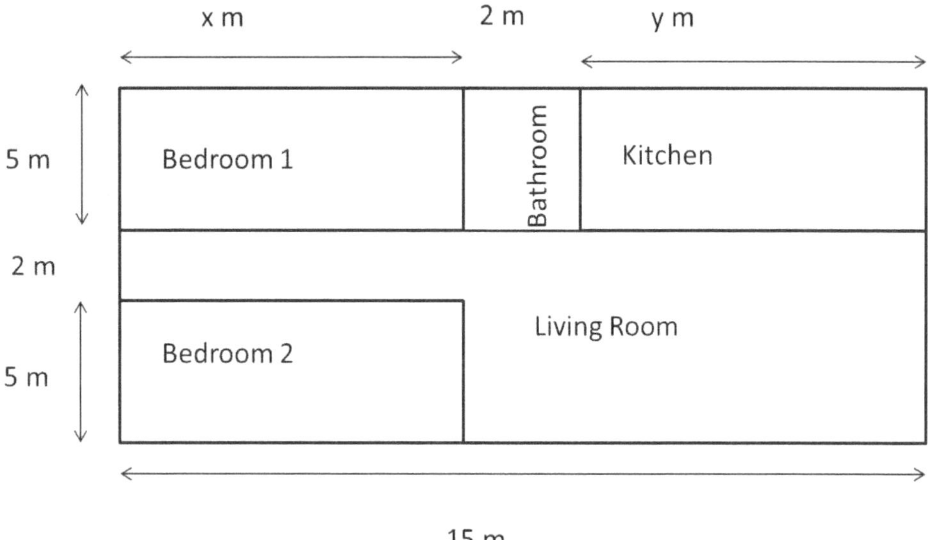

(i) The area of two bedrooms and kitchen are respectively equal to

(a) 5x, 5y (b) 10x, 5y (c) 5x, 10y (c) x, y

Area of one bedroom = 5x sq.m

Area of two bedrooms = 10x sq.m

Area of kitchen = 5y sq. m

(ii) Length of the outer boundary of the layout: (a) 27 m (b) 15 m (c) 50 m (d) 54 m

(iii) The pair of linear equation in two variables formed from the statements are

(a) x + y = 13, x + y = 9 (b) 2x + y = 13, x + y = 9

(c) x + y = 13, 2x + y = 9 (d) None of the above

(iv) Which is the solution satisfying both the equations formed in (iii)?

(a) x = 7, y = 6 (b) x = 8, y = 5 (c) x = 6, y = 7 (d) x = 5, y = 8

(v) Find the area of each bedroom.

(vi) What fraction of entire built up area is occupied by a living room?

(vii) Cost of floor tiles in kitchen at the rate of Rs 1,200 per square m will be Rs ....

(viii) What percentage of the entire built up area is occupied by bathroom and kitchen?

***

Factorisation

Factor is a number that divides a given number without leaving any remainder. Multiple is a number which is obtained by multiplying the given number by any other Natural number.

In the following expression we represent all possible factors of 72 in a table form.

72 = 1 X 72;	72 = 6 X 12;	72 = 18 X 4;
72 = 2 X 36;	72 = 8 X 9;	72 = 24 X 3;
72 = 3 X 24;	72 = 9 X 8;	72 = 36 X 2;
72 = 4 X 18;	72 = 12 X 6;	72 = 72 X 1;

Factors having only 2 subordinate factors are called prime factors. We can represent prime factorisation process in the following ways:

When the divisibility rules for 2, 3, 5, or 9 do not work, try dividing by other prime numbers. To find the prime factorization of 9009, start by trying 7, 11, 13, 17, and 19.

Method 1 Make a Factor Tree

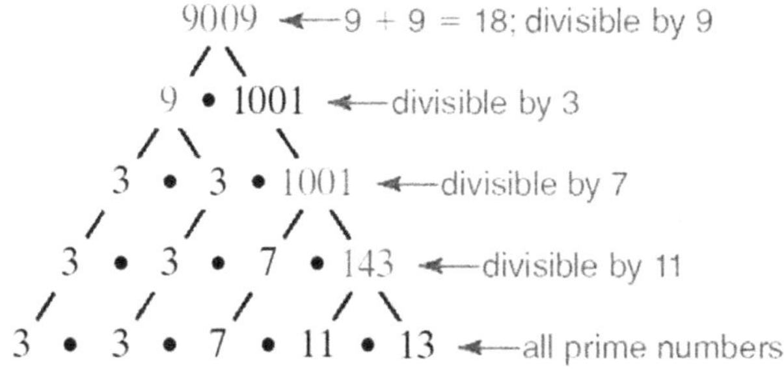

Method 2 Use Division

3	9009	←9 + 9 = 18; divisible by 3
3	3003	←3 + 3 = 6; divisible by 3
7	1001	←divisible by 7
11	143	←divisible by 11
13	13	←divisible by 13
	1	

So the prime factorization of 9009 is $3^2 \bullet 7 \bullet 11 \bullet 13$.

1 is the factor of all the natural numbers and all natural numbers are multiples of 1. All the even numbers are multiples of 2. All the odd numbers are not prime numbers.

Numbers having only 2 factors 1 and the number itself are called prime numbers. Lists of prime numbers between 1 to 200 are:

2, 3, 5, 7, 11, 13, 17, 19, 23, 29, 31, 37, 41, 43, 47, 53, 59, 61, 67, 71, 73, 79, 83, 89, 97, 101, 103, 107, 109, 113, 127, 131, 137, 139, 149, 151, 157, 163, 167, 173, 179, 181, 191, 193, 197, 199.

Q: On the basis of the given information work out the percentage of numbers from 1 to 200 which are prime numbers.

Composite numbers can have more than two factors. There is unlimited number of multiples of a given number.

We can have a definite pattern of factors, multiples and prime numbers if we arrange and categorise them in a definite fashion.

A list of Prime numbers from 1 to 500 is provided below.

2	3	5	7	11	13	17	19	23	29
31	37	41	43	47	53	59	61	67	71
73	79	83	89	97	101	103	107	109	113
127	131	137	139	149	151	157	163	167	173
179	181	191	193	197	199	211	223	227	229
233	239	241	251	257	263	269	271	277	281
283	293	307	311	313	317	331	337	347	349
353	359	367	373	379	383	389	397	401	409
419	421	431	433	439	443	449	457	461	463
467	479	487	491	499					

Try to categorise how many prime numbers are there in between following slabs of intervals:

1 to 100:

201 to 300

301 to 400

401 to 500

Is there any difference in the frequency of the occurrence of prime numbers in between the given intervals?

Q: Try to observe the following number pattern and complete the given steps.

(1 + 3 + 5)	=	3 X 3	=	3^2	=	9;
(1 + 3 + 5 + 7 + 9 + 11)	=	6 X 6	=	6^2	=	..........;
(Sum of 11 consecutive odd numbers)	=	... X	=	....^{2}	=	121;
(Sum of 111 consecutive odd numbers)	=	.... X	=	.....^{2}	=	........;
(Sum of 1111 consecutive odd numbers)	=	..... X	=	.....^{2}	=	........;

Q: Observe the following table of multiples of given numbers and answer the questions as follows.

2	4	6	8	10	12	14	16	18	20	22	24	26	28
3	6	9	12	15	18	21	24	27	30	33	36	39	42
4	8	12	16	20	24	28	32	36	40	44	48	52	56
5	10	15	20	25	30	35	40	45	50	55	60	65	70
6	12	18	24	30	36	42	48	54	60	66	72	78	84
7	14	21	28	35	42	49	56	63	70	77	84	91	98
8	16	24	32	40	48	56	64	72	80	88	96	104	112

How many multiples of 4 are also multiples of 2? How many multiples of 8 are also multiples of 2 and 4?

How many multiples of 2 are also multiples of 8? All multiples of .... And .... are not necessarily multiples of 8. All multiples of ...., ... and .... are all multiples of 2.

How many common multiles of 2, 4, 6, 8 and 12 are there in the given chart?

Basic Shapes

1. Shapes bounded by straight line segments are called polygons. There are different types of polygons which got their names according to the number of sides and also according to their relationships based on sides and angles.

Try to identify how many of the following shapes are polygons.

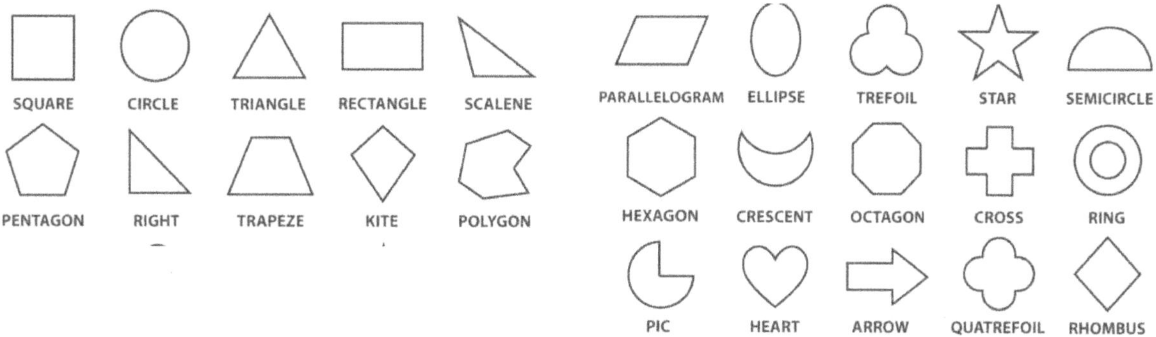

2. Observe statements regarding complementary and supplementary angles:

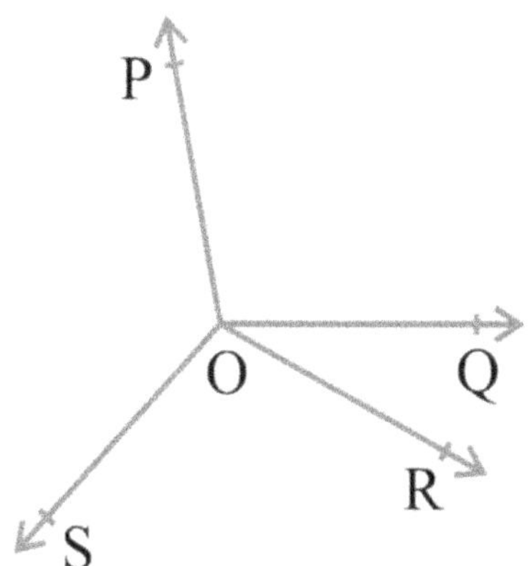

Two rays having a common origin make an angle. Interior of an angle is enclosed by two arms. The point at which rays meet is called vertex of an angle. Adjacent angles have a common arm and a common vertex. Such angles share an arm. If sum total of two adjacent angles make a right angle then such pair of angles are considered as complementary to each other.

If such pair makes a straight angle then we call such pair of angles as linear pair or supplementary to each other.

Identify some of such pairs in the given diagram.

3. There are different types of triangles on the basis of their sides and angles. Complete the following table.

Sl No	Properties	Names
1	All sides are equal to each other	
2	None of sides are equal to each other	
3	One of the interior angle is equal to a right angle.	
4	One of the interior angle is an obtuse angle.	
5	Any two sides are equal to each other.	

4. Find outer boundary of the following shapes.

(a)

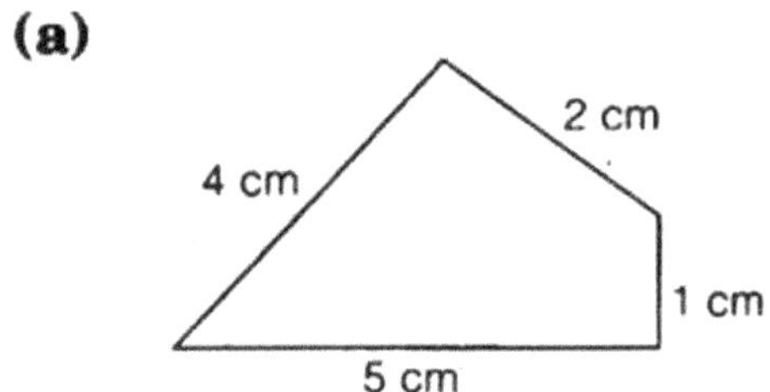

(b)

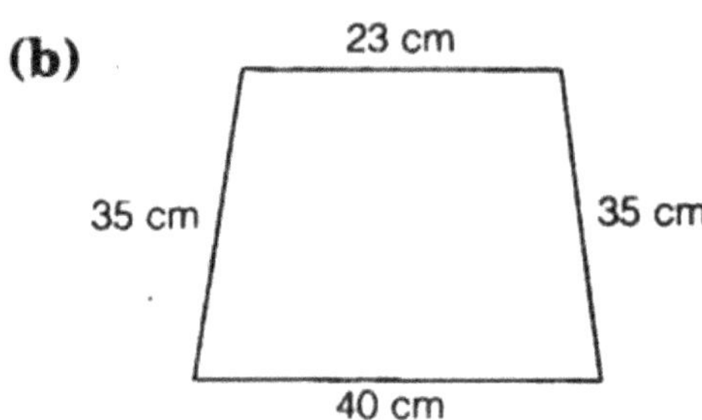

(c)

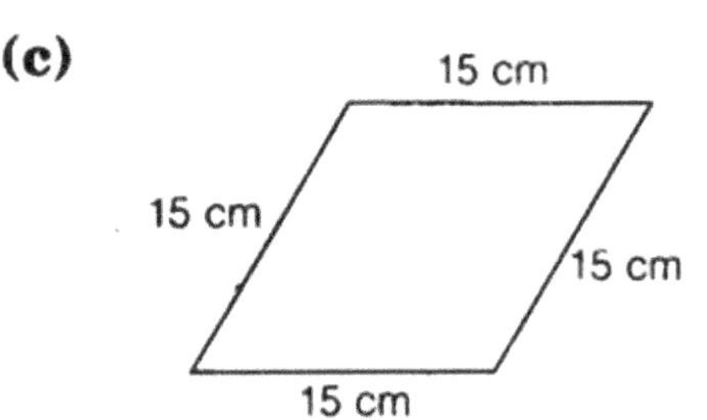

(d)

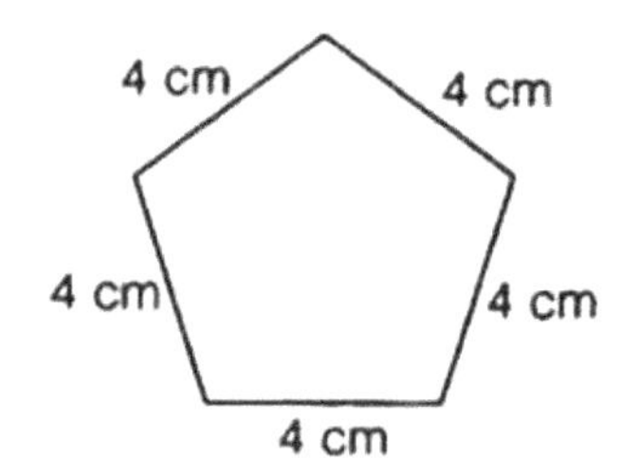

(e)

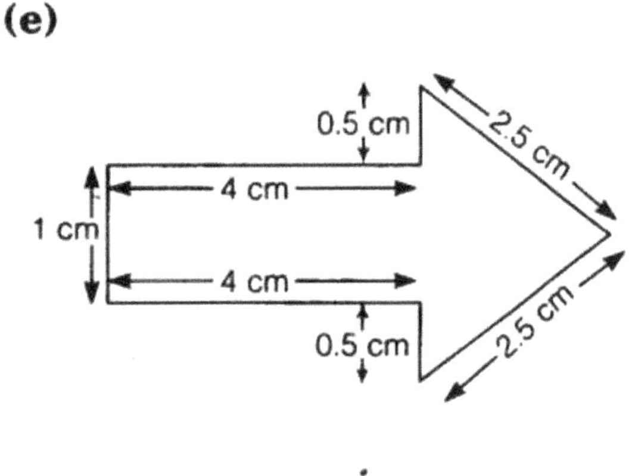

(f)

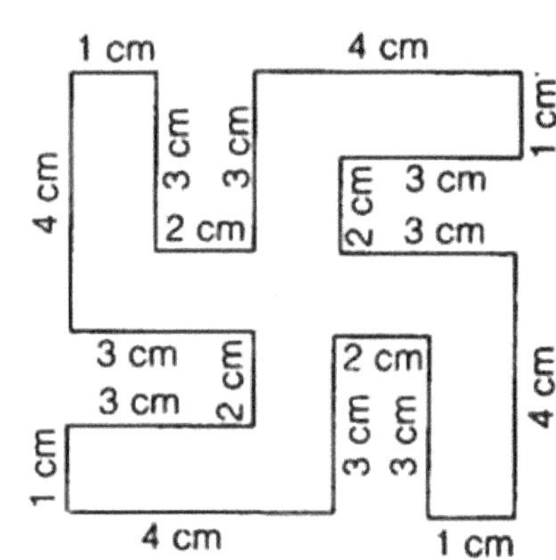

5. Find area of the following shapes

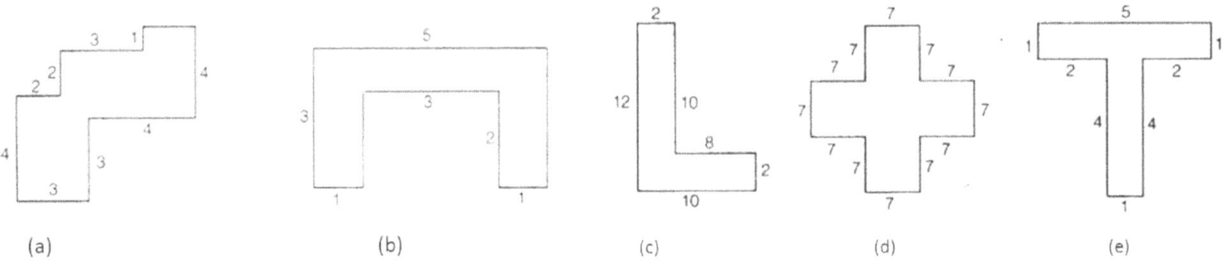

6. How many identical isosceles triangles are needed to make a hexagon by arranging them side by side in such a way that their bases become side of the hexagon?

7. How many diagonals can be drawn in a regular pentagon?

8. What will be the measure of interior angles of a regular heptagon?

***

Set of Selected Problems

1. Find the square with the help of the formulae :

(a) $2a+3b$ (b) $2ab+3bc$ (c) $x^2+\frac{2}{y^2}$ (d) $a+\frac{1}{a}$ (e) $4y-5x$ (f) $ab-c$

(g) $5x^2-y$ (h) $x+2y+4z$ (i) $3p+4q-5r$ (j) $3b-5c-2a$ (k) $ax-by-cz$

(l) $a-b+c-d$ (m) $2a+3x-2y-5z$ (n) 101 (o) 997 (p) 1007

2. Simplify :

(a) $(2a+7)^2+2(2a+7)(2a-7)+(2a-7)^2$

3. Multiply by using special property:

a) 1003 X 997 b) 3,003 X 2,997 c) 12,996 X 13,004

4. Arrange into ascending order:

11.11...., 11.0909....., 10.101101...., 11.0909..., 9.9090....

5. Express into simple fractions :

(a) $0\cdot\dot{2}$ (b) $0\cdot\dot{3}\dot{5}$ (c) $0\cdot1\dot{3}$ (d) $3\cdot7\dot{8}$ (e) $6\cdot2\dot{3}0\dot{9}$

6. Express into similar recurring fractions :

(a) $2\cdot\dot{3}$, $5\cdot2\dot{3}\dot{5}$ (b) $7\cdot2\dot{6}$, $4\cdot23\dot{7}$

(c) $5\cdot\dot{7}$, $8\cdot\dot{3}\dot{4}$, $6\cdot\dot{2}4\dot{5}$ (d) $12\cdot32$, $2\cdot1\dot{9}$, $4\cdot32\dot{5}\dot{6}$

7. Add :(a) $0\cdot4\dot{5}+0\cdot13\dot{4}$ (b) $2\cdot0\dot{5}+8\cdot0\dot{4}+7\cdot018$ (c) $0\cdot00\dot{6}+0\cdot\dot{9}\dot{2}+0\cdot0\dot{1}3\dot{4}$

8. Subtract :

(a) $3\cdot\dot{4}-2\cdot1\dot{3}$ (b) $5\cdot\dot{1}\dot{2}-3\cdot4\dot{5}$

(c) $8\cdot49-5\cdot3\dot{5}\dot{6}$ (d) $19\cdot34\dot{5}-13\cdot2\dot{3}4\dot{9}$

9. Multiply:

(a) $0\cdot\dot{3}\times0\cdot\dot{6}$ (b) $2\cdot\dot{4}\times0\cdot\dot{8}\dot{1}$ (c) $0\cdot6\dot{2}\times0\cdot\dot{3}$ (d) $42\cdot\dot{1}\dot{8}\times0\cdot2\dot{8}$

10. Divide :

(a) $0\cdot\dot{3}\div0\cdot\dot{6}$ (b) $0\cdot3\dot{5}\div1\cdot\dot{7}$ (c) $2\cdot3\dot{7}\div0\cdot4\dot{5}$ (d) $1\cdot\dot{1}8\dot{5}\div0\cdot\dot{2}\dot{4}$

11. Find the root (upto three decimal places) and write down the approximate values of the square roots upto two decimal places :

(a) 12 (b) $0\cdot\dot{2}\dot{5}$ (c) $1\cdot3\dot{4}$ (d) $5\cdot1\dot{3}0\dot{2}$

12. Find the rational and irrational numbers from the following numbers :

13. Solve the following:

A. Given a three digit number $x + 5 + y$ where x is the digit at hundreds place and y is the digit at ones. If the number $x + 5 + y$ is divisible by 9, find least positive value $x + y$?

B. Product of two numbers is 18.75. If one number is three times the other, then find larger number.

C. The sum of the squares of the digits constituting a certain positive three-digit number is 74. The hundreds digit of the number is equal to the doubled sum of the digits in the tens and units places. Find the number if it is known that the difference between that number and the number written by the same digits in the reverse order is 495.

D. Show that exactly one of the numbers n, $n + 2$ or $n + 4$ is divisible by 3.

E. $n(n + 1)(n + 5)$ is a multiple of 3.

F. The sum of the digits of a three-digit number is 11. If we subtract 594 from the number consisting of the same digits written in the reverse order, we shall get a required number. Find that three-digit number, if the sum of all pairwise products of the digits constituting that number is 31.

G. Pradeep gave away 8 sweets to his friends. This number was one-fifth of the number of sweets that he had with him at first. How many sweets did Pradeep have with him at first?

H. Some students planned a picnic. The budget for food was Rs. 480. But eight of these failed to go and thus the cost of food for each member increased by Rs. 10. How many students attended the picnic?

14. Sum total of cube root, square value and reciprocal of a number is equal to 66.125. Find the number.

15. Answer the following:

A. A number is 27 more than the number obtained by reversing its digits. If its unit's and ten's digit are x and y respectively. write the linear equation representing the above statement.

B. A three digit number 24 y is a multiple of 3, what might be the values of y?

C. Find the least number which must be added to 6203 to obtain a perfect square. Also, find the square root of the number so obtained.

D. Total number of 9 digit numbers that are divisible by 5, is equal to

E. How many numbers greater than 40000 can be formed using the digits 1, 2, 3, 4 and 5 if each is used only once in a number?

F. Find the number nearest to 110000 but greater than 100000 which is exactly divisible by each of 8,15 and 21.

G. If the number of all 4-digit number whose product of digits is divisible by 3, are N,the

H. Three normal AA_1, BB_1 and CC_1 are drawn from a point P(h, k) to the parabola $y^2 = 4ax$, at A, B and C points. The following conditions are satisfied by the three normals.(i) any two of three normals are coincide(ii) S(a, 0) be the focus of the parabola(iii) Three normals be real, then $h > 2a$(iv) Slopes of the normals are m_1, m_2 and m_3. If $m_1m_2 = \lambda$, then the locus of P is a parabola(v) P lies on the line $y = \mu$, then the sides of the triangle ABC touch the parabola $S' = 0$.
SA SB SC is equal to.

16. Chintawar can solve 49 mathematical problems while doing self-study for 1h 4 minutes. How many problems can be solved by Chintawar while doing self-study for 56 minutes? In such a way how many problems can be made by him in a fortnight?

17. A car driver increases the average speed of a car by 10% to save 40 minutes while moving through a highway of 120 km. What was the original speed of that car?

18. Consider p as a natural number. $(p^0 + p^1 + p^2 + \ldots\ldots p^{10,000}) = 10,000$; What is the value of p?

19: Answer the following...

Deepak bought 3 notebooks and 2 pens for Rs. 80. His friend Ram said that price of each notebook could be Rs. 25. Then three notebooks would cost Rs.75, the two pens would cost Rs.5 and each pen could be for Rs. 2.50. Another friend Ajay felt that Rs. 2.50 for one pen was too little. It should be at least Rs. 16. Then the price of each notebook would also be Rs.16.

Lohith also bought the same types of notebooks and pens as Aditya. He paid 110 for 4 notebooks and 3 pens. Later, Deepak guess the cost of one pen is Rs. 10 and Lohith guess the cost of one notebook is Rs. 30.

(i) Form the pair of linear equations in two variables from this situation by taking cost of one notebook as Rs. x and cost of one pen as Rs. y.

(a) $3x + 2y = 80$ and $4x + 3y = 110$ (b) $2x + 3y = 80$ and $3x + 4y = 110$

(c) $x + y = 80$ and $x + y = 110$ (d) $3x + 2y = 110$ and $4x + 3y = 80$

(iii) Find the cost of one pen? (a) Rs. 20 (b) Rs. 10 (c) Rs. 5 (d) Rs. 15

(ii) Which is the solution satisfying both the equations formed in (i)?

(a) $x = 10, y = 20$ (b) $x = 20, y = 10$ (c) $x = 15, y = 15$ (d) none of these

$3x + 2y = 3(20) + 2(10) = 60 + 20 = 80$ $4x + 3y = 4(20) + 3(10) = 80 + 30 = 110$

(iv) Find the total cost if they will purchase the same type of 15 notebooks and 12 pens.

(a) Rs. 400 (b) Rs. 350 (c) Rs. 450 (d) Rs. 420

(v) Find whose estimation is correct in the given statement.

(a) Deepak (b) Lohith (c) Ram (d) Ajay

20. Observe the process of locating Rational Numbers on a number line. On the basis of this mechanism locate three rational numbers in between 1.5 and 1.75.

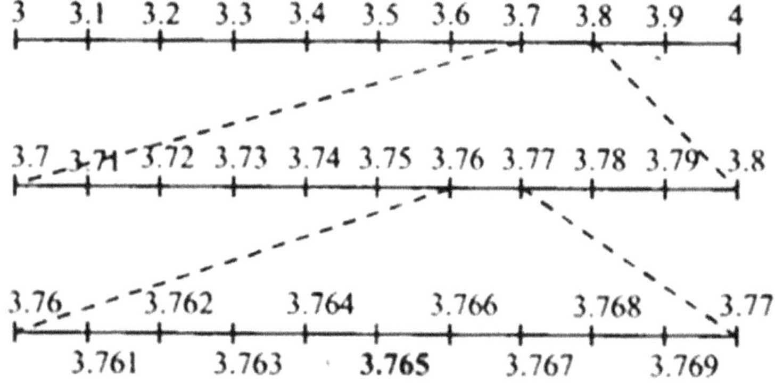

(i) 3.7 lies between 3 and 4

(ii) 3.76 lies between 3.7 and 3.8

(iii) 3.765 lies between 3.76 and 3.77

21. Solve the following:

A. In the formula $p^4 - q^3 = r^2 - s$, make p as the subject of the formula.

(a) $p = (r^2 - q^3 - s)^{\frac{1}{4}}$

(b) $p = (r^2 - q^3 + s)^{\frac{1}{4}}$

(c) $p = (r^2 + q^3 + s)^{\frac{1}{4}}$

(d) $p = (r^2 + q^3 - s)^{\frac{1}{4}}$

B. The total surface area of a cuboid is $S = 2\ (lb + bh + lh)$. Make l as the subject of the formula.

(a) $l = \dfrac{S}{2(b+h)}$

(b) $l = \dfrac{S}{b+h} + \dfrac{bh}{b+h}$

(c) $l = \dfrac{S-2bh}{2(b+h)}$

(d) $l = \dfrac{S-bh}{b+h}$

C. What are the auxiliary formulae of the statement "sum of the angles of a quadrilateral $ABCD$ is 360°" (If the four angles of the quadrilateral are A, B, C, and D)?

(a) $A = 360° - (B + C + D)$

D. If $S = \dfrac{a}{1-r^3}$, then express r in terms of S and a.

(a) $r = \sqrt[3]{1+\dfrac{a}{S}}$ (b) $r = \sqrt[3]{1+\dfrac{S}{a}}$

(c) $r = \sqrt[3]{1-\dfrac{S}{a}}$ (d) $r = \sqrt[3]{1-\dfrac{a}{S}}$

In $S = ut + \frac{1}{2}at^2$, $S = 96$, $t = 8$, and $a = 2$. Find u.

(a) 2 (b) 8

(c) 4 (d) 1

E. If $C = \dfrac{5}{9}\ (F - 32)$, then express F in terms of C.

(a) $F = \dfrac{9}{5}\ C - 32$ (b) $F = 32 - \dfrac{9}{5}\ C$

(c) $F = \dfrac{9}{5}\ (C + 32)$ (d) $F = \dfrac{9}{5}\ C + 32$

F. If $a = b - \sqrt{b^2 - 1}$, then express b in terms of a.

(a) $b = \dfrac{1}{2}\ (a^{-1} - a)$ (b) $b = \dfrac{1}{2}\ (a + a^{-1})$

(c) $b = \dfrac{1}{2}\ (a - a^{-1})$ (d) $b = \dfrac{-1}{2}\ (a + a^{-1})$

G. If $\dfrac{1}{a} + \dfrac{1}{b} = \dfrac{1}{c} + \dfrac{1}{d}$, then express a in terms of b, c, and d.

(a) $a = \dfrac{bcd}{bc + cd - bd}$ (b) $a = \dfrac{bcd}{cd + bd - bc}$

H. In $P = \dfrac{5x+2y}{3x-4y}$, if $x = 5$ and $P = 7$, then $y =$ ______.

(a) 3 (b) $\dfrac{3}{8}$

(c) $\dfrac{8}{3}$ (d) $\dfrac{1}{3}$

I. In the formula $x = y + \sqrt{y^2+1}$, make y as the subject of the formula.

(a) $y = \dfrac{1}{2}(x^{-1} - x)$ (b) $y = \dfrac{1}{2}(x - x^{-1})$

(c) $y = \dfrac{1}{2}(x^{-1} + x)$ (d) $y = \dfrac{1}{2}\left(x^2 + \dfrac{1}{x}\right)$

J. In the formula $E = 3k\ (1 - 2c)$, make c as the subject of the formula.

(a) $c = \dfrac{1}{2} + \dfrac{E}{6k}$ (b) $c = \dfrac{1}{2} - \dfrac{E}{3k}$

(c) $c = \dfrac{1}{2} - \dfrac{E}{6k}$ (d) $c = \dfrac{1}{2} + \dfrac{E}{3k}$

K. If $\dfrac{1}{f} = \dfrac{1}{u} + \dfrac{1}{v}$, then make v as the subject of the formula.

L. The sum of a^2 and cb^3 equals the sum of twice to d and thrice to c. Express b in terms of a, c, and d.

(a) $b = \sqrt[3]{\dfrac{1}{c}\left(2d + 3c - a^2\right)}$

(b) $b = \dfrac{1}{c}\sqrt[3]{2d + 3c - a^2}$

(c) $b = \dfrac{\sqrt[3]{a^2 - 2d - 3c}}{c}$

(d) $b = \sqrt[3]{\dfrac{1}{c}\left(2d + 3c + a^2\right)}$

M. In $c = \dfrac{22a+9b}{3a+2b}$, $c = 6$ and $a = 3$, find b.

(a) 6 (b) 2

(c) 4 (d) 8

The curved surface area (c) of a cone is πrl, where $l = \sqrt{r^2 + h^2}$, express h in terms of c and r.

(a) $h = \dfrac{1}{\pi r}\sqrt{c^2 - \pi^2 r^4}$ (b) $h = \dfrac{1}{\pi r}\sqrt{c - \pi^2 r^2}$

(c) $h = \dfrac{1}{\pi r}\sqrt{c^2 - \pi^2 r^2}$ (d) $h = \dfrac{1}{\pi r}\sqrt{c + \pi^2 r^4}$

22. Mathematics teacher of a school took her 9th standard students to show Red fort. It was a part of their Educational trip. The teacher had interest in history as well. She narrated the facts of Red fort to students. Then the teacher said in this monument one can find combination of solid figures. There are 2 pillars which are cylindrical in shape. There are two domes at the corners which are hemispherical. There are 7 smaller domes at the centre. Flag hoisting ceremony on Independence Day takes place near these domes.

I: Find lateral surface area of 2 pillars having height 7 m and base 1.4 m.

II: Volume of hemisphere having radius of base equal to 3.5 m.

23: Mathematics teacher of a school took her 9th standard students to show Gol Gumbaz. It was a part of their Educational trip. The teacher had interest in history as well. She narrated the facts of Gol Gumbaz to students. Gol Gumbaz is the tomb of king Muhammad Adil Shah, Adil Shah Dynasty. Construction of the tomb, located in Vijayapura , Karnataka, India, was started in 1626 and completed in 1656. It reaches up to 51 meters in height while the giant dome has an external diameter of 44 meters, making it one of the largest domes ever built. At each of the four corners of the cube is a dome shaped octagonal tower seven stories high with a staircase inside.

(a) What is the total surface area of a cuboid? (i) lb + bh + hl (ii) 2(lb + bh + hl) (iii) 2(lb + bh) (iv) $1^2 + b^2 + h^2$

(b) What is the curved surface area of hemispherical dome ?

(c) What is the height of the cubodial part ?

(d) Circumference of the base of the dome = ...

24: Following chart represents the score of few students in exam.

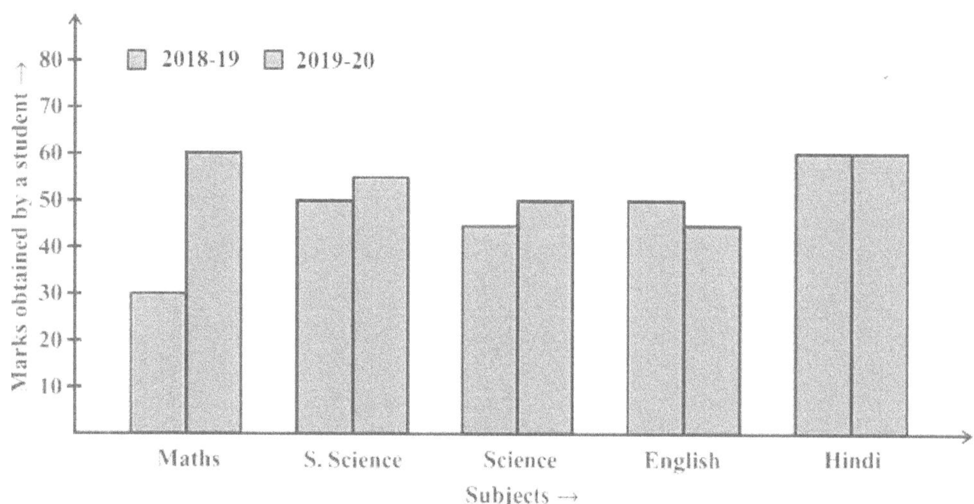

In which subject improvement of score during two consecutive examination was maximum?

1. Standard Worksheets

Number system that we use in mathematics is called decimal system as we are using 10 digits to represent a number. Some of the aspects related to fraction values are as follows:

Standard/ Lowest/ Simplest form of a fraction is that form in which the numerator and denominator have no factor in common. For example : $\frac{6}{13}, \frac{7}{9}, \frac{1}{8}$.

- To convert the given fraction in its standard/ lowest/ simplest form, divide both numerator and denominator by the common factors one by one. For example :

$$\frac{72}{96} = \frac{72 \div 12}{96 \div 12}$$

$$= \frac{6}{8}$$

$$= \frac{6 \div 2}{8 \div 2} = \frac{3}{4}$$

Equivalent Fractions : Two or more fractions which represent the same part of the whole are called equivalent fractions.

For example : $\frac{1}{2}, \frac{2}{4}, \frac{3}{6}$ are equivalent fraction.

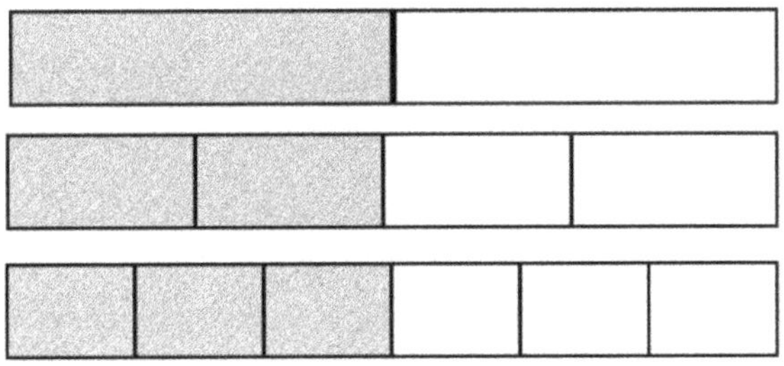

$\frac{1}{2}$

$\frac{2}{4}$

$\frac{3}{6}$

Fractions having different denominators and numerator as 1 are called unit fractions. We always add like fractions. A like fraction can be subtracted from another like fraction. Decimals are special types of fractions having denominators as multiples of 10. 0.1 is equal to one tenths. Fractions can be represented in number line if they represent a definite decimal value. One eighth is equal to 0.125, that is why it can be represented in a number line.

1. Whole thing is represented as 1.
2. A fraction indicates one or more equal parts of a whole.

This is a whole. It is written as 1.

If we divide the whole into 2 equal parts. Each part is called one-half. It is written as $\frac{1}{2}$.

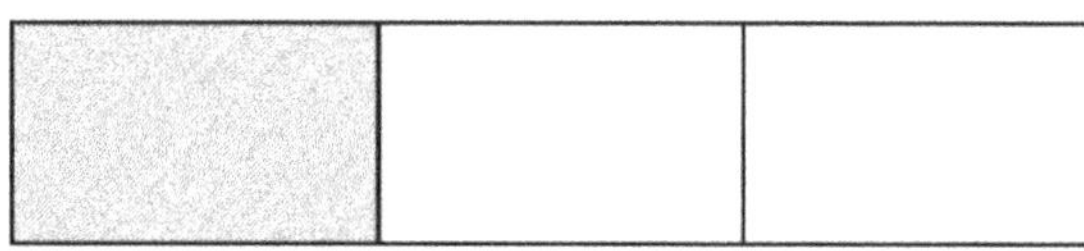

If we divide the whole into 3 equal parts, each part is called one-third. It is written as $\frac{1}{3}$.

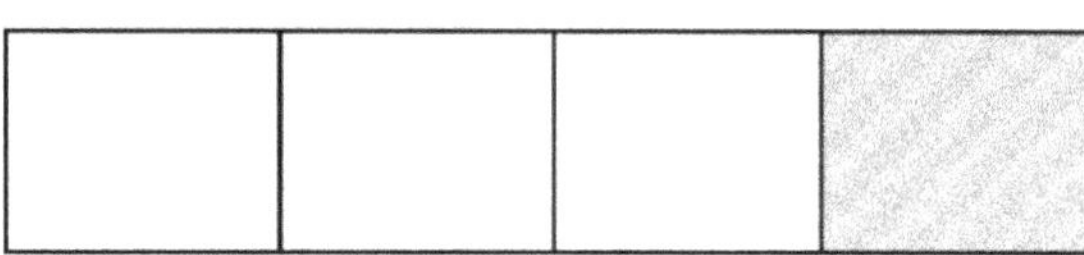

If we divide the whole into 4 equal parts, each part is called one-fourth or a quarter. It is written as $\frac{1}{4}$

3. The numbers such as quarter, half, one-fifth, two-thirds are called **Fractional numbers** and their symbols $\left(\frac{1}{4}, \frac{1}{2}, \frac{1}{5}, \frac{2}{3}\right)$ are called **Fractions**.

Fraction is a section which represents part of a whole and can be represented in the form of a rational number. Unit fractions have numerator 1. Fractions having identical denominators are called like fractions.

Before adding or subtracting we convert all the fractions into like fractions. Only like fraction can be subtracted from a fraction. Repeated decimal can be converted into a fraction.

Aid Box:

I: What fraction of all the numbers starting from 1 to 1000 are multiples of 50? How many oof all such multiples are also multiples of 100?

II: Half of a quarter of 8,064 is equal to p and quarter of one third of 12,096 is equal to q. Find the value of (p + q) ÷ 1,008

III: Cistern A can fill up quarter of a water tank in 10 minutes, cistern B can fill up 0.1 part of that tank in 8 minutes. Find the time taken by both the cisterns jointly to fill up four such water tanks.

IV: (0.5 – 0.5 + 0.5 – 0.5 …….. 1,009 times) X 2,008 = ……………….

Worksheet 1

1. Convert the following in fractions:

   a) 0.125 b) 1.25 c) 6.25 d) 1.125 e) 5.75 f) 3,75

2. Half of a whole number exceeds the greatest two digit number by 5. Find sixth fraction of that number.

3. Richardson got half of a cake. Pinto got another half slice from the remaining. Piskilla took rest of the cake and shared equally along with her other three friends. Share got by Piskilla in fraction is equal to ______.

4. Simbalco multiplies two unit fractions and got a value equal to one 21st . Two possible unit fractions are ______ and ________.

5. Rijuama covered up sixteen sheet papers with decoration works in 1 hour 20 minutes. While working with same pace she can cover up 100 such sheets with decoration works in ________.

Aid Box: --- [Understanding fraction and decimal]

Fraction is part of a whole. If we divide a spherical apple in two equal halves then each of the fraction will be considered as half of a whole.

Decimal is a special tye of fraction having denominator 10,100,1000, and so on.

Percentage is a special type of fraction having denominator 100.

For Example: 5% of 100 = 5/100 or 0.05;

I: 10% of 40% of a number is equal to 2,009. Find sum ttal of one fifth and 20% of that number.

II: A greatest number of five digits and a smallest number of six digits are formed without repeating any of the digits twice. Find sum total of both the digits.

III: Istuana can finish her assignment in 9 days while working at the rate of 2 hours a day. How many days can be saved if she prefer working at the rate of 3 hours a day?

IV: Mohanlal, Sampatlal and Ganpatlal preferred working jointly to finish a project activity in 20 days. They all work with working capacity at the ratio of 1: 2: 3 resectively. If Mohanlal and Sampatlal prefer working jjointly then find number of days they need to finish the same project work.

V: Dinkar Joshi preferred working in a farm at the maximum wage rate per day with a condition that there should be deduction of wage (as finialised per day) for the number of days he remain absent at the work station. After completion of the work he has received Rs 1331 and there was a deduction of Rs 605. Find the number of days he remained absent at the work place.

VI: What least number should be subtracted from the greatest number of six digits to make the number divisible by 8?

VII:

In questions **1** to **24**, change the fractions to decimals.

1. $\frac{1}{4}$ **2.** $\frac{2}{5}$ **3.** $\frac{4}{5}$ **4.** $\frac{3}{4}$ **5.** $\frac{1}{2}$ **6.** $\frac{3}{8}$

7. $\frac{9}{10}$ **8.** $\frac{5}{8}$ **9.** $\frac{5}{12}$ **10.** $\frac{1}{6}$ **11.** $\frac{2}{3}$ **12.** $\frac{5}{6}$

13. $\frac{2}{7}$ **14.** $\frac{3}{7}$ **15.** $\frac{4}{9}$ **16.** $\frac{5}{11}$ **17.** $1\frac{1}{5}$ **18.** $2\frac{5}{8}$

19. $2\frac{1}{3}$ **20.** $1\frac{7}{10}$ **21.** $2\frac{3}{16}$ **22.** $2\frac{2}{7}$ **23.** $2\frac{6}{7}$ **24.** $3\frac{19}{100}$

In questions **25** to **40**, change the decimals to fractions and simplify.

25. 0·2 **26.** 0·7 **27.** 0·25 **28.** 0·45

29. 0·36 **30.** 0·52 **31.** 0·125 **32.** 0·625

33. 0·84 **34.** 2·35 **35.** 3·95 **36.** 1·05

37. 3·2 **38.** 0·27 **39.** 0·007 **40.** 0·000 11

Evaluate, giving the answer to 2 decimal places:

41. $\frac{1}{4}+\frac{1}{3}$ **42.** $\frac{2}{3}+0{\cdot}75$ **43.** $\frac{8}{9}-0{\cdot}24$ **44.** $\frac{7}{8}+\frac{5}{9}+\frac{2}{11}$

45. $\frac{1}{3}\times 0{\cdot}2$ **46.** $\frac{5}{8}\times\frac{1}{4}$ **47.** $\frac{8}{11}\div 0{\cdot}2$ **48.** $\left(\frac{4}{7}-\frac{1}{3}\right)\div 0{\cdot}4$

Arrange the numbers in order of size (smallest first)

49. $\frac{1}{3}$, 0·33, $\frac{4}{15}$ **50.** $\frac{2}{7}$, 0·3, $\frac{4}{9}$ 51. 0·71, $\frac{7}{11}$, 0·705 **52.** $\frac{4}{13}$, 0·3, $\frac{5}{18}$

Some number facts:

An *integer* is a whole number. e.g. 2, −3 ...
A *prime* number is divisible only by itself and by one.
e.g. 2, 3, 5, 7, 11, 13 ...
The *multiples* of 12 are 12, 24, 36, 48 ...
The *factors* of 12 are 1, 2, 3, 4, 6, 12.
A *square number* is the result of multiplying a number by itself.
e.g. $5 \times 5 = 25$ so 25 is a square number.
A *cube number* is the result of multiplying a number by itself three times. e.g. $5 \times 5 \times 5 = 125$, so 125 is a cube number.

53: Find the greatest number of six digits which is also divisible by 4, 8 and 12.

54: What least number of five digits is divisible by 21, 42 and 63 leaving remainder 13 in each case?

55: Find the smallest possible seven digit numbers which is divisible by 12, 18, 36 and 72 leaving remainder 11 in each case.

56: What least number should be subtracted from 20,089 to obtain a multiple of 11, 22 and 55?

57: Find sum total of the greatest number of five digits and smallest number of six digits in such a way that the number will be a common multiple of 12, 24 and 36.

58: What least number should be subtracted from 45,089 to obtain a common multiple of 13,26 and 65?

Worksheet 2

Complete each expanded form.

1. 38,500,000,700,000 (3 × _?_) + (8 × _?_) + (5 × _?_) + (7 × _?_)

2. 4.0008 (_?_ × 1) + (_?_ × 0.0001)   3. 0.000009 (_?_ × 0.000001)

Write each expanded form in two ways.

4. 5,042,102   5. 201,407,090,000   6. 15,000,087,000

7. 0.045678   8. 3.050904   9. 78.5009

Write each expanded form in standard form.

10. (9 × 10,000,000,000,000) + (3 × 100,000) + (4 × 100)

11. (4 × 1,000,000,000,000) + (5 × 10,000) + (2 × 1000) + (9 × 1)

12. 4 + 0.1 + 0.07 + 0.000009   13. 20 + 0.008 + 0.0001 + 0.00005

Write each number in standard form and in expanded form.

14. 95 trillion, 700 million   15. 8 trillion, twelve million, five

16. 13 billion, 7 hundred   17. 14 hundred thousandths

18. 80 and 13 ten thousandths   19. 907 millionths

20. The distance around Earth's equator is approximately 24,900 miles. How is this number written in expanded form using powers of 10? .

21. Write each in expanded form using exponents.

a. 3 millionths   b. 6 hundredths   c. 9 thousandths   d. 4 hundred thousandths

22. What fraction of a year is equal to 2 fortnights?

23. What smallest number should be subtracted from 5 digit greatest number to make the value divisible by 11?

24. Nandanwar can cover a distance of 60 m in 6 seconds and Sangitika runs at an average speed of 36 km per hour. If they start running together then who will finish the race of 200 m first ?

25. 20 tens + 20 hundredths + 20 thousands = ________________.

26. 20% of 30% of one sixth of 1,100 = _____________.

27. 30% of 50% of 2,008 = ……………………

Worksheet 3

Write the place of the underlined digit. Then write its value.

1. 2242 2. 63,666 3. 199,999 4. 880,888

Place a comma where needed in each. Then write the period name for the underlined digit.

5. 3 4 2 5 _9 6. 1 6 4 3 2 7. 2 0 0 0 6 0 8. 8 0 5 0 2 7

Write the number in standard form.

9. forty-five thousand, seven hundred sixty-two 10. five thousand, six

11. nine hundred thousand, seven 12. ten thousand, nineteen

Write the word name for each number.

13. 217,046 14. 737,008 15. 16,231,075 16. 12,923,780

Round to the nearest hundred.

13. 158 14. 426 15. 375 16. 896 17. 719 18. 950

19. 1047 20. 3888 21. 5942 22. 6891 23. 3098 24. 8762

25. 37,405 26. 62,345 27. 88,088 28. 65,097 29. 58,706 30. 66,636

Round to the nearest thousand.

31. 9155 32. 7983 33. 4550 34. 6237 35. 8396

36. 33,888 37. 15,942 38. 93,192 39. 87,983 40. 46,237

41. 326,150 42. 145,706 43. 357,029 44. 563,498 45. 807,476

46. 821,593 47. 450,513 48. 435,127 49. 205,120 50. 761,604

51. Find the six digit greatest multiple of 8.

52. Write in standard form: 2,000,000 + 3 X 10^5 + 400,000 + 3 tens + 15 tenths + 4

53. Arrange the following from greatest to least:

21 million, 43X 10^7, 4.3 X 10^6 , 2 million + 3 hundred thousand;

54. Anasthesia observed that a train miving with a uniform speed of 36 km/h crosses a light post in 45 seconds. Is this information sufficient for calculating length of that train? If yes, try to calculate length of that train.

55. (0.5 – 0.5 + 0.5 – 0.5 …… 1,209 times) = ...

Worksheet 4

Compare. Write <, =, or >.

1. 0.46 _?_ 0.39	**2.** 0.709 _?_ 0.921	**3.** 0.06 _?_ 0.60
4. 9.8 _?_ 9.80	**5.** 0.509 _?_ 0.510	**6.** 0.623 _?_ 0.627
7. 0.4286 _?_ 0.4190	**8.** 0.5691 _?_ 0.5690	**9.** 0.53 _?_ 0.536
10. 0.8 _?_ 0.78	**11.** 7.610 _?_ 7.61	**12.** 7.3 _?_ 7.301
13. 2.34 _?_ 2.3513	**14.** 91.42 _?_ 90.425	**15.** 0.059 _?_ 0.59

Write in order from greatest to least.

16. 0.75, 0.39, 0.2, 0.35

17. 0.484, 0.495, 0.523, 0.54

18. 8.63, 8.6, 8.65, 7.99

19. 9.21, 9.0, 9.2, 9.06

20. 0.5478, 0.546, 0.5462, 0.5593

21. 8.134, 8.215, 8.2152, 8.2052

Write in order from least to greatest.

22. 2.7054, 0.9832, 1.2396, 0.9276

23. 2.7993, 0.0803, 0.0779, 0.2396

24. 0.1211, 0.12, 0.121, 0.0911

25. 0.052387, 0.52386, 0.05023, 0.0523

26. Niharika wants a pencil. It costs Rs. 10. She gives nine one rupee coin, one-half rupee coin and one-quarter rupee coin. Is it enough?

27. Comlete the following number patterns:

Look at the patterns and complete them.

3, 6, 9, 12 ____,____,_____.	2, 4, 6,____,____,_____.
8, 16, 24, 32,____,____,_____.	4, 8, 12, 16, ____,____,_____.
5, 10, 15,____,____,_____.	30, 60, 90,____,____,_____.
A1, B2, C3, D4,____,____,_____.	12A, 13B, 14C,____,____,_____.
51, 56, 61, 66, ,____,____,_____.	1, 2, 3, 4, 5 ,____,____,_____.
10, 20, 30,____,____,_____.	1, 3, 6, 10, 15, ____,____,_____.
2, 4, 8, 16, 32,____,____,_____.	12, 24, 36, 48, ____,____,_____.

28. If 11 X 11 = 121 and 111 X 111 = 12321 then 1111 X 1111 = __________________.

29. Rajat can finish half of a project in 12 days and Meena alone can finish quarter of the same project in 6 days. They jointly can finish entire project in _____ days.

Worksheet 5

Estimate by rounding. Then multiply.

1. 25 × 3
2. 62 × 4
3. 58 × 5
4. 42 × 6
5. 19 × 7
6. 956 × 5
7. 619 × 8
8. 534 × 4
9. 519 × 5
10. 348 × 9

Find the product.

11. 87 × 6
12. 93 × 7
13. 79 × 8
14. 41 × 5
15. 32 × 4
16. 759 × 3
17. 825 × 4
18. 329 × 6
19. 478 × 8
20. 976 × 9
21. 9 × 49
22. 8 × 93
23. 7 × 358
24. 5 × 953

Estimate the product:

25. 1021 X 984 = _____ X 10^5 ;

26. Nine students gave oral reports for their science project. Of those reports, three were each 18 minutes 7 seconds long and the rest were each 5 minutes 15 seconds long. How long did it take for all the reports to be given?

27. Find outer boundary and area of the shaded portion.

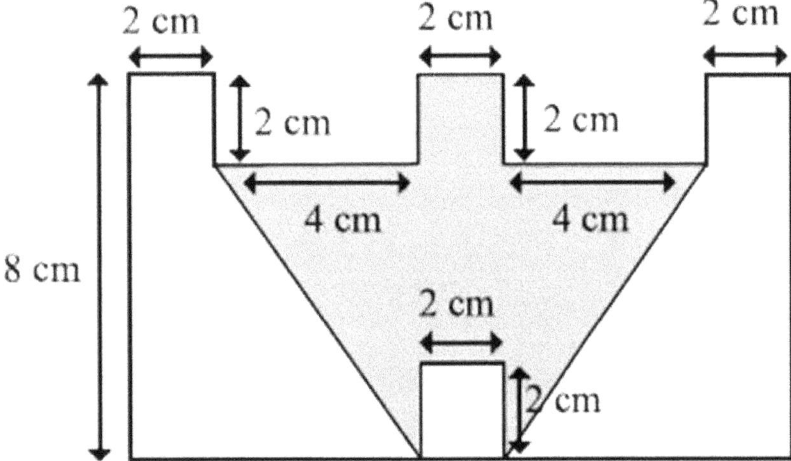

Worksheet 6

Estimate using front-end digits. Then find the difference.

1.	800 − 526	**2.**	700 − 439	**3.**	300 − 124	**4.**	902 − 514	**5.**	600 − 78
6.	9000 − 4572	**7.**	8000 − 2333	**8.**	6006 − 1737	**9.**	8060 − 5274	**10.**	3000 − 543
11.	$7.00 − 5.21	**12.**	$6.00 − 3.92	**13.**	$8.00 − 2.97	**14.**	$5.09 − 1.35	**15.**	$4.00 − 0.83
16.	$87.00 − 64.27	**17.**	$93.00 − 78.42	**18.**	$60.03 − 14.59	**19.**	$48.00 − 7.03	**20.**	$30.20 − 4.53

Align and subtract.

21. 4000 − 784 **22.** 9000 − 8762 **23.** 5003 − 1784

24. 7020 − 4721 **25.** 7200 − 6548 **26.** 5081 − 329

27. 8700 − 421 **28.** 9300 − 7842 **29.** 4800 − 703

Find the missing minuend.

30.	? − 764 = 136	**31.**	? − 459 = 241	**32.**	? − 623 = 278	**33.**	? − 596 = 257	**34.**	? − 861 = 263
35.	? − 5278 = 2722	**36.**	? − 4927 = 1073	**37.**	? − 3452 = 3548	**38.**	? − 1777 = 1226	**39.**	? − 2182 = 1848

Find the value.

40. 504 – *n* when *n* =113 **41.** 6097 + *n* when *n* = 9362 **45.**

42. *n* – 309 when *n* = 519 43. 9002 + *n* when *n* = 2754

44. Every cubic millimeter of human blood contains near about about 7500 white blood cells. A count less than 1500 above this number is still considered healthy. Is a white cell count of a person reaching 8750 considered healthy?

45. Earth's total surface area is about 19,956 X 10^{4} square miles. Approximately 139,692 X 10^{3} square miles of the Earth surface are covered with water. About how much of Earth's surface is covered by land? Estimate your finding to the nearest million?

46. 46th multiple of 1/92 of 121,121 = _______________.

47: 12th multiple of 10th multiple of 240,360 + 11th multiple of 13th multiple of 143,286 = ………………

48: 12th multiple of 100 + 13th multiple of 1,000 + 23rd multiple of 10,000 = …………………..

Worksheet 7

Use rounding to estimate. Then add or subtract. (Watch for + or −.)

1. 36,587 87,943 + 13,156	**2.** 28,764 64,537 + 35,936	**3.** 65,446 1,915 + 47,291	**4.** 49,765 18,976 + 7,359
5. 26,542 − 17,986	**6.** 34,896 − 15,984	**7.** 41,132 − 17,545	**8.** 62,764 − 58,685
9. 115,609 205,399 + 411,111	**10.** 356,789 141,217 + 222,888	**11.** 471,009 180,007 + 277,777	**12.** 365,786 274,982 + 186,214
13. 672,244 − 456,688	**14.** 681,337 − 278,456	**15.** 524,700 − 316,672	**16.** 938,400 − 619,711

17. 125 X 8 = 1,000 and 40 X 25 = 1,000. Now complete the following expressions:

a) 1005 X 125 X 100 X 8 = 1.005 X 10^{n} . Find the value of n.

b) 40 X 9003 X 8 = 125 X 9003 X ______.

c) 21021 X 25 X 125 X ___ X 40 = 21.021 X 10^{9} ;

18. Each necklace uses 72 cm of wire. Will a 5000 cm roll of wire be enough to make 75 necklaces? If not, how much more wire will be needed?

19. Palady rented a shop at Town Hall Market. It sold 18 pairs of earrings at Rs. 5,500 each and 8 belts at Rs 350.75 each. How much money did the shopkeeper collect from the sales?

20. On Saturday morning there were 1,205 people at the Shopping Mall Market. There was double that number in the afternoon. How many people came to the Market on Saturday?

21. Fancy belts are made of braided cords. Each belt uses 96 cm. of cord. Will a 12 m roll of cord be enough to make a dozen belts?

22. Last year Tuna sold 204 necklaces which was 15 more than her sale of two years back. This year she sold twice that number. How many necklaces did Kelly sell in the past three years?

Worksheet 8

Estimate the quotient. Use compatible numbers.

1. 2164 ÷ 43 **2.** 5838 ÷ 28 **3.** 7842 ÷ 37

4. 3984 ÷ 19 **5.** 82,461 ÷ 41 **6.** $51,206 ÷ 53

7. 13,642 ÷ 206 **8.** 85,136 ÷ 409 **9.** $485,725 ÷ 520

10. 672,385 ÷ 710 **11.** 879,500 ÷ 425 **12.** $972,360 ÷ 325

Choose the best estimate.

13. $32\overline{)2940}$ ≈ ? **a.** 1 **b.** 10 **c.** 100 **d.** 1000

14. $19\overline{)6248}$ ≈ ? **a.** 3 **b.** 30 **c.** 300 **d.** 3000

15. $210\overline{)380{,}493}$ ≈ ? **a.** 2 **b.** 20 **c.** 200 **d.** 2000

16. $389\overline{)792{,}432}$ ≈ ? **a.** 2 **b.** 20 **c.** 200 **d.** 2000

17. A rural village's population is between 800 and 1000. The sum of the digits in its population is 21, and the digits in the ones and the hundreds places are the same. What might be the population of the village?

18. Tamanna has 10 pieces of gum to share with her friends. There wasn't enough gum for all her friends, so she went to the store and got 70 pieces of strawberry gum and 12 packs each containing10 pieces of bubble gum. How many pieces of gum does Adrianna have now?

19. Chintu started back counting by 5 starting from 200. He stopped after counting for 19 times. Find the value that he has obtained at this step.

20. Tokino is painting a portrait of her best friend, Mona. To make it easier, she divides half of the portrait into 6 equal parts. What fraction represents each part of the portrait?

21. Ruchika observed that we can construct different three digit numbers by using digits 4, 3 and 2 only once. Arrange all these numbers in ascending order.

22. ____________ is the smallest possible five digit number divisible by 9. It exceeds the smallest five digit number by ______________.

23. 30% of 40% of one sixth of 11,011 = ______________.

24. There are _____ prime numbers located in between 10 and 30.

Worksheet 9

Observe the chart showing some oof the Roman Numerals:

I	II	III	IV	V	VI	VII	VIII	IX	X
1	2	3	4	5	6	7	8	9	10
V	X	XV	XX	XXV	XXX	XXXV	XL	XLV	L
5	10	15	20	25	30	35	40	45	50
X	XX	XXX	XL	L	LX	LXX	LXXX	XC	C
10	20	30	40	50	60	70	80	90	100
C	CC	CCC	CD	D	DC	DCC	DCCC	CM	M
100	200	300	400	500	600	700	800	900	1000

Complete each to write the Roman numeral in standard form.

1. CCLXIII = 100 + _?_ + 50 + _?_ + _?_ + _?_ + _?_ = _?_

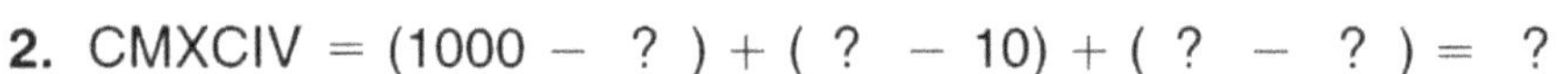

2. CMXCIV = (1000 − _?_) + (_?_ − 10) + (_?_ − _?_) = _?_

Write the Roman numeral in standard form.

3. XXXIV **4.** MVII **5.** LV **6.** DXXI

7. CCLXX **8.** DCCXC **9.** XCIX **10.** MDIII

11. XLVII **12.** MCCLVI **13.** CXLV **14.** MDCCXCI

15. MMCLI **16.** MMDCCCIII **17.** MDCCLXXXV **18.** MDCCCXLV

Write each as a Roman numeral.

19. 18 **20.** 24 **21.** 31 **22.** 52 **23.** 14 **24.** 73

25. 180 **26.** 193 **27.** 387 **28.** 504 **29.** 919 **30.** 623

31. 731 **32.** 876 **33.** 415 **34.** 327 **35.** 613 **36.** 287

37. DCCXC + CXLV = ____________________.

38. Product of sixth and eighth value obtained in the following number series is _______________.

1, 1, 2, 3, ____, _____, _____, ______, ______;

39. Product of predecessor and successor of four digit greatest number = __________________.

40. Half a dozen banana costs Rs 20. Cost of 50 banana = Rs ________________.

Worksheet 10

I: Fill in the blanks:

(i) A _____________ is a simple closed curve.

(ii) _____________ is a line segment that runs between the circle and its centre.

(iii) _____________ is a chord that goes through the centre of the circle.

(iv) ____________ is a line segment that joins two points on the circle.

(v) __________________ is the distance around the circle, it is in the length of a circle.

(vi) Diameter is equal to ___________ of radius

(vii) Radius is equal to ________ of diameter.

(viii) The relation between diameter(d) and radius(r) is ________

(ix) A circle has ______ corners

II: Find the fraction which is shaded.

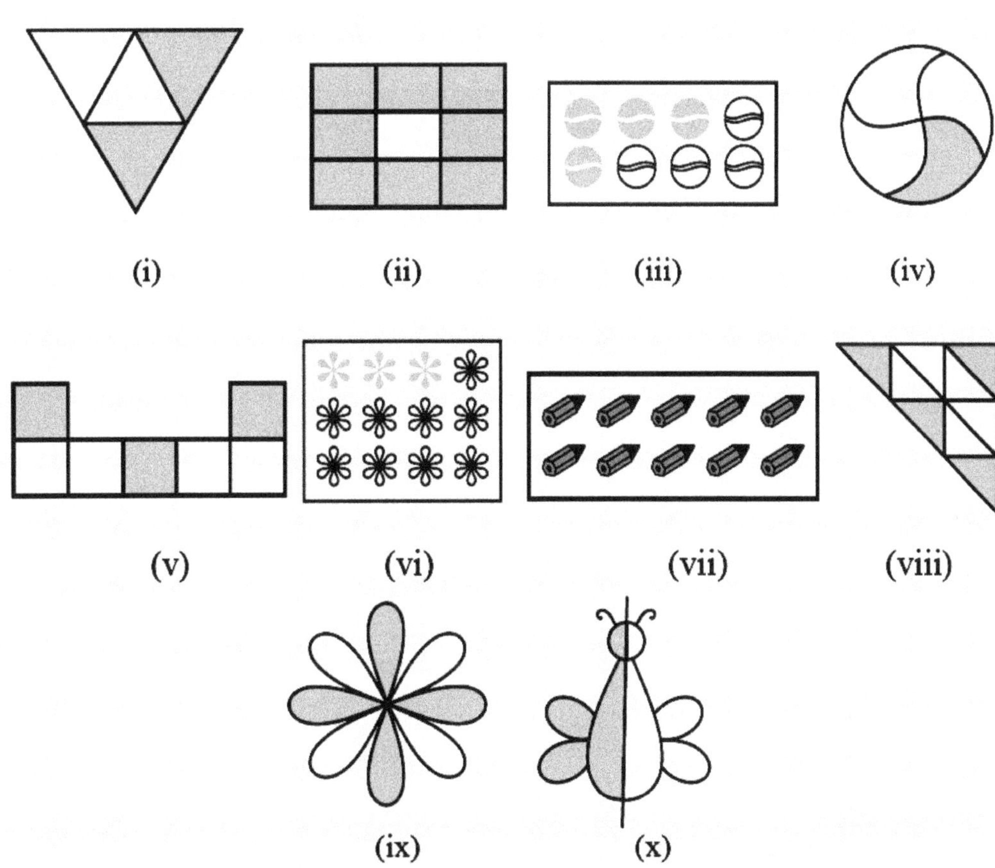

III: What fraction of 3 weeks is Sunday?

IV: One fifth of three twentieth of 15,000 = _____________.

V: Represent the following fractions:

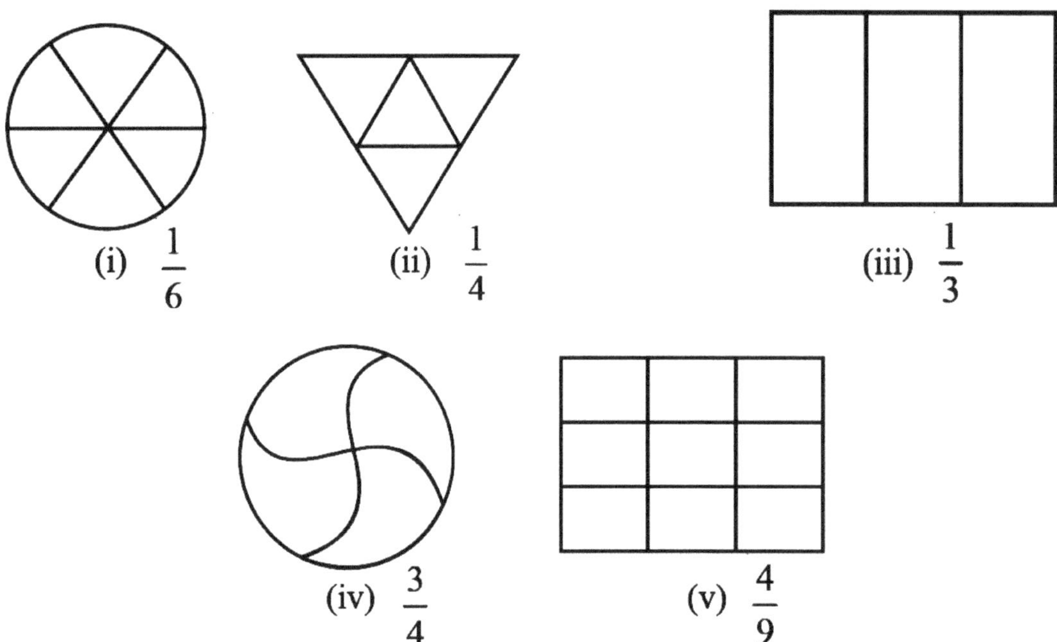

VI: There are 400 mangoes. 1/8th of them are ripe. How many mangoes are ripe?

Aid Box: ---

In the number 308,610,547,823, write the digit in the:

1. ten-billions place **2.** millions place **3.** hundred-thousands place

Write the number in standard form.

4. three hundred four billion, six hundred thousand **5.** CCLXI

6. 1,000,000,000 + 40,000 + 80 + 3 **7.** eight and twelve thousandths

Write the word name for each number.

8. 360,071 **9.** 1,009,124,008 **10.** 6.71 **11.** 0.531 **12.** CMLXI

Compare. Write <, =, or >.

13. 185,035,013 ? 185,503,013 **14.** 10.09 ? 10.1 **15.** 9.63 ? 9.630

Write in order from least to greatest.

16. 6,135,936; 6,315,396; 6,531,639; 6,153,693 **17.** 3.12; 31.2; 0.312

Worksheet 11

1. Richimon painted half of a wall in 1 hour 46 minutes. Bheema painted quarter of similar sized wall in 7 minutes less than an hour. Who works faster? If they work jointly then calculate the time taken by them to finish the painting of six such walls.
2. Find values of x in each of the following figures:

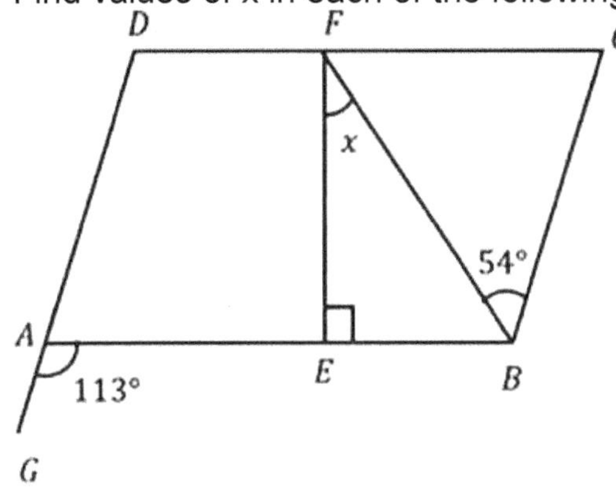

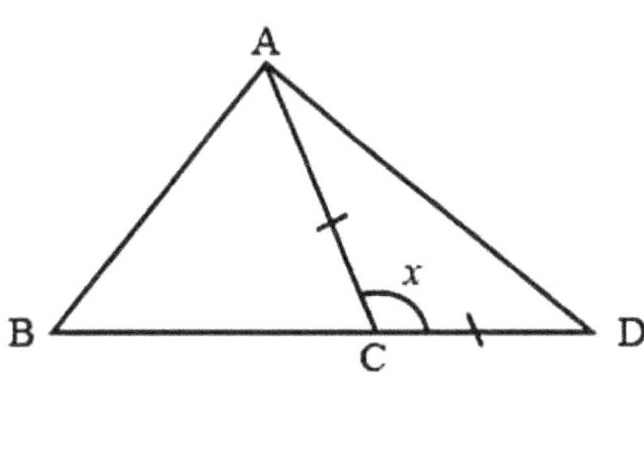

____________________ ____________________

3. A frog jumps 3 steps at a time starting from 0. Count the jumps he takes to reach 27. So, he has taken 27÷ 3 = ______ jumps. He has taken _________ jumps, if he is at 36. If he is at 42, he has taken _______ jumps.

4. Pandelonia wants 1850 sacks of cement for making a house. A truck carries the maximum load of 250 sacks at a time. How many trips will the truck make for carrying all the sacs of cement? The fellow driver charges ` Rs 900 for a trip. How much will Pandelonia pay the driver for all the trips?

5. Meera made 204 candles to sell in the market. She makes packets of 6. How many packets will she make? If she packs them in packets of 12, then how many packets will she make?

6. Tamanna used a box having capacity of holding 16 sweets for packing all the 3280 sweets. She needs _____ boxes of such types for packing all the sweets.

7. Complete the following:
   a. 3 x 4 = 12 Division facts = ___________
   b. 36 ÷ 4 = 9 Multiplication facts = _____________
   c. 12 x 3 = 36 Division facts = _________ Multiplication facts = _____________
   d. Repeated addition is __________________
   e. Repeated subtraction is _________________
   f. Division Rule: Dividend = ___________ x _____________ + _______________
   g. 8 x 3 = 24, 24 is ___________ of 3 and 8. 3 and 8 are __________ of 24

8. Some letters are given which are numbered 1, 2, 3, 4 and 5. Find that combination of numbers so that letters arranged accordingly form a meaningful word.

E L P T A

1 2 3 4 5

(A) 5, 2, 3, 4, 1 **(B)** 5, 2, 3, 1, 4 **(C)** 3, 1, 4, 5, 2 **(D)** 5, 4, 1, 2, 3

---

9. Find a figure from the options which completes the Fig. (X).

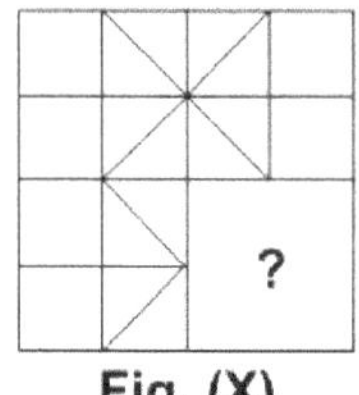

Fig. (X)

(A) 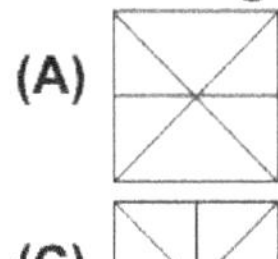

(B) 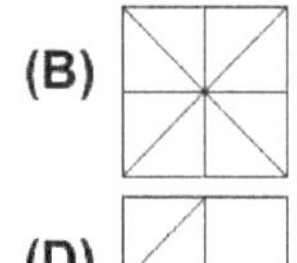

(C)

(D)

---

10. Standing on a platform, Amit told Sonia that Delhi was more than 10 km but less than 15 km from there. Sonia knew that it was more than 12 km but less than 14 km. If both of them were correct, which of the following could be the distance of Delhi from there?

(A) 11 km **(B)** 12 km **(C)** 13 km **(D)** 15 km

---

11. In the following series one term is wrong. Find the wrong term.

2, 18, 4, 20, 8, 22, 16, 25, 32, 26

(A) 18 **(B)** 16 **(C)** 25 **(D)** 32

---

12. How many unit cubes are there in the given figure?

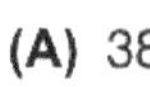

(A) 38

(B) 48

(C) 51

(D) 46

---

13. The given question consists of figures (i), (ii), (iii) and (iv). There is a definite relationship between figures (i) and (ii). Establish a similar relationship between figures (iii) and (iv) by selecting a suitable figure from the options that would replace (?) in figure (iv).

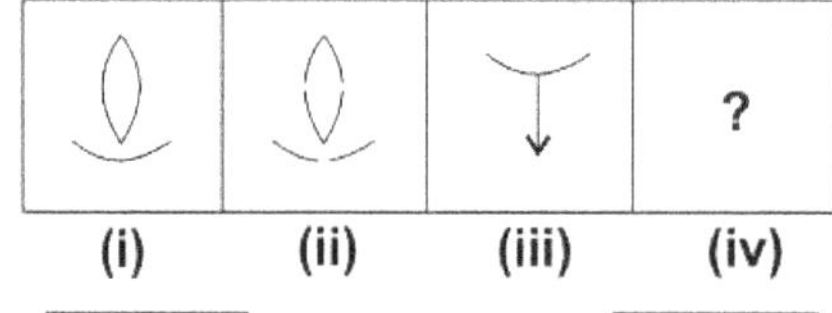

(A) 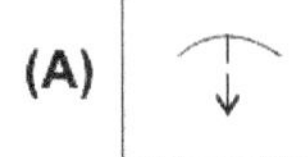 **(B)** 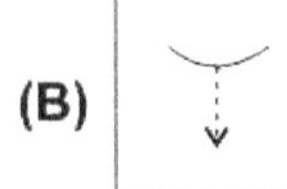 **(C)** 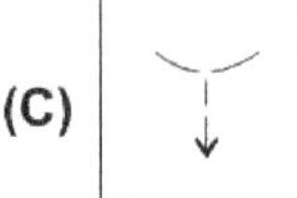 **(D)** 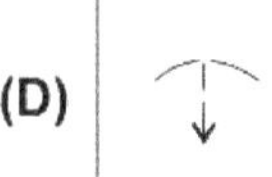

Worksheet 12

Use rounding to estimate. Then multiply.

1. 1109 × 3
2. 6043 × 4
3. 5180 × 7
4. 9205 × 5
5. 6089 × 8

6. 4009 × 5
7. 8400 × 8
8. 3090 × 6
9. 7008 × 9
10. 9060 × 4

11. 23,016 × 5
12. 68,509 × 8
13. 40,243 × 7
14. 52,050 × 4
15. 80,403 × 6

16. 83,600 × 3
17. 90,053 × 5
18. 40,070 × 8
19. 80,003 × 7
20. 89,000 × 9

Find the product. You may use the Distributive Property.

21. 6 × 9081
22. 9 × 3014
23. 7 × 4209
24. 5 × 4870
25. 4 × 20,859
26. 8 × 68,806
27. 5 × 70,042
28. 3 × 68,006
29. 8 × 25,070
30. 9 × 90,506
31. 6 × 76,080
32. 7 × 58,004
33. 9 × 91,006
34. 4 × 78,500
35. 5 × 90,003
36. 8 × 79,000
37. 3 × 70,008
38. 7 × 90,098
39. 4 × 170,009
40. 6 × 703,007

41. Find outer boundary of each of the following figures:

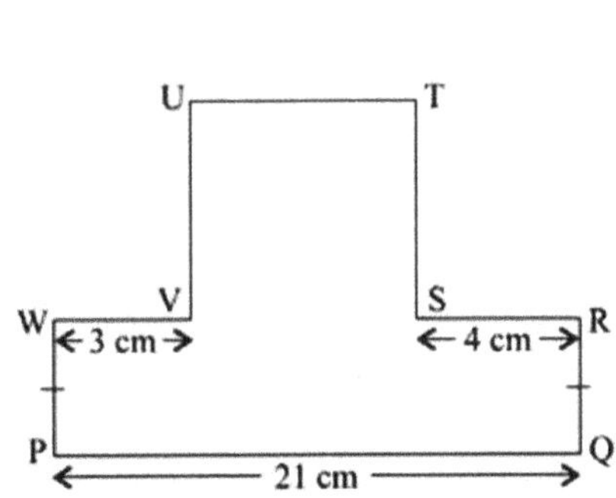

____

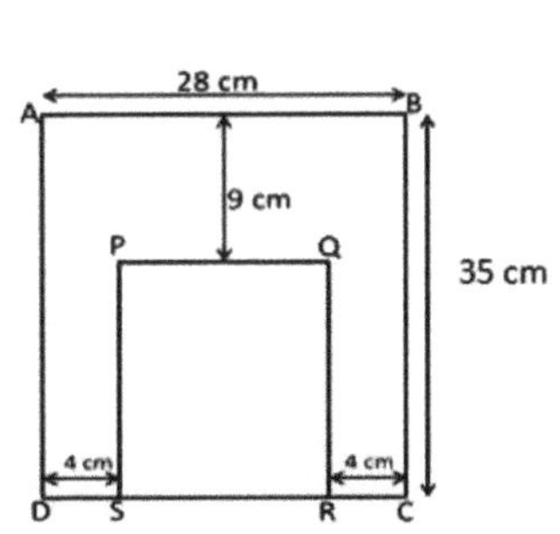

____

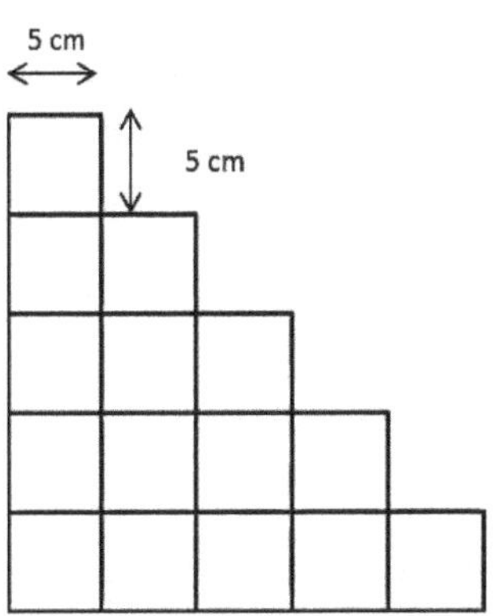

____

42. 43% of 1/96 X 10^4 = ______________.

Worksheet 13

1. Which of the following shows correct descending order?

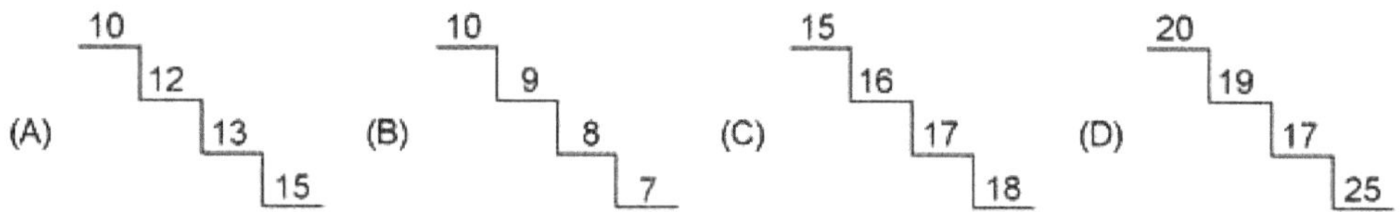

2. Latika, Monika and Sonika are sitting in a row. Latika is sitting between Monika and Sonika. Which of the following is the correct order?

(A) 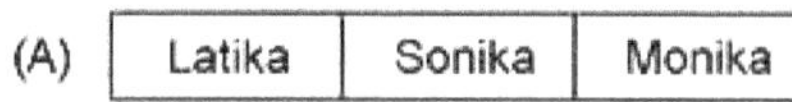

Latika	Sonika	Monika

(B) 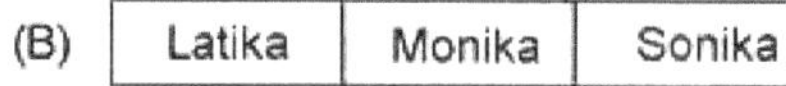

Latika	Monika	Sonika

(C) 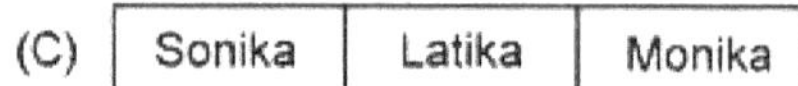

Sonika	Latika	Monika

(D) 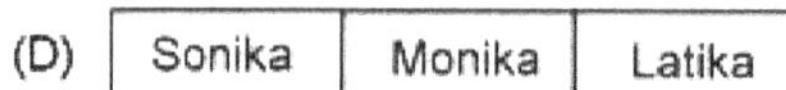

Sonika	Monika	Latika

3. The [frog] can jump two steps at a time. If it is at 5th step, where will it be after 2 jumps?

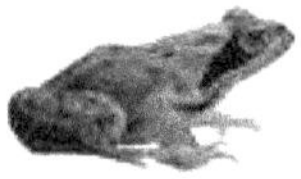

(A) 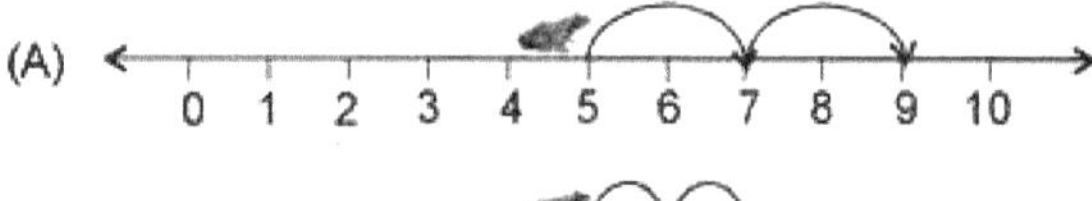

(B) 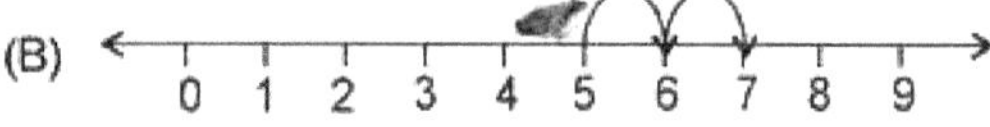

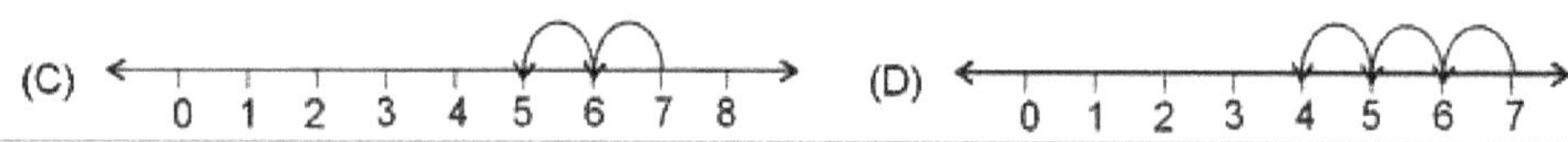

4. Four friends are celebrating their birthdays. The candles on cake shows their ages. Who is the eldest?

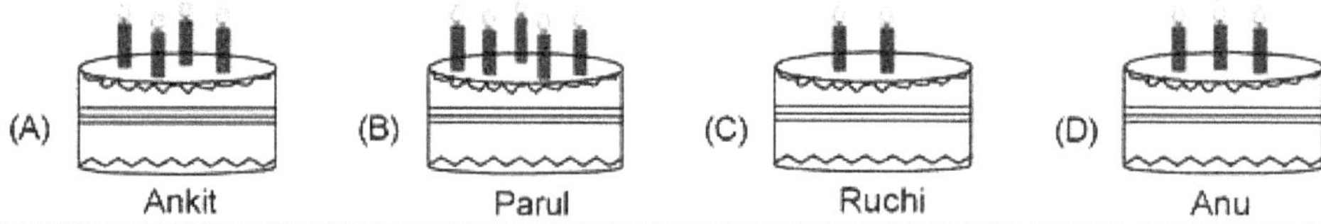

5. Given two baskets shows the number of apples.

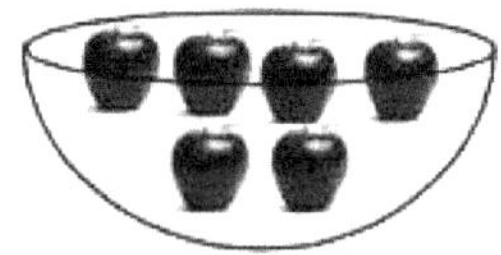

Yellow basket

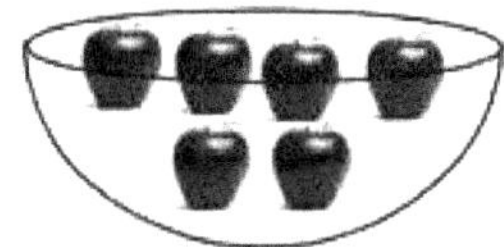

Red basket

Which is correct statement?

(A) Yellow basket has more apples than red basket.

(B) Red basket has more apples than yellow basket.

(C) Both red and yellow baskets have equal apples.

(D) Red basket has less apples than yellow basket.

6. Which number in the following number pattern is just before 30?

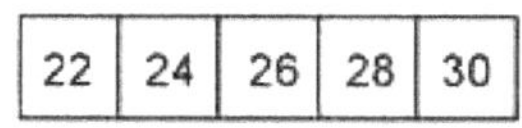

22	24	26	28	30

(A) 26 (B) 28 (C) 24 (D) 22

7. What fraction of each of the following figure is shaded?

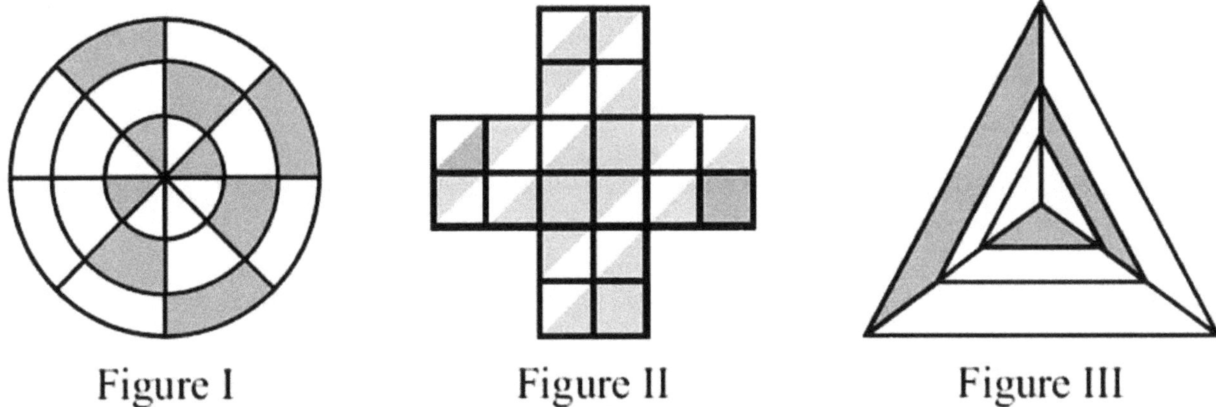

8. Marks obtained by different students in an examination is displayed below:

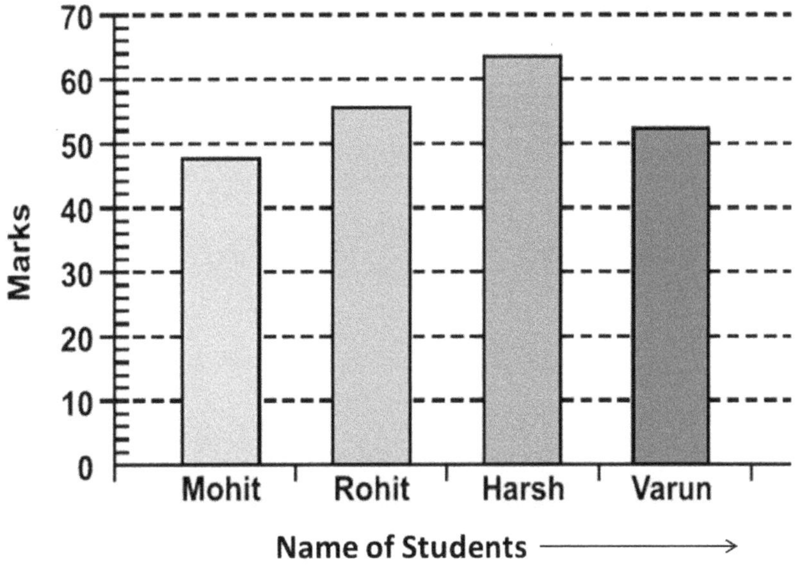

a) Who scored maximum marks?
b) How many students scored below 60?
c) Students scoring below 50 are considered as bad scorer. How many of the fellow students were in the list of bad scorers?
d) What percent of all the students scored above 60 marks?

9. Complete the following number pattern:

1 + 3	= 2 X 2	= 2^2	= 4;
1 + 3 + 5	= 3 X 3	= 3^2	= 9;
1 + 3 + … + 21	= __ X __	= $\_\_\_^2$	= ___;

Worksheet 14

1. Tilottama bought 16 cakes by paying Rs sixteen hundred ninetysix. She wanted to collect another four cakes at the same rate. The total amount payable by her at the cash counter will be Rs. _____________.

2. A supermarket receives 625 cases of oranges. Each case holds 135 oranges. How many oranges in all does the supermarket receive?

3. Mr Bandarnayake got an assignment which can be finished by employing 13 workers for 12 days. New work order came for finishing the similar assignment in 13 days. Number of workers to be appointed at the new site will be ________.

4. 12% of 12% of $\frac{1}{144}$ X 13,013 = __________.

Use rounding to estimate. Then multiply.

5. 541×122 **6.** 345×211 **7.** 217×115 **8.** 431×134 **9.** 501×272

10. 244×152 **11.** 420×135 **12.** 305×271 **13.** 360×417 **14.** 742×343

Find the product.

15. 354×120 **16.** 417×131 **17.** 252×204

18. 475×218 **19.** 624×382 **20.** 728×618

21. 683×4234 **22.** 527×6049 **23.** 482×2979

24. 236×1143 **25.** 962×4085 **26.** 819×2709

27. $n \times 328$ when $n = 274$ **28.** $n \times 853$ when $n = 418$

29. $275 \times n$ when $n = 362$ **30.** $415 \times n$ when $n = 672$

30. Continue the patterns:

a) 550, 560, 570, , , , .

b) 910, 920, 930, 940, , , , .

c) 209, 207, 205, , , , .

d) 401, 402, 403, , , , .

2. Selected Assignments

Assignment A

1. Find areas enclosed by the following figures:

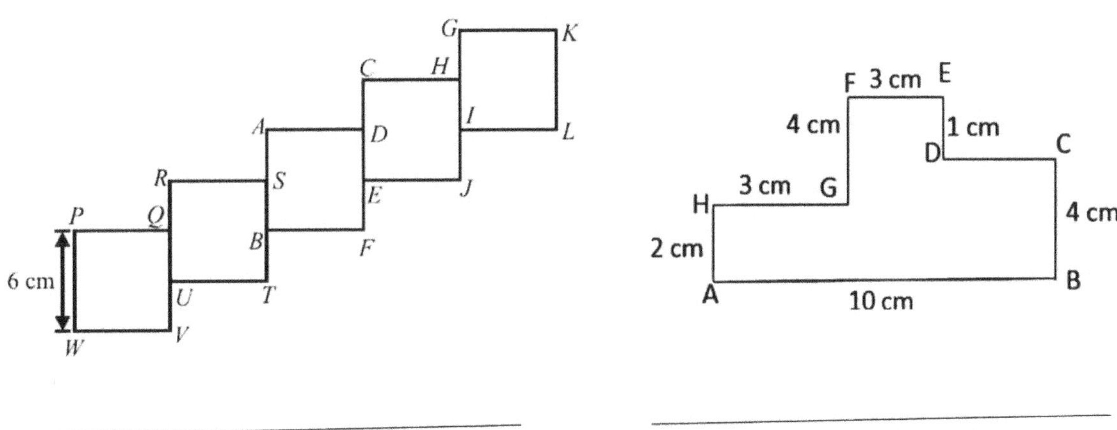

2. Write times displayed in the following wall mount clocks:

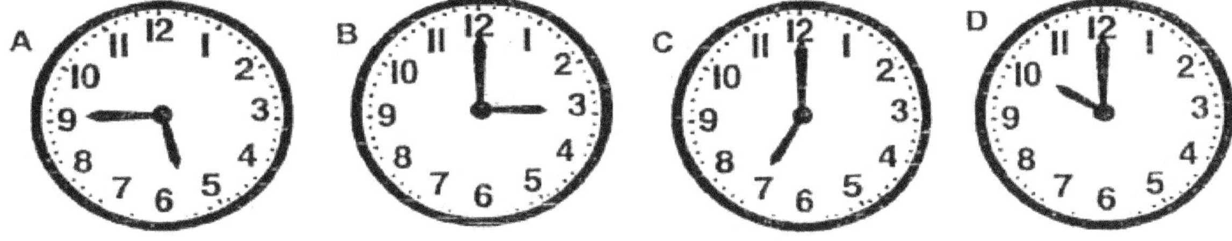

3. Harpreet observed that a wall mount clock strikes 4 bells at 4 O'Clock in 4 seconds. It will strike 10 bells at 10 O'Clock in ____ seconds.

4. Bandarnayake observed that a Goods Train covered a distance of 100 m in ten seconds. Another Mail train covers 72 km in one hour. Compare speed of both the train.

5. Mr. Bandarnayake finishes his journey of 120 km in 2 and half hours. While moving with same speed he has visited his native place and it took him 45 minutes to drive to and fro his native place from his home of countryside. Find the distance of his native place from the countryside.

6. What least number must be subtracted from a seven digit greatest number to make the number divisible by 11?

7. Dhanu has the longest jump of 3 metres 40 cm. Gurjeet is second. His jump is 20 cm less than Dhanu's. Gopi comes third.

His jump is only 5 cm less than Gurjeet's jump.

How long are Gurjeet's and Gopi's jumps?

Try and see how far you can jump.

How far can you throw a ball? ___________ metres.

Look for a big ball, like a football or volleyball. How far can you kick it? ___________

CONVERSION

4 m 55 cm = _____ cm	7 m 6 cm = _____ cm	8 m 89 cm = _____ cm
7 m 45 cm = _____ cm	3 m 16 cm = ______ cm	18 m 8 cm = _____ cm
8 km 45 m = ____ km	5 km 520 m = _____ km	44 km 660 m = ____ km
18 km 425 m = ____ km	5 km 50 m = _____ km	23 km 166 m = ____ km

8. Observe the table depicted below and aanswer questions as follows: ---

Sports	World Record	Indian Record
High Jump (Men)	Javier S. (2m 45 cm)	Chandra Pal (2m 17 cm
Long Jump (Men)	Mike P. (8m 95 cm)	Amrit Pal (8m 8 cm)
High Jump (Women)	Stefka K. (2m 9 cm)	Bobby A. (1m 91 cm)
Long Jump (Women)	Galina C. (7m 52 cm)	Anju G. (6m 83 cm)

A. How many centimetres more should Chandra Pal jump to equal the Men'sWorld Record for high jump?

B. How many centimetres higher should Bobby A. jump to reach 2 metres?

Remember that 1m= 100 cm; Half metre = ______ cm; one and half metre = _______;

C. Galina's long jump is nearly

a) 7 metres b) 7 and a half metres c) 8 metres

D. Look at the Women's World Records. What is the difference between the longest jump and the highest jump?

E. If Mike P. could jump ______ centimetres longer, his jump would be full 9 metres.

F. Whose high jump is very close to two and half metres?

a) Stefka K. b) Chandra Pal c) Javier S. d) Bobby A

9. Make 3 different 3 digit numbers using 1, 9 and 8, where each digit can be used only once.

   Check which of these numbers are divisible by 9.

10. Which numbers among 2, 3, 5, 6, 9 divides 12345 exactly? Write 12345 in reverse order and test now which numbers divide it exactly?

11. Write different 2 digit numbers using digits 3, 4 and 5. Check whether these numbers are divisible by 2, 3, 5, 6 and 9?

12. Write the smallest digit and the greatest possible digit in the blank space of each of the following numbers so that the number formed are divisible by 3.

    i. __ 6724 ii. 4765__ 2 iii. 7221__ 5

13. Find the smallest number that must be added to 123, so that it becomes exactly divisible by 5?

14. Find the smallest number that has to be subtracted from 256, so that it becomes exactly divisible by 10?

15. Prasad and Raju met in the market on 1st of this month. Prasad goes to the market every 3rd day and Raju goes every 4th day. On what day of the month will they meet again?

16. During an experiment Dana recorded the following temperatures: 22°C, 12°C, 15°C, 5°C, 8°C. If this pattern continues, predict the tenth temperature in the series.

17. Scientists built earthquake stations at different elevations. One station is 75 m above sea level, and a second is 35 m below sea level. What is the difference in height between the two stations?

18. A diamond-mine entrance begins at 75 ft above sea level. Workers discover diamonds 48 ft below sea level. How deep is the mine at that point?

19. A parachutist opens her parachute at an altitude of 5000 ft. Her change in altitude is 25 ft per second.

    a. Write an equation to find her altitude h at a time after she opens her parachute.

    b. How far, written as an integer, has she descended in 12 seconds?

    c. What is her altitude 12 seconds after she opens her parachute?

20. Observe the pattern and complete it:

    a) 112 + 9 = 112 + 10 − 1 = 122 − 1 = 121
    b) 112 + 99 = 112 + 100 − 1 = 212 − 1 = 211
    c) 112 + 999 = 112 + 1000 − 1 = _____ − 1 = ________;

21. One sixteenth of 8,080 + one nineteenth of 38038 = ____________.

Assignment B

1. What percent of 12.5 is 0.25?
2. 5% of 5 + 15% of 300 + 20% of 600 = ____________.
3. Weight of all the three balls shown in the figure is same. Weight of a ball = __________.

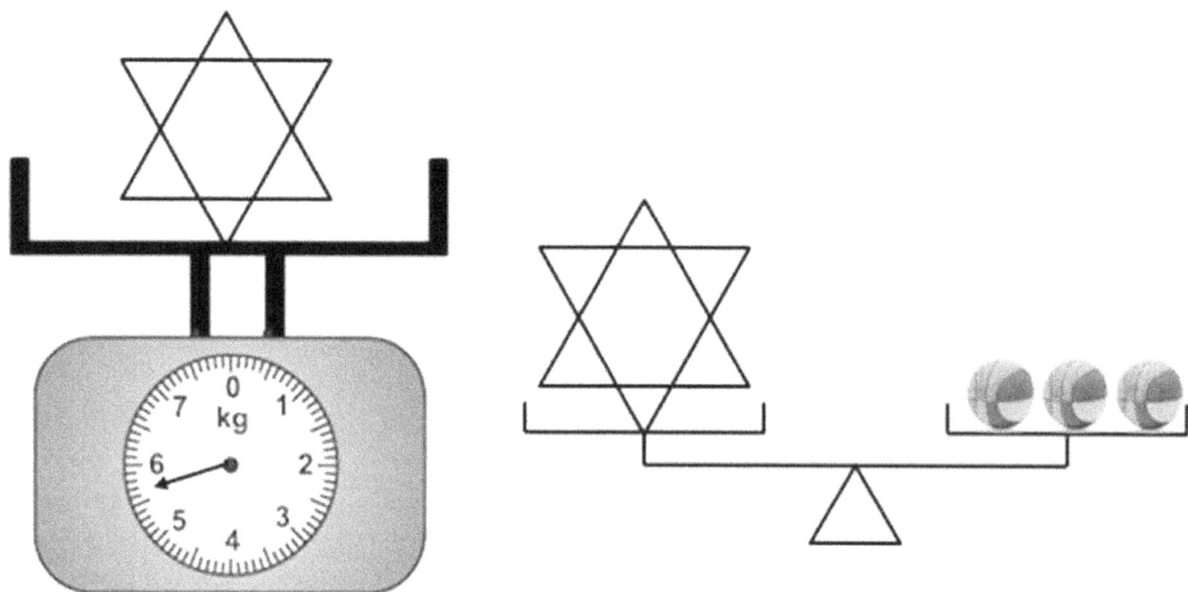

4. What is the value of the following expression?

$$84{,}000 \times 10 + 24{,}000 \div 2 + (1{,}80{,}000 \div 3)$$

5. Draw top portion of the following figures.

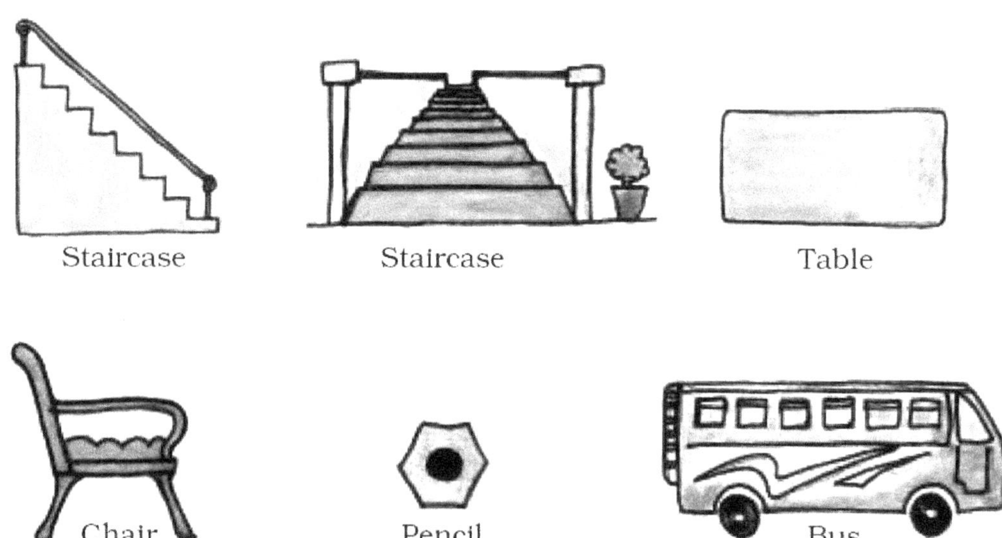

6. 20% of 30% of $100\frac{1}{6}$ = ___________.

7. Find outer boundary of the following figure.

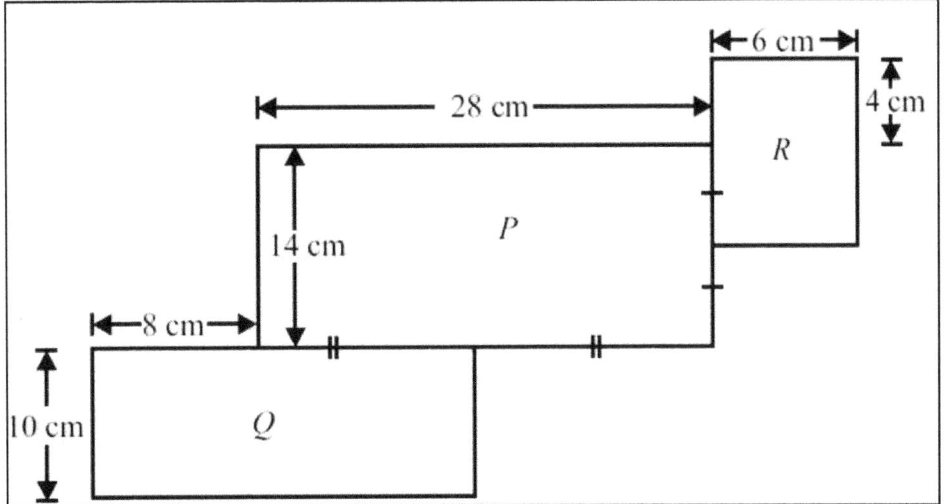

8. What fraction of the following figures are shaded?

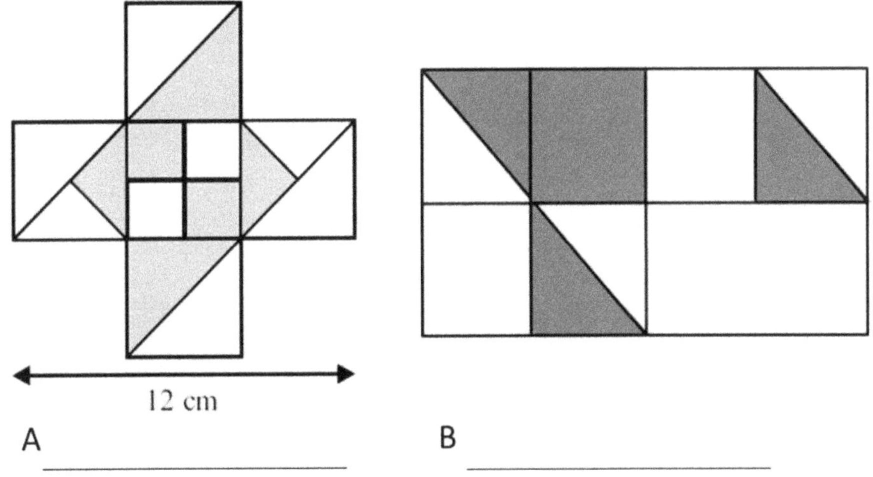

A ____________________ B ____________________

9. Find the missing character.

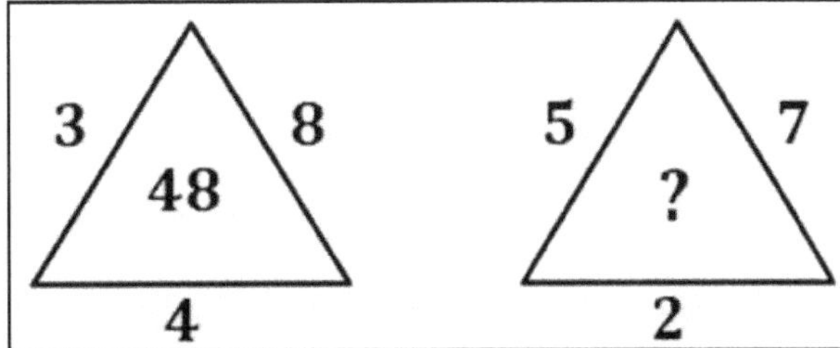

10. Solve the following:

a. What fraction of a day is equal to three hours?

b. Find the greatest possible divisor of 125, 625 and 3125 which can divide all these numbers leaving no remainder.

Find the product.

11. 8×30 **12.** 6×20 **13.** 40×9 **14.** $80{,}500 \times 7$

15. 15×67 **16.** 3023×83 **17.** 215×356 **18.** 605×4582

19. $372 \times \$1.59$ **20.** $625 \times \$4.37$ **21.** $394 \times \$7.85$

Use rounding to estimate. Then multiply.

22. 86×24 **23.** 246×26 **24.** 607×47 **25.** 318×64 **26.** 215×31

27. 416×258 **28.** 346×517 **29.** 237×608 **30.** 6289×413 **31.** 7385×329

32. $\$4.29 \times 32$ **33.** $\$7.48 \times 62$ **34.** $\$26.42 \times 104$ **35.** $\$72.48 \times 320$ **36.** $\$6.75 \times 342$

37. How many of the following shapes must be shaded to kee one fifth of the entire figure unshaded?

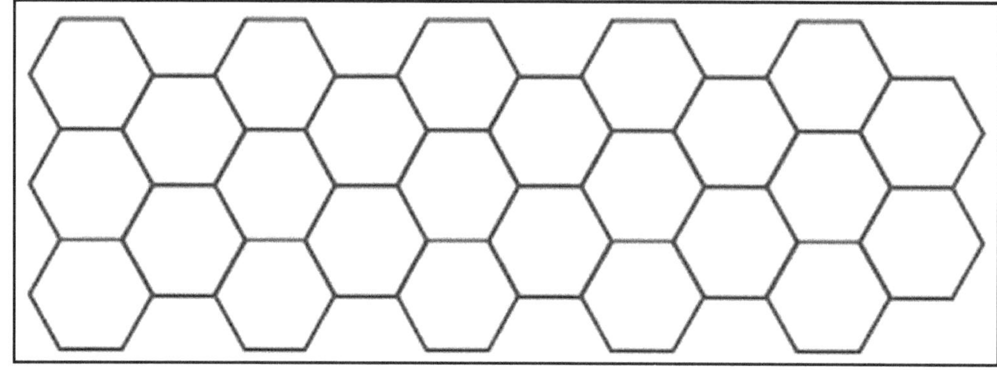

38. A zoo purchased 50 parrots during the month of July. How many of them died before the month of November?

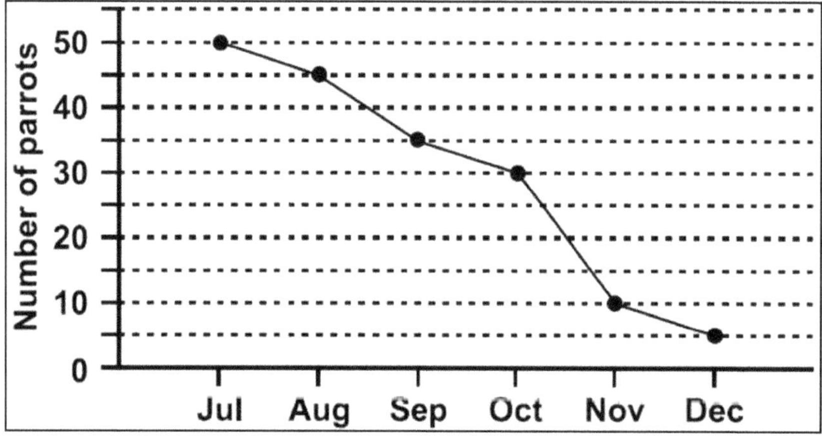

39. four fifth of six nineteenth of 95,095 = ______________.

Assignment C

1. Solve the following:

   Find the value of $(P+Q+R)\times S$ in the following addition problem.

$$\begin{array}{cccccccc} 2 & \boxed{P} & 0 & 6 & 8 & 4 & 1 & 5 \\ +3 & 1 & 2 & \boxed{Q} & 4 & 2 & 2 & 6 \\ \hline \boxed{S} & 0 & 2 & 7 & 2 & \boxed{R} & 4 & 1 \end{array}$$

2. Value of decimal in the box = ____________.

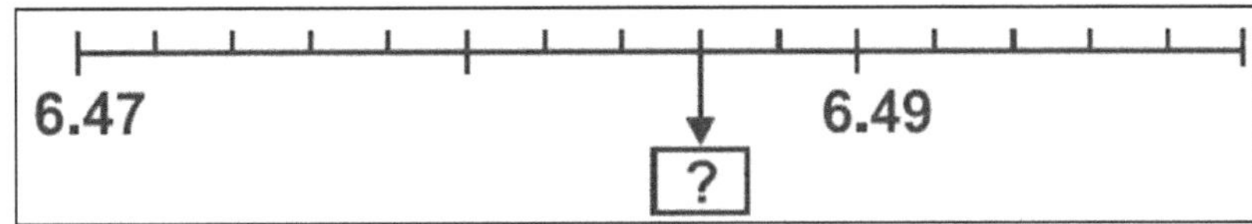

3. Divisibility rules for cerain prime numbers are explained. These rules can be used differently to solve mathematical problems.

   Tests of Divisibility :

   (a) Divisibility by 10 – The number should have 0 (Zero) in its ones place. For example - 70, 1050 are divisible by 10.

   (b) Divisibility by 5 :– The number should have either 0 or 5 in its ones place. For example - 20, 35 are divisible by 5.

   (c) Divisibility by 2 :– The number should have 0, 2, 6 or 8 in its ones place. For example - 124, 238 are divisible by 2.

   (d) Divisibility by 3 :– The sum of the digits of the number must be a multiple of 3. For example - 765 is divisible by 3 as 7+6+5 = 18, which is a multiple of 3.

   (e) Divisibility by 9 :– The sum of the digits of the number must be a multiple of 9. For example - 26541 is divisible by 9, as the sum of its digits, 2+6+5+4+1 is 18 which is a multiple of 9.

   Numbers having only two factors 1 and the number it-self are called prime numbers. Numbers having more than two prime factors are called Composite numbers.

   Set of Prime Numbers in between 1 and 200 is given below:

   2, 3, 5, 7, 11, 13, 17, 19, 23, 29, 31, 37, 41, 43, 47, 53, 59, 61, 67, 71, 73, 79, 83, 89, 97, 101, 103, 107, 109, 113, 127, 131, 137, 139, 149, 151, 157, 163, 167, 173, 179, 181, 191, 193, 197, 199.

4. What least number should be subtracted from the greatest dive digit number to make the value divisible by 8?

Aid Box I:

Divide and check.

1. $5\overline{)47}$	**2.** $4\overline{)39}$	**3.** $3\overline{)25}$	**4.** $7\overline{)59}$	**5.** $8\overline{)76}$
6. $6\overline{)51}$	**7.** $9\overline{)87}$	**8.** $6\overline{)49}$	**9.** $7\overline{)60}$	**10.** $4\overline{)23}$
11. $4\overline{)31}$	**12.** $6\overline{)38}$	**13.** $5\overline{)33}$	**14.** $8\overline{)79}$	**15.** $7\overline{)68}$

Find the quotient and the remainder.

16. $58 \div 6$	**17.** $65 \div 8$	**18.** $29 \div 4$	**19.** $62 \div 7$
20. $32 \div 7$	**21.** $49 \div 5$	**22.** $75 \div 8$	**23.** $89 \div 9$
24. $26 \div 3$	**25.** $51 \div 9$	**26.** $47 \div 6$	**27.** $53 \div 8$

28. Coomplete each of the following division ---

1.
```
     7 8 ? ?
  6)4 7,1 3 0
   -4 2
      5 1
     -? ?
        ? 3
       -? ?
          ? 0
         -? ?
            ?
```

2.
```
     9 5 ? ? R ?
  8)7 6,4 3 8
   -7 2
      4 4
     -? ?
        ? 3
       -? ?
          ? 8
         -? ?
            ?
```

3.
```
     ? ? ? ? ? R ?
  9)8 2 7,4 3 8
   -8 1
      1 7
     -  ?
        ? 4
       -? ?
          ? ?
         -? ?
            ? ?
           -? ?
              ?
```

29. The British Library's General Catalogue of Printed Books to 1995 contains about six million records from three files: British Library Catalogue, Humanities and Social Sciences Catalogue, and Science Reference and Information Service Catalogue. A typical reader would need 6 months to scan 198,000 catalog pages. If a typical reader can scan an equal number of catalog pages each month, how many catalog pages can he scan in one month?

30. Julia stores 3,535 cans of juice on 7 shelves in a stockroom. Each shelf has the same number of cans of juice stored on it. How many cans of juice are stored on each shelf?

31. A vendor packs 12,784 apricots in 6 cases. Each case holds the same number of apricots. How many apricots are in each case? How many apricots are left over?

Aid Box II:

Write each division using compatible numbers.

1. 1758 ÷ 4 **2.** 3951 ÷ 5 **3.** 7453 ÷ 8 **4.** 8326 ÷ 9

5. 9875 ÷ 23 **6.** 4282 ÷ 34 **7.** 63,792 ÷ 59 **8.** 84,796 ÷ 78

Estimate the quotient.

9. 1957 ÷ 4 **10.** 4893 ÷ 5 **11.** 6397 ÷ 8 **12.** 3319 ÷ 9

13. 2679 ÷ 83 **14.** 8529 ÷ 92 **15.** 4813 ÷ 68 **16.** 7945 ÷ 94

17. 83,592 ÷ 94 **18.** 39,125 ÷ 58 **19.** 61,958 ÷ 75 **20.** 38,958 ÷ 49

Estimate to compare. Write <, =, or >.

21. 27,903 ÷ 7 _?_ 35,903 ÷ 9 **22.** 5798 ÷ 3 _?_ 11,938 ÷ 6

23. 2829 ÷ 23 _?_ 4173 ÷ 13 **24.** 12,636 ÷ 24 _?_ 15,296 ÷ 32

25. 46,879 ÷ 18 _?_ 49,362 ÷ 19 **26.** 69,135 ÷ 27 _?_ 56,238 ÷ 16

27. For which of the following conditions would you use a histogram to represent data?

(i) The number of letters for different areas in a postman's bag.

(ii) The height of competitors in an athletics meet.

(iii) The number of cassettes produced by 5 companies.

(iv) The number of passengers boarding trains from 7 a.m to 7 p.m at a station.

28. The following list records the shoppers who visited during the first hour in the morning.

W W W G B W W M G G M M W W W W

G B M W B G G M W W M M W W W

M W B W G M W W W W G W M M W

W M W G W M G W M M B G G W

Make a frequency distribution table using tally marks. Draw a bar graph to illustrate it.

29. The weekly wages (in ₹) of thirty workers working in a definite factory are:

830, 835, 890, 810, 835, 836, 869, 845, 898, 890,

820, 860, 832, 833, 855, 845, 804, 808, 812, 840,

885, 835, 835, 836, 878, 840, 868, 890, 806, 840

Using tally marks make a frequency table with intervals as 800-810, 810-820 and so on.

Assignment D

I. Match the columns:

Match each definition with a term in the box.

a the written form of a number that shows the place value of each of its digits

b one of two or more numbers that are multiplied to form a product

c an approximate answer; to find an answer that is close to the exact answer

d to find addends that are nearly alike in order to estimate their sum

standard form
estimate
expanded form
clustering
factor

II. Evaluate:

1. $12 + 7 \times 9^2$ **2.** $6 \times (7 - 4)^2 + 13$ **3.** $14 \times (6 + 79) \div 7$

4. $19^4 - 100 + (85 - 4 \times 2)$ **5.** $156 \div 3 \times 7^3 + 19$ **6.** $(19 \times 6)^4 + 214 \div 2$

Evaluate. Use a calculator to check your work.

7. $12 + 7 \times 9^2$ **8.** $6 \times (7 - 4)^3 + 13$ **9.** $10^4 \times (6 + 78) \div 7$

10. $19^2 - 100 + (85 - 4 \times 2)$ **11.** $156 \div 3 \times 7^2 + 19$ **12.** $(20 \times 6)^2 + 214 \div 2$

13. $(4 \times 7 + 5)^2 \div 11 + 1$ **14.** $87 - 54 + 12 \times 5^3$ **15.** $3^3 \times (15 + 19 - 10) \div 9$

16. $(9^2 - 19) + 42 \div 6 \times 2^3$ **17.** $51 + 5^2 \times 31 + 18^2 - 9 \times 7$

Compare. Write <, =, or >.

18. $16^2 \times 5 - 90$ _?_ $90 \times 5 - 16^2$ **19.** $(64 + 192) \div 8^2$ _?_ $64 + 192 \div 8^2$

20. $195 \div 5 \cdot 9^2$ _?_ $195 \div (5 \cdot 9)^2$ **21.** $17(3)^2 \cdot (18 - 3)$ _?_ $17 \cdot 3^2 \cdot (18 - 3)$

III. Which least number of six digit is divisible by 3, 5 and 11 leaving remainder 2 in each case?

IV. If 7236 people visit the zoo in 12 days, what is the average number of people who visit the zoo in three consecutive days?

V. A number between 130 and 140 when divided by 12 has a quotient that contains the same two digits and has no remainder. Find the number.

VI. Write each of the following fractions:

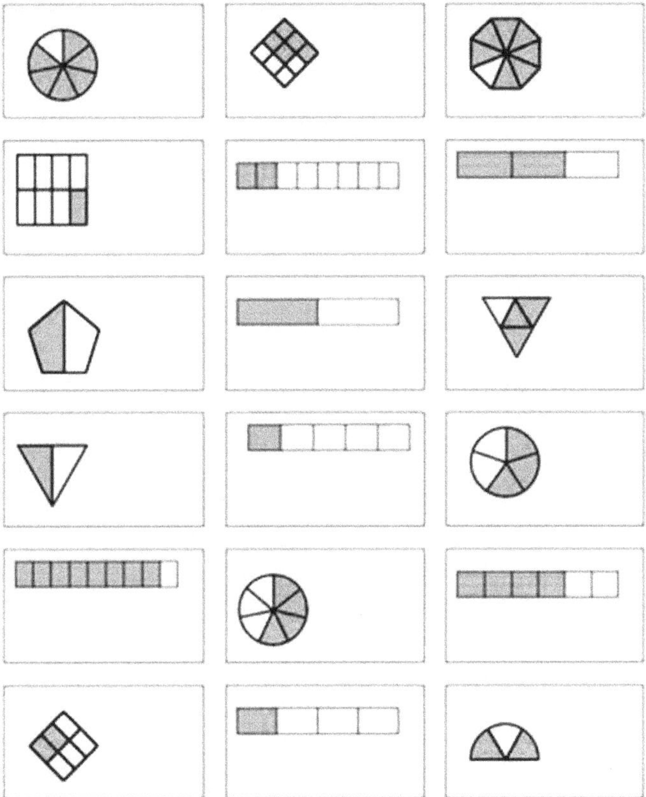

VII. What fraction of all the numbers starting from 1 to 50 are prime numbers?

VIII. Arya, Abhimanyu, and Vivek shared lunch. Arya has brought two sandwiches, one made of vegetable and one of jam. The other two boys forgot to bring their lunch. Arya agreed to share his sandwiches so that each person will have an equal share of each sandwich.

(a) How can Arya divide his sandwiches so that each person has an equal share?

(b) What part of a sandwich will each boy receive?

IX. Kristin received a CD player for her birthday. She bought 3 CDs and received 5 others as gifts. What fraction of her total CDs did she buy and what fraction did she receive as gifts?

X. Is there similarity in between following fractions? What types of fractions are there in the following list?

$$\frac{3}{9}, \frac{9}{27}, \frac{103}{309}, \frac{3009}{9027}, \frac{21063}{63189};$$

XI. 0.1 X 0.002 X 0.0003 = 6 X 10 ^{n} ; Value of n = _______;

XII. Find the representative fraction for the following figures:

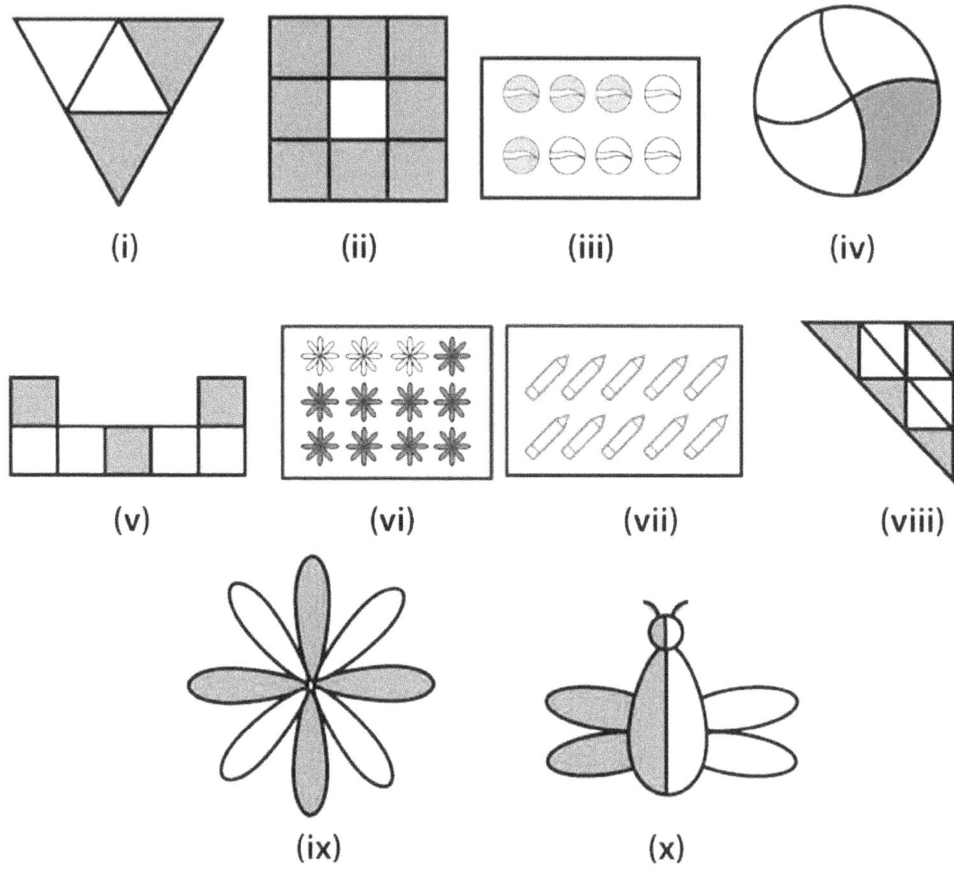

XIII. What types of fractions are there in the following set?

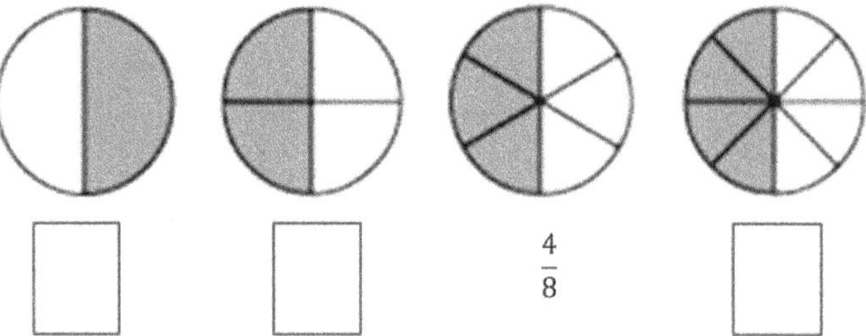

XIV. Rijuana finishes half of her assignment in 16 days and Spondelina can finish quarter of the same project in 8 days. They jointly participated in the project to complete it before time. Calculate the time they take to finish the project if they work jointly.

XV. Ramesh had 20 pencils, Sheelu had 50 pencils and Jamaal had 80 pencils. After 4 months, Ramesh used up 10 pencils, Sheelu used up 25 pencils and Jamaal used up 40 pencils. What fraction did each use up? Check if each has used up an equal fraction of her/his pencils?

Aid Box : ---

Compute.

1. $8 \times 2 \div 4$ **2.** $4 \times 6 + 3$ **3.** $2 \times 7 - 4$

4. $81 \div 9 - 3$ **5.** $64 \div 8 + 5$ **6.** $8 + 3 \times 4 - 5$

7. $9 + 45 \div 5 - 3$ **8.** $9 \times 4 \div 6 + 7$ **9.** $48 \div 6 \times 3 - 5$

10. $27 - 16 \div 4 + 2$ **11.** $18 - 3 \times 2 + 9$ **12.** $81 \div 9 - 2 \times 3$

Use the order of operations to compute.

13. $4 - 9 \div 3 - 1$ **14.** $16 \div 4 + 2 \times 6$

15. $(3 \times 7) + (64 \div 8)$ **16.** $(18 - 9) \div (1 + 2)$

17. $20 + 6 \div 3 - 7$ **18.** $24 - 8 \div 4 \times 3$

19. $18 \times (11 - 6)$ **20.** $7 + (19 - 2) \times 3$

21. $3 + 5 \times 10 \div 2 + 8$ **22.** $17 + 63 \div 3 \times 6 - 9$

23. $59 - 45 \div 5 \times 3 + 41$ **24.** $134 - 8 \div 4 \times 2$

25. $10 \times 4 + (49 \div 7) \times 2$ **26.** $(35 \div 5) \times 2 + 3 \times 6$

27. $18 - 3 \div 3 + (63 \div 3) - 6$ **28.** $19 - 4 \times 2 + (19 - 3) \div 4$

29. $(28 \div 7) + 5 - 3 + (7 \times 2)$ **30.** $4 + (29 - 2) \div 9 + (16 + 2)$

31. $(4 \times 8) - 5 + (0 \div 6)$ **32.** $(24 \div 6) - 3 + (2 \times 4)$

33. $2 + (3 \times 6) + n$ when $n = 10$ **34.** $(12 + 72) \div n$ when $n = 6$

35. $(28 + n) \times 4$ when $n = 32$ **36.** $(9 \times 8) - (n \times 6)$ when $n = 3$

37. $n \times 2 \div 2 + 24$ when $n = 8$ **38.** $6 + n - 3 \times 6 \div 9$ when $n = 2$

39. Calculate the value of A X B + C X D

A = $y + 48 \div n$ when $n = 6$; $y = 12$ C = $a \times b - 12$ when $a = 13$; $b = 29$

B = $4 \times (a + b) + 2$ when $a = 6$; $b = 3$ D = $(n - y) \div (2 \times y)$ when $n = 200$; $y = 40$

40. 20% of 30% of 0.11 = 11×10^{n} ; Value of n = _____.

Assignment E

Write four related facts using the given numbers.

1. 6, 7, 42
2. 5, 9, 45
3. 8, 9, 72
4. 3, 4, 12

Find the quotients.

5. 63 ÷ 9, 630 ÷ 9, 6300 ÷ 9, 63,000 ÷ 9
6. 54 ÷ 6, 540 ÷ 60, 5400 ÷ 600, 54,000 ÷ 6000
7. 35 ÷ 7, 350 ÷ 70, 3500 ÷ 70, 35,000 ÷ 70

Use basic facts to find the value of *n*.

8. $64{,}000 \div 80 = n$
9. $150{,}000 \div n = 3000$
10. $n \div 60 = 400$

Divide and check.

11. $9\overline{)3027}$
12. $8\overline{)5866}$
13. $24\overline{)49}$
14. $41\overline{)984}$
15. $31\overline{)1836}$
16. $15\overline{)945}$
17. $86\overline{)68{,}906}$
18. $73\overline{)78{,}146}$
19. $28\overline{)\$56.56}$
20. $17\overline{)\$35.02}$
21. $26\overline{)\$286.26}$
22. $64\overline{)\$204.80}$

Write whether each number is divisible by 2, 3, 4, 5, 6, 9, and/or 10.

23. 90
24. 795
25. 4152
26. 6252
27. 70,320

Estimate the quotient.

28. 845 ÷ 9
29. 1015 ÷ 29
30. 1836 ÷ 15

Use the order of operations to compute.

31. $36 - 3 \times 7 + 10 \div 5$
32. $(35 \div 7) + 2 \times 3 - 4$

33. Solve the following –

How much does each box of each kind of card cost?

Thank you cards =

Get well cards =

Birthday cards =

Anniversary cards =

Quantity	Item	Total Cost
25 boxes	Thank you cards	$ 86.25
32 boxes	Get well cards	$155.20
46 boxes	Birthday cards	$273.70
18 boxes	Anniversary cards	$125.10

34. Score of an examination is calculated on the basis of full marks assigned for a particular examination. Score is calculated in the form of a fraction having denominator 100. Sanjana got 67 out of 80 in an examination. Score of Lina was 78 out of 90 and that of Mohini was 83 out of 100. Who scored better in the examination?

Aid Box ---

I: Find the perimeter ---

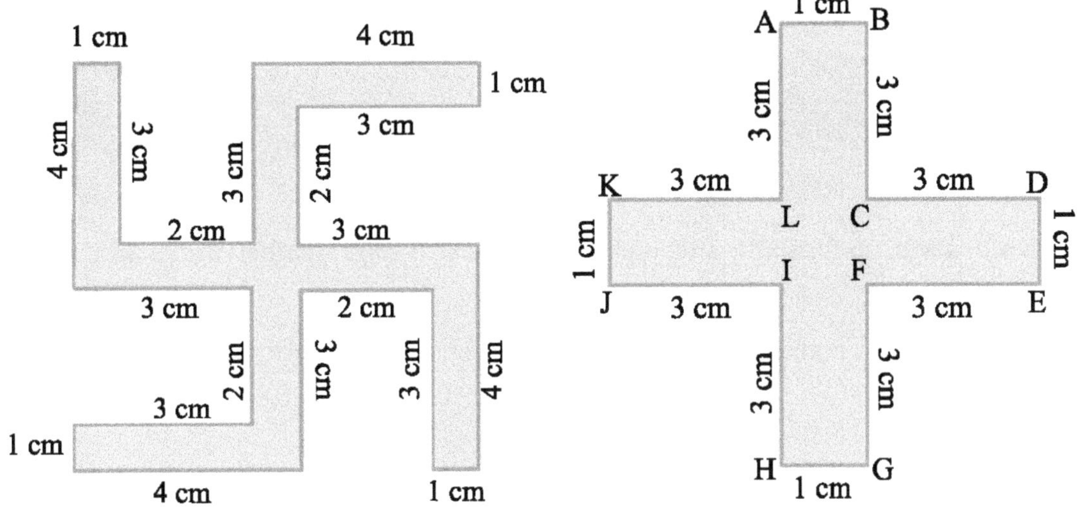

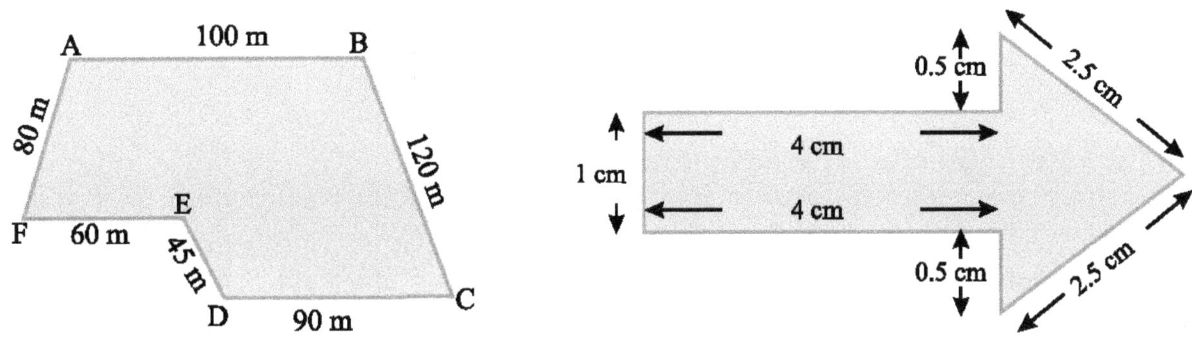

II: How many non-overlapping triangles can be accommodated inside a pentagon?

III: What fraction of all the natural numbers from 1 to 100 are multiples of 5?

IV: Rounak observed that a goods train crosses a light post in 45 seconds. It was moving with a uniform velocity of 36 km/h. It that train continues moving with same velocity then the time taken by the train to cross a 1 km 40 m long platform is ______________.

V: If we add all the consecutive odd numbers then the product obtained will be the square of the number of values added. For example, 1 + 3 = 2 X 2 = 4. During one such computation a square value 12321 is obtained. Hoow many consecutive odd numbers were added?

Aid BoX 1:

1. Find the biggest and smallest number:

a) 27,645 64,393 39,760 41,647 b) 7,35,326 7,38,709 7,37,425 7,31,294

c) 8,24,269 6,45,796 9,38,400 7,50,424 d) 37,78,284 60,78,390 76,78,740 49,78,676

e) 4,68,30,240 5,70,39,520 3,62,47,840 5,76,28,580

2. The following cards with digits 0,7,9,4 and 5 are given. 0 7 9 4 5

The students are asked to form the smallest and greatest 5 digit number using all the cards. Find difference of these two numbers duly formed by students.

3. Form the biggest 6 digits number using all the digits given below: 6 , 4 , 0, 2, 5 and 9;

4. Complete the following:

___,494	fifty eight thousand four hundred ninety four
327,067	___ thousand sixty seven
908,____	908 thousand six hundred seventy four
_,743,475	5 million, 743 thousand four hundred seventy five
36,207,650	36 million, ___ thousand six hundred fifty
247,384,812	___ million 384 thousand eight hundred twelve
5,490,000,500	5 billion 490 million five hundred
6,742,165,000	6 billion 742 million 165 thousand.

5. Complete the following:

a. One complete circle covers _______ degrees

b. 60 minutes =_______ degrees.

c. Angle between two consecutive numbers in clock = _______ degrees

d. _______________lakhs = 1 crore

e. Right angle = ________ degrees

f. An obtuse angle is more than a ______ angle but less than _____ angle.

g. 2 x Right angle = _____ degrees.

h. ______ thousand makes 2 lakhs.

6. Write in standard form: 13 thousandth + 13 thousand + 13 ones = ____________________.

7. A ____________ has no definite length and no end points.

8. 5% of 5% of one fifth of 10^6 = ___________.

9. Do as instructed ---

1. Fill in the blanks by using laws under multiplication of whole numbers.

(i) 2 × _______ = 3 × ______

(ii) 112 × 528 = _______ × ______

(iii) 5 × (3 × 8) = (5 × 3) × _______

(iv) _______ × 7 = 7 × _______ = 0

(v) 9 × (2 + 16) = _______ × 2 + _______ × 16

(vi) (20 + 4) × 1 = _______ × 1 + 4 × _______

(vii) 17 × (8 – 3) = 17 × _______ – _______ × 3

(viii) (12 – 6) × 32 = 12 × _______ – 6 × _______

2. Fill in the blanks.

(i) 5 × 4 = □ × 5

(ii) 15 × (10 × 6) = (□ × 10)

(iii) 10 × (15 + 6) = (10 × 15) + (□ × 6)

(iv) 10 × (100 + 60) = (□ × 100) + (10 × □)

10. Write the value of fraction displayed in the following figure:

11. Complete the following:

Number	Sum of the digits at odd places (from the right)	Sum of the digits at even places (from the right)	Difference Is the given number divisible by 11
29843			
90002			
80927			
19091908	8+9+9+9=35	0+1+0+1=2	35-2=33 Yes
83568			

12. What least number should be added to seven digit smallest odd number to make it divisible by 11?

13. How many prime factors are there in the following number?

a)13013 b) 1690 c) 9797

Aid Box 2: ---

Simplify the following:

1. $\frac{1}{5} - \left\{ \frac{2}{5} \div \frac{4}{15} \times \frac{1}{2} - \left(\frac{1}{2} + \frac{2}{5} \right) \right\}$

2. $\frac{3}{4} + \left(\frac{4}{3} - \overline{\frac{1}{2} + \frac{2}{3}} + \frac{4}{5} \right)$

3. $\frac{7}{8} + \left\{ \frac{5}{7} + \left(\frac{1}{2} + \frac{1}{3} \right) \div \frac{5}{6} \right\}$

4. $\frac{5}{2} \times \left(\frac{5}{6} - \frac{2}{3} \right) \div \frac{2}{5} \times \left(\frac{3}{5} + \frac{6}{25} \right)$

5. $\left(\overline{\frac{2}{3} - \frac{3}{4}} \times \frac{1}{8} \right) \div \left(\frac{2}{3} - \overline{\frac{3}{4} + \frac{5}{8}} \right)$

6. $1\frac{1}{2} + \left[\frac{1}{3} \div \left\{ \frac{2}{5} \div \left(\frac{4}{5} - \overline{\frac{1}{10} + \frac{3}{5}} \right) \right\} \right]$

7. $\left[\frac{1}{2} + \left\{ \left(\frac{3}{4} \div \frac{9}{16} \right) \times 1\frac{1}{2} \right\} - 2\frac{1}{4} \right]$

8. $3\frac{1}{2} + \left\{ \left(10\frac{2}{5} - 5\frac{1}{3} \right) \div 3\frac{2}{3} \right\} - 1\frac{1}{5}$

9. $\left[\left(2\frac{3}{4} + 1\frac{2}{6} \right) \times \left(1\frac{1}{5} \div \frac{2}{5} \right) \right]$

10. $\left\{ \left(\frac{1}{2} - \frac{1}{3} \right) + \left(1\frac{2}{3} \div \frac{1}{9} \right) \right\} - \left\{ \left(\frac{5}{3} - \frac{1}{6} \right) \div \frac{9}{6} \right\}$

11. $\left[2\frac{1}{4} \times \left\{ 3\frac{1}{3} - \frac{1}{2} + \left(\frac{5}{3} - \frac{1}{6} \right) \right\} \right] + \frac{5}{6}$

Observe the following number papttern and complete the given steps:

24 × 9	= 24 × (10 – 1)
24 × 99	= 24 × (100 – 1)
24 × 999	= 24 × (1000 – 1)
12: 24 X ____	= 24 X (10000 – 1)
13: 24 X 999999	= ___ X (__________– 1) ;

14. Rijuana completed typing a letter in 25 minutes. She shared typing 20 such letters with her fellow partner working in the same office. They can finish typping all the letters in ____ hours.

15. 20 % of 20 % of 1000.001 = _____________.

16. Multiple Lines of Symmetry:

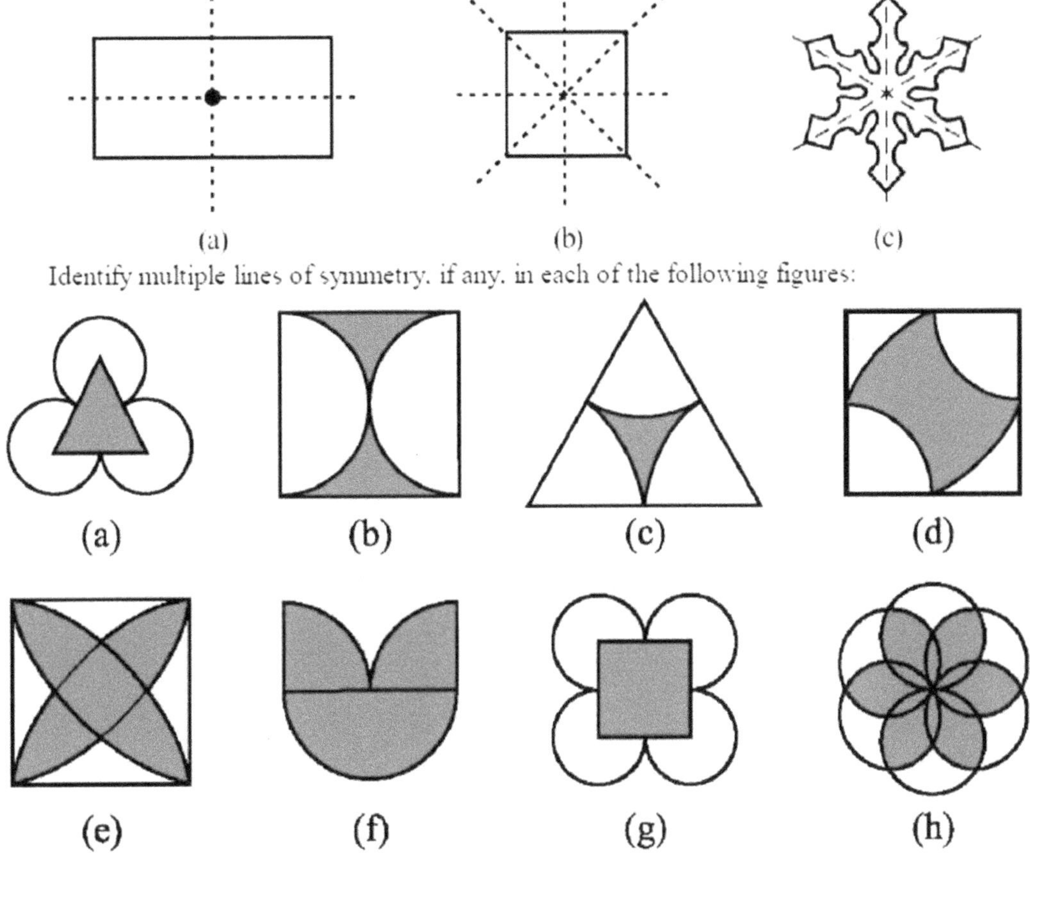

16. Fill in the blanks:

- The digits having only two lines of symmetry are_________ and __________.
- The digit having only one line of symmetry is __________.
- The number of digits having no line of symmetry is_________.
- The number of capital letters of the English alphabets having only vertical line of symmetry is________.
- The number of capital letters of the English alphabets having only horizontal line of symmetry is________.
- The number of capital letters of the English alphabets having both horizontal and vertical lines of symmetry is________.
- The number of capital letters of the English alphabets having no line of symmetry is__________.
- The line of symmetry of a line segment is the ________ bisector of the line segment.
- The number of lines of symmetry in a regular hexagon is __________.
- The number of lines of symmetry in a regular polygon of n sides is_______.
- A protractor has __________ line/lines of symmetry.

16. How many lines can be drawn passing through any two out of three non—collinear points?

18. Draw lines of symmetry.

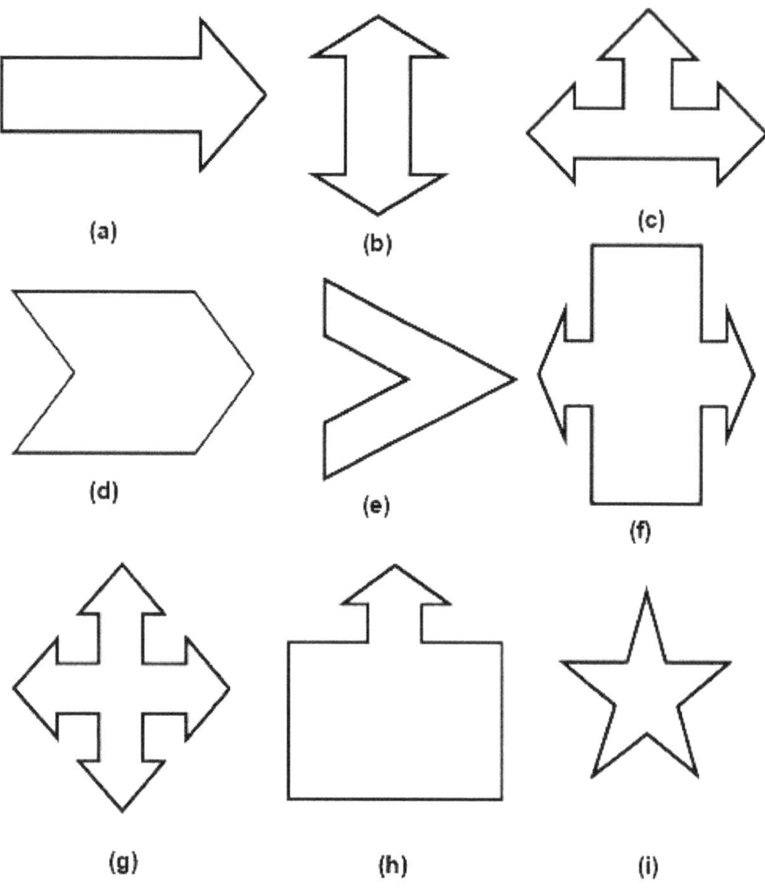

19. Comlete the following number pattern:

37 × 3 = 111

37 × __ = 222

37 × ___ = 333

37 × 12 = ___

37 × ___ = 555

37 × 18 = ___

37 × 21 = 777

37 × ___ = 888

37 × 27 = 999

20. Anum's family purchased 5 packets of cooking oil at the rate of Rs 121.80 per packet, 3 bags of rice at the rate of Rs 235.50 per bag and 40 kg flour at the rate of Rs 42.70 per kg. Find the total amount paid by her.

21. Sonalika purchased the following items for her home.

i. Two electric bulbs at the rate of Rs 80.95 each.
ii. Four small stools at the rate of Rs 105.50 each.
iii. Three tables at the rate of Rs 530.95 each.
iv. Six chairs at the rate of Rs 458.30 each.

Find the total amount paid by her.

Assignment F

I. Evaluate yourself: --

Tell whether the number is divisible by 2, 3, 4, 5, 6, 8, 9, and/or 10.

1. 333	**2.** 128	**3.** 225	**4.** 7535	**5.** 8289
6. 9410	**7.** 99,483	**8.** 67,704	**9.** 67,713	**10.** 67,722
11. 23,918	**12.** 35,932	**13.** 85,446	**14.** 40,620	**15.** 90,990
16. 17,934	**17.** 49,708	**18.** 77,075	**19.** 13,104	**20.** 486,890
21. 207,984	**22.** 352,860	**23.** 607,712	**24.** 581,889	**25.** 270,228

Find the missing digit or digits that would make each number divisible by the given number.

26. 3,95□; by 10

Think
The last digit must be **0** to be divisible by 10.

27. 17,84□; by 3	**28.** 243,05□; by 9	**29.** 698,39□; by 3 and by 9
30. 17,39□; by 5	**31.** 14,5□2; by 8	**32.** 13,□12; by 8 and by 3
33. 27,1□8; by 6	**34.** 20,71□; by 4	**35.** 502,7□5; by 3 and by 5
36. 37,6□3; by 9	**37.** 98□,124; by 6	**38.** 109,83□; by 4 and by 8

II: Application of divisibility rules:

Tell which numbers are divisible by 2.

1. 24	2. 47	3. 98	4. 436	5. 569	6. 760
7. 6135	8. 9842	9. 7764	10. 57,961	11. 79,778	12. 490,893
13. 65	14. 90	15. 873	16. 745	17. 4000	18. 9154
19. 35,960	20. 45,782	21. 73,590	22. 94,615	23. 870,520	24. 791,621

Some of the divisibility rules are as follows:

Divisibility rules of 5 : Digit at the unit place of number should be 5 or 0;

Divisibility rule of 10: Digit at ones place of the number should be 0;

Divisibility rule of 4: Number formed by digits at tens place and ones place of the given number should be a multiple of 4;

Divisibility rule of 3: Number formed by sum total of all the digits should be a multiple of 3;

Divisibility rule of 9: Number formed by sum total of all the digits should be a multiple of 9;

Tell which numbers are divisible by 4.

25. 96 **26.** 82 **27.** 324 **28.** 422 **29.** 3820 **30.** 9416

31. 79,131 **32.** 83,536 **33.** 20,904 **34.** 72,072 **35.** 131,616 **36.** 806,300

Tell which numbers are divisible by 3. Tell which numbers are divisible by 9.

37. 69 **38.** 87 **39.** 135 **40.** 159 **41.** 4320 **42.** 3519

43. 71,415 **44.** 83,721 **45.** 95,580 **46.** 81,693 **47.** 100,512 **48.** 560,373

Tell which numbers are divisible by 6.

49. 84 **50.** 93 **51.** 204 **52.** 396 **53.** 1029 **54.** 5415

55. 11,712 **56.** 30,609 **57.** 28,514 **58.** 72,144 **59.** 503,640 **60.** 712,820

Write whether each number is divisible by 2, 3, 4, 5, 6, 9, and/or 10.

61. 1425 **62.** 2360 **63.** 4390 **64.** 6570 **65.** 8735 **66.** 9822

III: Compatible Numbers:

Compatible numbers are numbers that are easy to compute mentally.

Compatible-number estimation may use different sets of

numbers to estimate a quotient.

Estimate: 17,452 ÷ 4 = 16,000 ÷ 4 = 4,000;

17,452 ÷ 4 = 20,000 ÷ 4 = 5,000; both the values are correct ;

Study following examples: --

63,356 ÷ 56 is about 1000. and 83,25 ÷ 41 is about 200.

Example 1: Seven Siberian tigers at the city zoo eat 2075 pounds of meat each week. If the tigers eat equal amounts, about how many pounds of meat does each tiger eat each week?

Solution: This problem can be solved mentally by using compatible numbers.

2075 can be rounded u to 2100;

Therefore 2075 ÷ 7 = 2100 ÷ 7 = 300;

Answer: Each tiger eats about 300 pounds of meat each week.

Exampple 2: 500 + 300 = 800. The numbers 500 and 300 are compatible for addition. Justify.

Solution: The numbers 500 and 300 are compatible for addition, since the sum of 800 can be easily calculated mentally.

Self Study: ---

Write each division using compatible numbers.

1. 1758 ÷ 4 **2.** 3951 ÷ 5 **3.** 7453 ÷ 8 **4.** 8326 ÷ 9

5. 9875 ÷ 23 **6.** 4282 ÷ 34 **7.** 63,792 ÷ 59 **8.** 84,796 ÷ 78

Estimate the quotient.

9. 1957 ÷ 4 **10.** 4893 ÷ 5 **11.** 6397 ÷ 8 **12.** 3319 ÷ 9

13. 2679 ÷ 83 **14.** 8529 ÷ 92 **15.** 4813 ÷ 68 **16.** 7945 ÷ 94

17. 83,592 ÷ 94 **18.** 39,125 ÷ 58 **19.** 61,958 ÷ 75 **20.** 38,958 ÷ 49

Estimate to compare. Write <, =, or >.

21. 27,903 ÷ 7 _?_ 35,903 ÷ 9 **22.** 5798 ÷ 3 _?_ 11,938 ÷ 6

23. 2829 ÷ 23 _?_ 4173 ÷ 13 **24.** 12,636 ÷ 24 _?_ 15,296 ÷ 32

25. 46,879 ÷ 18 _?_ 49,362 ÷ 19 **26.** 69,135 ÷ 27 _?_ 56,238 ÷ 16

27. While hunting, a cheetah can cover 1310 ft of ground in as few as 60 strides. About how many feet does it travel in 5 strides?

28. Bamboo is so low in nutrients that a giant panda eats as much as 175 kg of it in 20 hours. About how many pounds can it eat in a couple of hour?

29. A book covers 2370 pages with 24 lines on every page. If we make the same book of 2000 pages with increasing number of lines in each page then how many lines would be there on each page?

30. 513 + 299 = 812. 513 and 299 are not compatible for addition. Justify.

Answer: The numbers 513 and 299 are not compatible for addition, since the sum (812) cannot be easily calculated mentally. To estimate 513 + 299, replace 513 and 299 with the compatible numbers 500 and 300. An estimate of 513 + 299 is found by mentally calculating 500 + 300 = 800.

31. Consider the multiplication: 19.4 × 3.8 = 73.72. Are 19.4 and 3.8 are compatible for addition?

32. Estimate the following using compatible numbers:

A.72 × 78 B. 288 × 415 C. 398 X 511

Aid Box: Extreme and Mean

1. **Identify means and extremes in the following:**

   (i) $2:5 = 8:20$ (ii) $3:4 = 6:8$ (iii) $a:b = c:d$

2. **Decide whether the four numbers given in each of the following are in proportion or not:**

   (i) 18, 24, 30 and 40 (ii) 14, 19, 3 and 4
   (iii) 6, 8, 12 and 16 (iv) 15, 20, 16 and 21
   (v) 20, 30, 40 and 50 (vi) 21, 57, 28 and 76

3. **Find the value of x if the proportion $2 : x = 3 : 7$.**

4. **Find the fourth proportional in the following:**

   (i) 2, 3 and 6 (ii) $\frac{11}{24}$, $\frac{7}{15}$ and $\frac{5}{8}$ (iii) 16, 12 and 8
   (iv) 76, 28 and 57 (v) 36, 45 and 4 (vi) 40, 30 and 24

5. **Find the mean proportion in the following:**

   (i) 15 and 60 (ii) 18 and 32 (iii) 28 and 63
   (iv) 27 and 12 (v) 40 and 90 (vi) 44 and 99

Find proportion (direct and inverse)

(1) Direct proportion:

Consider the following chart.

Quantity of Pencils	Cost
4	Rs 20
3	Rs 15
2	Rs 10
1	Rs 5

What is the proportion of number of pencils and their cost.

In this chart, we can easily observe that the cost of pencils increases or decreases with the corresponding increase or decrease in the quantity of pencils.

6. Identify inverse proportion:

   a) The number of copies you buy and their total cost.
   b) The number of men doing a job and the time taken to finish it.
   c) The amount of time taken in a journey and speed of the vehicle.
   d) The number of boxes and the number of Pencils packed in them.

Assignment G

Use rounding to estimate. Then multiply.

5. 219 × 304 **6.** 391 × 104 **7.** 604 × 206 **8.** 508 × 709 **9.** 760 × 306

10. 360 × 703 **11.** 362 × 202 **12.** 937 × 209 **13.** 846 × 407 **14.** 928 × 607

15. 457 × 320 **16.** 936 × 430 **17.** 869 × 650 **18.** 947 × 730 **19.** 898 × 860

Find the product.

20. 600 × 739	**21.** 900 × 846	**22.** 700 × 4004	**23.** 500 × 8009
24. 720 × 365	**25.** 740 × 438	**26.** 860 × 549	**27.** 930 × 714
28. 507 × 367	**29.** 604 × 863	**30.** 708 × 905	**31.** 403 × 870
32. 230 × 1258	**33.** 470 × 2479	**34.** 605 × 4059	**35.** 209 × 7086
36. 601 × 3583	**37.** 807 × 7859	**38.** 920 × 7003	**39.** 640 × 8705

40. What fraction of the following shapes are shaded?

(i) 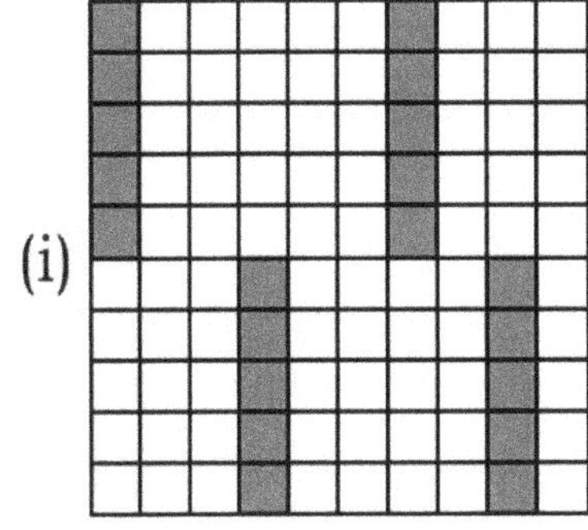 (ii) 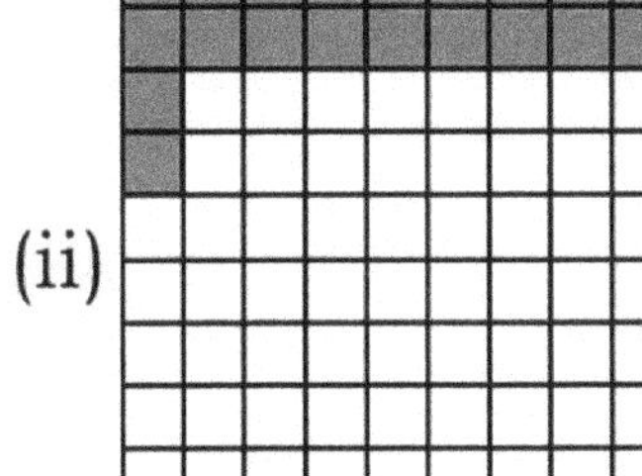 (iii) 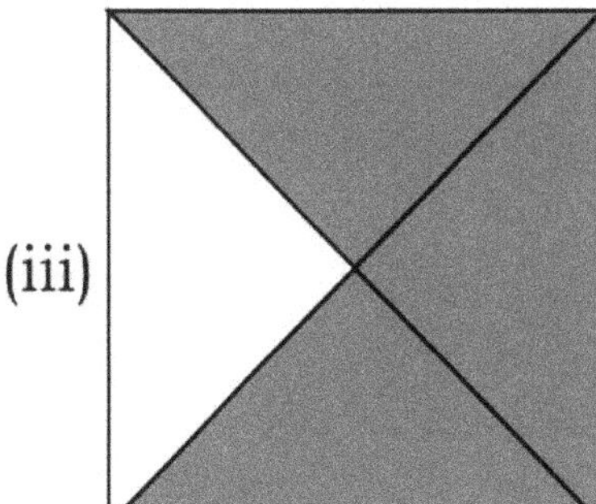

41. What percent of a day is equal to 4 hours?

42. A tank containing 336 gallons of fuel can be emptied in 12 minutes. How many gallons of fuel can be emptied in one minute?

43. There are 540 children enrolled in Valley School. If there are 18 classrooms in the school, what is the average number of students in each classroom?

Aid Box:

1. **Reduce the following into lowest equivalent form.**

(i) 4 : 50 (ii) 0.8 : 72 (iii) 3.5 : 4.9

(iv) $\frac{13}{60} : \frac{7}{15}$ (v) $\frac{5}{6} : \frac{3}{10}$ (vi) $\frac{2}{3} : 5$

(vii) $2\frac{1}{2} : 4$ (viii) $\frac{1}{3} : \frac{1}{6} : \frac{1}{9}$ (ix) 1.5 : 5 : 5.8

(x) $3\frac{2}{5} : 0.6 : 3.5$ (xi) $\frac{1}{5} : \frac{1}{10} : \frac{1}{15}$ (xii) $\frac{1}{7} : \frac{1}{14} : \frac{1}{21}$

2. **Find ratio of the following and write in lowest form.**

(i) Rs 150 and Rs 180 (ii) 250 cm and 1 m

(iii) 700 g and 2 kg (iv) 3 hours and 210 minutes

(v) 5 years and 3 months

(vi) 15 days, 2 weeks and 1 month

3. **Convert the following fractions into ratio form.**

(i) $\frac{2}{9}$ (ii) $\frac{5}{6}$ (iii) $\frac{1}{75}$ (iv) 3 (v) $\frac{p}{q}$

4. **Represent the following into fractions.**

(i) 1:5 (ii) 2:19 (iii) 8:1 (iv) 75:76 (v) $x : y$

5. In a Science test, 25 students out of 45 students of class VI were passed. Find the ratio between the passed students and total students.

6. Arshad earns Rs 20,000 per month. Find the ratio of his monthly income and expenditure if he saves Rs. 5000 per month.

7. The measures of sides of two squares are 2 cm and 5 cm. Find the ratio of their perimeters.

8. Weight of a sack of flour is 16 kg and the weight of another sack is 14kg 400g. Find the ratio among their weights.

9. Measures of angles of a triangle are 30°, 60° and 90°. Find the ratio of these angles according to the given order.

10. Albert traveled 4000 miles in 16 days. If he traveled the same number of miles each day, how many miles did he travel each day?

11. Roy feeds the birds in the zoo 6500 ounces of birdseed in 52 weeks. How many ounces of birdseed does he feed the birds each week?

12. 0.5 X 0.006 X 0.00008 = 24 X 10^n ; value of n = ________;

Assignment H

206

1. Write True or False :

(i) $5 - 3 = 3 - 5$ (ii) $3 \times 1 + 7 = 3 \times 8$

(iii) $2 - (0 - 8) = (2 - 0) + 8$ (iv) $9 + (7 + 5) = (9 + 7) + 5$

(v) $4 \times (35 \times 2) = (4 \times 35) \times 2$

(vi) $24 - (50 - 6) = (24 - 50) - 6$

(vii) $14 \div 0 = 14$ (viii) $0 \div 125 = 0$

(ix) $18 \div 18 = 0$ (x) $75 \div 75 = 1$

4. Write the predessor and successor of the following numbers:

(i) 671 (ii) 245

5. Choose the correct answer:

(i) The smallest natural number is ______.
(a) 0 (b) 1 (c) 2 (d) 100

(ii) The predecessor of 1 in the set of whole numbers is _______.
(a) 0 (b) 2 (c) 3 (d) none

(iii) The smallest seven digit number is _______.
(a) 1234567 (b) 9999999
(c) 1111111 (d) 1000000

(iv) The greatest six digit number is ___________
(a) 876543 (b) 999999 (c) 111111 (d) 100000

(v) The numbers divisible by 2 are called______numbers.
(a) prime (b) even (c) odd (d) whole

6. Draw a number line to represent the following whole numbers.

(i) 0, 1, 3, 9 (ii) Whole numbers > 3

(iii) Whole numbers ≤ 8

(iv) Whole numbers > 5 but < 10

(v) Whole numbers ≥ 1 but ≤ 8

7. What percentage of all the numbers starting from 1 to 50 are prime numbers?

8. A smallest seven digit number divisible by both 3 and 9 is ________________.

Factors :

- A factor of a number is a number which divides the number leaving no remainder.

  For example - 3 divides 9 leaving no remainder. So, 3 is a factor of 9.
- 1 is a factor of every number.
- Every number, except 1, has at least two factors – 1 and the number itself.
- A number has limited number of factors.

  For example – The factors of 18 are 1, 2, 3, 6, 9 and 18.
- A factor of a number is either less than or equal to the number.

Multiples :

- Multiples of a given number are those numbers which when divided by the given number leave no remainder.
- Multiple of a number is obtained by multiplying the number by another number.

  For example – Multiples of 2 are obtained by multiplying 2 with 1, 2, 3, 4 and so on.
- Every number is a multiple of itself.
- Every number is a multiple of 1.
- Every multiple of a number is either greater than or equal to the number.
- A number can have unlimited number of multiples.

  For example – The multiples of 7 are 7, 14, 21, 28, 35 . . . . . so on.

Classification of Factors and Multiples : On the basis of divisibility, factors and multiples of numbers can be classified into various types.

(a) Even Number – A number exactly divisible by 2 is called an even number. For example - 2, 4, 96, 288 are all even numbers.

(b) Odd Number – A number when divided by 2 leaves remainder 1, is called an odd number. For example - 1, 3, 73, 245 are all odd numbers.

(c) Prime Numbers – Numbers which have exactly two factors, 1 and the

Now find the following:

A: The smallest prime number is ___.

B: Product of first three consecutive prime numbers is ____ more than the fifth PPrime number.

3. Second Level Worksheets

Selected Worksheets

Worksheet 1

I. Add or Subtract

1. $\frac{7}{12}+\frac{7}{24}$
2. $-\frac{3}{4}+\frac{7}{8}$
3. $\frac{2}{5}+\left(-\frac{2}{7}\right)$
4. $-\frac{3}{5}-\left(-\frac{5}{6}\right)$
5. $\frac{5}{24}-\frac{3}{8}$
6. $-\frac{7}{12}-\frac{3}{4}$
7. $-\frac{3}{8}+\left(-\frac{4}{5}\right)$
8. $\frac{2}{15}+\left(-\frac{3}{10}\right)$
9. $-\frac{2}{9}-\left(-\frac{2}{3}\right)$
10. $-\frac{7}{15}-\frac{5}{12}$
11. $\frac{3}{8}+\frac{7}{12}$
12. $-2\frac{1}{4}+\left(-1\frac{1}{3}\right)$
13. $3\frac{2}{5}-3\frac{1}{4}$
14. $\frac{3}{4}+\left(-\frac{4}{15}\right)$
15. $-1\frac{2}{3}+4\frac{3}{4}$
16. $-\frac{1}{8}-2\frac{1}{2}$
17. $3\frac{2}{5}-1\frac{1}{3}$
18. $5\frac{1}{3}+\left(-8\frac{3}{7}\right)$
19. $\frac{3}{5}-\frac{2}{3}$
20. $1\frac{1}{3}-2\frac{5}{6}$

21. $\left(\frac{1}{43}-\frac{1}{43}+\frac{1}{43}-\frac{1}{43}+\ \ldots\ldots 1{,}000\ times\right) X \left(1+\frac{1}{1000}\right) X\ 1720$ = ……………………

II. ılve each equation. Check your solution.

1. $434=-31y$
2. $6x=-4.2$
3. $\frac{3}{4}a=-12$
4. $-10=\frac{b}{-7}$
5. $7.2=\frac{3}{4}c$
6. $r+0.4=1.4$
7. $-2.4n=7.2$
8. $7=\frac{1}{2}d$
9. $n-0.64=-5.44$
10. $\frac{t}{3}=2$
11. $\frac{3}{8}=\frac{1}{2}x$
12. $\frac{1}{2}h=-14$
13. $k-1.18=1.58$
14. $4\frac{1}{2}s=-30$
15. $\frac{2}{3}f=\frac{8}{15}$
16. $\frac{2}{3}m=22$
17. $\frac{2}{3}g=4\frac{5}{6}$
18. $7=\frac{1}{3}v$
19. $\frac{g}{1.2}=-6$
20. $z-4\frac{5}{8}=15\frac{3}{8}$
21. $-12=\frac{1}{5}j$

22. (m – 1) m (m + 1) = 300 ; $(m^3\ -\ m^2\ +1)=$ ……….. and $m^2(m^4-2m^2+1)$ = ………..

23. What fraction of all the numbers from 1 to 1,200 are multiples of 111?

24. What least number should be subtracted from 121,230,549 to make the value divisible by 11?

***.

Worksheet 2

1. When a number is multiplied by itself, the product is said to be _______ of that number.
2. The number of zeroes at the end of the square of a number is _______ the number of zeroes at the end of the number.
3. When a 'n' digit number is squared, then the number of digits in the square, thus, obtained is _______.
4. If $7^2 = 49$ and $0.7^2 = 0.49$, then $0.007^2 =$ _______.
5. The smallest number with which 16 should be multiplied to make it a perfect cube is _______.
6. The cube root of 125 is _______.
7. The square of a proper fraction is always _______ than itself.
8. The square of an odd number is always odd. Is the given statement true?
9. The square of a prime number is always prime. Is the given statement true?
10. The square root of a 4 digit or a 3 digit (perfect square) number is a _______ digit number.
11. If the units digit of a number is 2, then it does not have a square root. Is the given statement true?
12. If the units digit of a perfect square is 5, then the units digit of its square root is _______.
13. The square root of a prime number can be obtained approximately but not exactly. Is the given statement true?
14. If x is a non-zero number, then $x \times x \times x$, written as _______ is called the _______ of x.
15. A number n is a perfect cube only if there is an integer m such that $n =$ _______.
16. The smallest number by which 81 should be divided to make it a perfect cube is _______.
17. The cubes of the digits 1, 4, 5, 6, and 9 are the numbers ending in the same digits 1, 4, 5, 6, and 9, respectively (True/False).
18. Cubes of the numbers for which the digits in the units place are 2, 8 and 3, 7 ends in _______ and _______, respectively.
19. If a number ends in two 9's, then its cube ends in _______ number of 9's.
20. What is the digit in the units place of the cube of 31?
21. Number of digits in the cube of a two-digit number may be _______.
22. Cube root of a perfect even cube is _______ and the perfect odd cube is _______.
23. The cube root of $\frac{27}{8}$ is _______.
24. $3\sqrt[3]{\frac{3.43}{10}} =$ _______
25. $\sqrt[3]{a^6 \times b^9} =$ _______
26. The cube root of (-125) is _______.
27. 216 is the cube of _______.
28. If m is a cube root of n, then we write $m =$ _______.
29. $\sqrt[3]{0.125} + \sqrt[3]{0.729} =$ _______
30. $\sqrt[3]{-m^6} =$ _______

31. Find Square root: $(30 + 2\sqrt[2]{90} + \sqrt{440} + \sqrt[3]{792\sqrt{99}}$

32. How many times do 7 occur if we start writing all the natural numbers starting from 1 to 200?

33. How many even multiples of 3 are there in between 1 and 1,999?

34. Few saplings were planted beside a highway at a uniform interval of 16 $\sqrt{3}$ m to cover up a length of 2 km 560 m. How many saplings were used for this work?

35. (1.001 X 10.01 X 100.1 X 0.1001 X 0.001001) = ... X 1,001

Worksheet 3

1. $11x^2 - 88x^3 + 14x^4$ is called a ______ polynomial.
2. The degree of the polynomial $7x^3y^{10}z^2$ is ______.
3. The expression is a polynomial. (True/False)
4. If $A = 3x^2 + 5x - 3$ and $B = 5x^2 - 7$, then $2A - B$ is ______.
5. If $a + b + c = 0$, then $a^3 + b^3 + c^3 =$ ______.
6. Factors of $x^6 - y^6$ is ______.
7. The LCM of $\sqrt{2}x, \sqrt{8}x^7y^2$ is ______.
8. The HCF of $44a^3$ and $66b^pa^4$ is $22a^3$, then p can be ______.
9. One of the factor of $x^3 - x^2 + x - 1$ is ______ .
10. The quotient of $8x^3 - 7x^2 + 5x + 8$ when divided by $2x$ is ______.
11. The remainder obtained when $80x^3 + 55x^2 + 20x + 172$ is divided by $x + 2$ is ______.
12. Factorize $6x^2 + x - 2$.
13. Find the LCM and HCF of the polynomials $15x^2y^3z$, $3x^3yz^2$.
14. Find the remainder when x^{15} is divided by $x - 2$.
15. Find the remainder if $x^5 - 3x^3 + 5x + 1$ is divided by $2x - 1$.
16. $\sqrt{a + b - 2\sqrt{ab}}$ is ______ where $\sqrt{a} > \sqrt{b}$.
17. The product of two symmetric expressions is a/an ______ expression.
18. The square root of $a^{m^2} \cdot b^{n^2}$ is ______.
19. The value of a if $x^3 - 8x^2 + 2x + a$ is divisible by $x - 2$ is ______.
20. Factorize $a^5b - ab^5$.
21. The degree of a polynomial A is 7 and that of polynomial AB is 56, then find the degree of polynomial B.
22. If $A = x^3$, $B = 4x^2 + x - 1$, then find AB.
23. Factorize $m^7 + m^4$.
24. Factorize $\frac{1}{6}a^2 - a + \frac{4}{3}$.
25. If $3x^2 + 8ax + 3$ is a perfect square, then find the value of a.
26. The factors of $a^3 + b^3 + c^3 - 3abc$ are ______.
27. The HCF of $(a^2 + 1)(a + 11)$ and $(a^2 + 1)^2 (a + 11)^2$ is ______.
28. The value of $81^3 - 100^3 + 19^3$ is ______.
29. If $A = 4x^3 - 8x^2$, $B = 7x^3 - 5x + 3$ and $C = 3x^3 + x - 11$, then find $(A + C) - B$.
30. $8x^2 + 11xy + by^2$ is a symmetric expression, then b = .
31. The HCF of $(a - 1)(a^3 + m)$ and $(a + 1)(a^3 - n)$ and $(a + 1)(a^2 - n)$ is $a^2 - 1$, then the values of m and n are ______.
32. Expand $\underset{a,b,c}{\pi}\ a^2(b + c)$.
33. The factors of $(a - b)^3 + (b - c)^3 + (c - a)^3$ is ______.
34. Expand $\sum c^2(a^2 - b^2)$.
35. If $A = 4x^3 - 8x^2$, $B = 7x^3 - 5x + 3$ and $C = 3x^3 + x - 11$, then find $2A - 3B + 4C$.
36. If $A = x^3$, $B = 4x^2 + x - 1$, $C = x + 1$, then find $(A - B)(A - C)$.
37. Find the quotient and remainder when $x^4 + 4x^3 - 31x^2 - 94x + 120$ is divided by $x^2 + 3x - 4$.
38. Factorize $a^3 + \frac{3ax}{8} + \frac{x^3}{64} - \frac{1}{8}$.
39. Find the LCM and HCF of the following polynomials.
    $36(x + 2)^2 (x - 1)^3 (x + 3)^5$, $45(x + 2)^5 (x - 1)^2 (x + 3)^5$ and $63(x - 1)^5 (x + 2)^5 (x + 3)^4$.
40. The LCM of the polynomials $(x^2 + x - 2)(x^2 + x - a)$ and $(x^2 + x - b)(x^2 + 5x + a)$ is $(x - 1)(x + 2)^2 (x + 3)$, then find the values of a and b.
41. Find the remainder when x^{23} is divided by $x^2 - 3x + 2$.

***.

Worksheet 4

Write the place of the underlined digit. Then write its value.

1. 131,24$\underline{1}$,920,057
2. $\underline{6}$70,901,230,001,400
3. $\underline{8}$0,270,310,000
4. 0.42$\underline{9}$7
5. 0.8152$\underline{3}$
6. 7.01432$\underline{5}$
7. 1$\underline{6}$.1876
8. 17.927$\underline{4}$3
9. 0.1976$\underline{0}$8

Use the number 64,310,420,069,346.789125. Name the digit in the given place.

10. millions
11. ten trillions
12. hundred billions
13. trillions
14. millionths
15. hundredths
16. tenths
17. ten thousandths
18. hundred thousandths

Write the word name for each number.

19. 201,000,006,400
20. 20,030,010,000
21. 6,000,121,000,015
22. 0.004
23. 8.0408
24. 0.00062
25. 0.000079
26. 5.042019
27. 1.568970

Write each number in standard form.

28. thirteen million, five thousand
29. three hundred eight billion
30. one hundred twelve trillion
31. ninety-one billion, fifty
32. eleven millionths
33. two thousand ten hundred thousandths
34. 750 trillion
35. 42 ten thousandths

***.

Worksheet 5

► To express a number in expanded form, multiply each digit by its value. Then express the products as a sum.

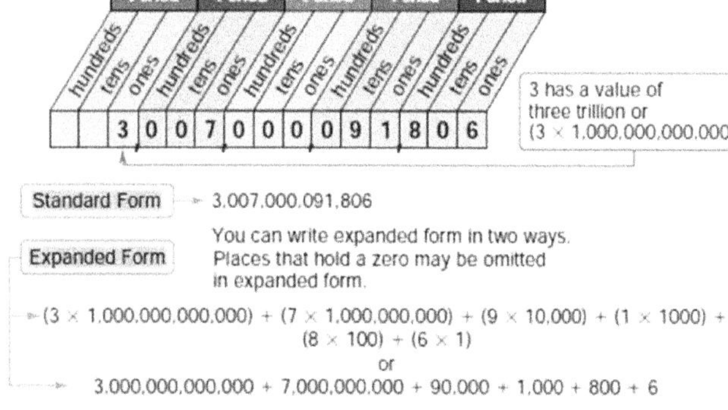

► Decimal numbers can also be written in expanded form. For decimals, the digits are multiplied by 0.1, 0.01, 0.001, and so on.

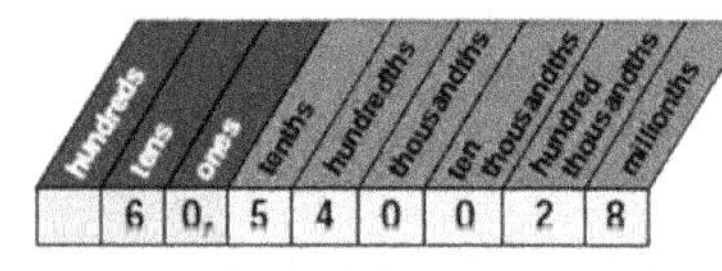

Standard Form	Expanded Form

Complete each expanded form.

1. 38,500,000,700,000 (3 × _?_) + (8 × _?_) + (5 × _?_) + (7 × _?_)
2. 4.0008 (_?_ × 1) + (_?_ × 0.0001)
3. 0.000009 (_?_ × 0.000001)

Write each expanded form in two ways.

4. 5,042,102
5. 201,407,090,000
6. 15,000,087,000
7. 0.045678
8. 3.050904
9. 78.5009

Write each expanded form in standard form.

10. (9 × 10,000,000,000,000) + (3 × 100,000) + (4 × 100)
11. (4 × 1,000,000,000,000) + (5 × 10,000) + (2 × 1000) + (9 × 1)
12. 4 + 0.1 + 0.07 + 0.000009
13. 20 + 0.008 + 0.0001 + 0.00005

Write each number in standard form and in expanded form.

14. 95 trillion, 700 million
15. 8 trillion, twelve million, five
16. 13 billion, 7 hundred
17. 14 hundred thousandths
18. 80 and 13 ten thousandths
19. 907 millionths

Solve each problem.

20. In 2005, the population of the
21. In 2005, the population of the world

Worksheet 6

- An **exponent** tells how many times to use the base as a factor.

$10^2 = 10 \times 10$ Read 10^2 as "ten to the second power" or "ten squared."	$10^3 = 10 \times 10 \times 10$ Read 10^3 as "ten to the third power" or "ten cubed."

- **Positive powers of 10** are used to show whole number place value.

$10^5 = 10 \times 10 \times 10 \times 10 \times 10 = 100{,}000$
$10^4 = 10 \times 10 \times 10 \times 10 = 10{,}000$
$10^3 = 10 \times 10 \times 10 = 1{,}000$
$10^2 = 10 \times 10 = 100$
$10^1 = 10 \times 1 = 10$ ← Any number raised to the first power equals that number.
$10^0 = 1$ ← Any nonzero number raised to the zero power is equal to 1.

In positive powers of ten, the exponent indicates the number of zeros in the product.

- **Negative powers of 10** are used to show decimal place value.

In negative powers of ten, the exponent indicates the number of decimal places.

$10^{-1} = 0.1$
$10^{-2} = 0.01$
$10^{-3} = 0.001$

Read 10^{-1} as "ten to the negative first power."

- You can write numbers in standard form in expanded form using exponents.

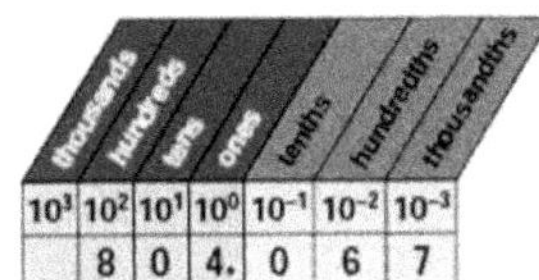

Standard Form Expanded Form

Write each power of ten in standard form.

1. 10^8 2. 10^2 3. 10^{-2} 4. 10^{-4}
5. 10^{-1} 6. 10^{-3} 7. 10^0 8. 10^7

Write each as a power of ten.

9. $10 \times 10 \times 10$ 10. $10 \times 10 \times 10 \times 10 \times 10$ 11. 10
12. 0.0001 13. 0.1 14. 0.001

Write each number in expanded form using exponents.

15. 1005 16. 218 17. 52.905 18. 840.500
$(1 \times 10^3) + (5 \times 10^0)$
19. 2.0006 20. 9.107 21. 77.04 22. 7.0034

Write each in standard form.

23. $(5 \times 10^4) + (8 \times 10^3) + (3 \times 10^1)$ 24. $(1 \times 10^6) + (6 \times 10^3) + (2 \times 10^0)$
25. $(6 \times 10^2) + (8 \times 10^{-2}) + (2 \times 10^{-4})$ 26. $(9 \times 10^2) + (9 \times 10^0) + (9 \times 10^{-2})$

27. 0.01 X 0.001 X .001001 X 0.00011 = ...

28. 201 tens + 201 tenths + 201 thousandths + 2001 hundredths = ...

29. $10^9 + 100^4 + 1000^3 + 10000^4 + 1000000^2 = 10^{8}$ X

30. 1.01 X 1.0100 X 101 X 10.1 X 0.101 X 0.00101 X101^3 = ...

II: Answer the following....

1: How many times do digits 3 occur if we write all the numbers from 1 to 100?

2. (2.005 X 20.05 X 200.5 X 2,005 X 0.02005) X 2005^{-1} X 10^{-3} = ...

3. Three fifth of ten eleventh of 33,077 =...............;

4. Half of a quarter of x = 16,096. X = ...

5. $\frac{1}{2} X \frac{2}{3} X \frac{3}{4} \ldots\ldots\ldots\ldots . X \left(1 - \frac{1}{1000}\right)$ = ...

6. $\left(1 + \frac{1}{10}\right)\left(1 + \frac{1}{11}\right) \ldots\ldots\ldots \left(1 + \frac{1}{10{,}001}\right)$ = ...

7. 20% of 60% of 100,400,600 = ...

8. (2.345 + 23.45 + 234.5 + 2345) = ...

9. $\frac{2}{3} \times 2\frac{1}{2}$ **10.** $\frac{3}{4} \times 2\frac{2}{3}$ **11.** $3\frac{1}{7} \times 4\frac{2}{3}$ **12.** $2\frac{2}{5} \times 3\frac{1}{6}$

13. $2\frac{1}{10} \times \frac{6}{7}$ **14.** $5\frac{5}{8} \times \frac{5}{9}$ **15.** $1\frac{1}{6} \times 9$ **16.** $3\frac{1}{8} \times 12$

17. $8\frac{1}{6} \times 3\frac{3}{7}$ **18.** $3\frac{1}{9} \times 2\frac{1}{7}$ **19.** $\frac{3}{4}$ of $2\frac{2}{3}$ **20.** $\frac{5}{9}$ of $2\frac{1}{4}$

21. $6 \times 5\frac{3}{5} \times 1\frac{2}{3}$ **22.** $6\frac{2}{3} \times 7 \times 1\frac{1}{5}$ **23.** $2\frac{1}{6} \times 5\frac{1}{3} \times 1\frac{7}{8}$

Compare. Write <, =, or >.

24. $2\frac{1}{2} \times 3\frac{1}{4}$? $2\frac{1}{4} \times 3\frac{1}{2}$ **25.** $1\frac{2}{3} \times 3\frac{1}{4}$? $3\frac{1}{4} \times 1\frac{2}{3}$

26. $3\frac{3}{5} \times 1\frac{1}{2}$? $2\frac{1}{2} \times 1\frac{3}{4}$ **27.** $6\frac{1}{4} \times 2\frac{1}{4}$? $3\frac{1}{2} \times 4\frac{1}{8}$

Find the value of *n*. Use the properties of multiplication.

28. $n \times 1 = 3\frac{1}{2}$ **29.** $n \times 4\frac{1}{5} = 4\frac{1}{5} \times 5$ **30.** $1\frac{1}{3} \times n = 0$

31. $(n \times \frac{1}{2}) \times 4 = \frac{1}{3} \times (\frac{1}{2} \times 4)$ **32.** $25(\frac{2}{5} + \frac{8}{15}) = (25 \times \frac{2}{5}) + (25 \times n)$

Worksheet 7

I. Solve the following...

1. 0.46 ? 0.39 **2.** 0.709 ? 0.921 **3.** 0.06 ? 0.60

4. 9.8 ? 9.80 **5.** 0.509 ? 0.510 **6.** 0.623 ? 0.627

7. 0.4286 ? 0.4190 **8.** 0.5691 ? 0.5690 **9.** 0.53 ? 0.536

10. 0.8 ? 0.78 **11.** 7.610 ? 7.61 **12.** 7.3 ? 7.301

13. 2.34 ? 2.3513 **14.** 91.42 ? 90.425 **15.** 0.059 ? 0.59

Write in order from greatest to least.

16. 0.75, 0.39, 0.2, 0.35

17. 0.484, 0.495, 0.523, 0.54

18. 8.63, 8.6, 8.65, 7.99

19. 9.21, 9.0, 9.2, 9.06

20. 0.5478, 0.546, 0.5462, 0.5593

21. 8.134, 8.215, 8.2152, 8.2052

Write in order from least to greatest.

22. 2.7054, 0.9832, 1.2396, 0.9276

23. 2.7993, 0.0803, 0.0779, 0.2396

24.21 thousandths, 201 hundredths, 2001 tenths, 12 hundredths, 102 tens, 12.9 ones

25. 1.001×10^5, 10.01×10^6, 100.1×10^7, 1001×10^4, 0.1001×10^6, 100100×10^9

II. **Round to the nearest cent.**

1. $4.368 **2.** $5.472 **3.** $35.476 **4.** $12.525

5. $.463 **6.** $.085 **7.** $1.5971 **8.** $99.9943

Round each number to the underlined place.

9. $9\underline{4},329$ **10.** $1\underline{7},721$ **11.** $0.1\underline{9}716$ **12.** $3.14\underline{1}59$

13. $2.71\underline{8}28$ **14.** $10\underline{0}.5003$ **15.** $9\underline{9}.59$ **16.** $0.666\underline{6}6$

Round each number in the table to its greatest place.

17.

Ocean	Average Depth (feet)
Pacific	12,925
Atlantic	11,730
Indian	12,598
Arctic	3,407

18.

Continent	Area in Square Miles
Europe	3,800,000
Asia	17,200,000
Africa	11,700,000
Australia	3,071,000

III. Estimate the sum or difference. Use front-end estimation with adjustments.

1. 31.6 + 18.1
2. 68.7 − 63.9
3. 7.5 − 2.9
4. 9.1 − 3.6
5. 0.87 − 0.54
6. 0.74 − 0.15
7. 76.67 + 23.89 + 69.47
8. 16.34 + 44.59 + 39.07
9. 0.66 + 0.7 + 0.19
10. 0.84 + 0.59 + 0.8

Estimate the sum or difference by rounding.

11. 18.1534 + 7.0901
12. 4.8359 − 0.7473
13. 0.45601 + 0.06428
14. 4371.5902 − 127.3246
15. 386,002,444 − 49,624,973
16. 2.361912 − 0.19008
17. 952.0667 + 232.608 + 351.03991
18. 7.30267 + 45.37 + 0.84652

19. (1 + 2 + 3 + ... 1000) X $(1001)^{-1}$ X 500 = 5^p X 10^q ; p = ... ; q = ...;

20. (10,001 + 101,101 + 1101100 + 10,11,001) - (20,002 + 101,101) = ...

21. (10 + 10 + 10 + ... 1000 times) X 10^{-1} 1001^{-1} X 2500 = a^b ; a = ... ; b = ...;

IV. Estimate using rounding. Then find the sum.

1. 7 + 8.56
2. 6.4922 + 15.58
3. $11,873.52 + 4,906.09
4. 2,527,004,609 + 38,211,073
5. 3,465,892 + 2,396,087
6. 1.6902333 + 0.7197807
7. 526,381,485 + 574,626,009
8. 3,245,840,900 + 80,059,275
9. 3.905 + 4.96
10. 0.4791 + 1.085
11. 0.10907 + 0.092
12. 0.2613 + 0.45 + 0.852
13. 0.5441 + 9.3 + 0.4637
14. 567,074 + 96,132 + 8650
15. 9,732,785 + 13,820,465

Choose the correct addends for each sum. Use estimation to help you. Explain in your Math Journal the method you used for each exercise.

	Sum	Addends			
16.	6.0108	0.6	4.321	2.1408	3.27
17.	1.4868	0.814	0.143	0.6293	0.7145

V. Find the sum

1. $\begin{array}{r} 3.12 \\ +9.94 \\ \hline \end{array}$

2. $\begin{array}{r} 0.51 \\ 0.0029 \\ +0.0018 \\ \hline \end{array}$

3. $\begin{array}{r} 0.008 \\ 0.11 \\ 0.5 \\ +0.993 \\ \hline \end{array}$

4. $\begin{array}{r} 497.386 \\ +556.22 \\ \hline \end{array}$

5. $\begin{array}{r} 390.809 \\ 905.5 \\ 8.87064 \\ +330.008 \\ \hline \end{array}$

Find the difference.

6. $\begin{array}{r} \$100 \\ -\ \$55.99 \\ \hline \end{array}$

7. $\begin{array}{r} 0.1 \\ -0.0001 \\ \hline \end{array}$

8. $\begin{array}{r} 412.009 \\ -228.4 \\ \hline \end{array}$

9. $\begin{array}{r} 1.2 \\ -0.772 \\ \hline \end{array}$

10. $\begin{array}{r} \$50 \\ -\ 23.75 \\ \hline \end{array}$

Align and add.

11. 0.67 + 39 + 7.5 + 58.22
12. 4,509.88 + 430.618 + 777.1
13. 0.49 + 0.006 + 0.213 + 0.1
14. 8.02029 + 28.98 + 617.7
15. 629.55 + 401.39201
16. 4,040 + 3,049.89 + 2057.52

Align and subtract.

17. 30 − 28.735
18. 9,002 − 4,887.56
19. 30.801 − 17.91
20. 497.1 − 437.805
21. 3,108.77 − 2,974.557
22. 1,001.1 − 802.22

VI. Write the following as numerical expressions...

1. the sum of two and seven
2. 14 less than 100
3. ten decreased by 0.5
4. 70 more than 350

Write each word expression as an algebraic expression. Use *x* as your variable.

5. the sum of a number and 45
6. 12 more than a number
7. the difference of 1 and a number
8. 13 subtracted from a number
9. a number decreased by five
10. eleven less than a number
11. a number added to sixteen
12. a number increased by fifty
13. eight more than a number
14. 45 decreased by a number

Write each mathematical expression as a word expression.

15. $100 - 5$
16. $10 - x$
17. $u + 7.99$
18. $95 + y$
19. $m - 65$
20. $35 - 18.3$
21. $7 + 8$
22. $a + 1$
23. $\$16.02 - c$

Worksheet 8

Write each number in standard form.

1. three ten thousandths , seventeen thousands and 15,021

2. nine trillion, four hundred thousand, 232 tens and twenty one hundred

3. sixty-seven, six hundred seventeen, five hundred fifty and sixty-eight millionths

Write each number in expanded form using exponents.

4. four and eighty-three thousandths 5. 200,070,040,333

6. 734 7. 329,050 8. 24,082,006

Write in order from greatest to least.

9. 0.3014; 3.014; 0.0314; 0.314 10. 0.031289; 3.001289; 33.1289, 34.3202

Round each number to its underlined place.

11. 6,745,199 12. 399.97022 13. 11,542,391.956

Estimate. Use front-end estimation with adjustments. Then use rounding.

14. 3.45 + 6 + 1.02 15. 39.28 + 46.91 +12.24 16. 98 – 44.01

Add or subtract.

17. 0.97 – 0.426 18. $500.58 _ $3.79 19. 99.0152 + 400 + 3.9848

Write each as an algebraic expression. Use *n* as your variable.

20. 8 more than a number 21. a number decreased by 200

Evaluate each expression.

22. $y - 52$, for $y = 96$ 23. $17.96 + m$, for $m = 50.42$

Write each number in expanded form two ways.

24. 46,000,000 2. eight thousand, eighty and eighty-three millionths

Write each number in standard form.

25. 10^5 4X (2 X 10^3) X (5 X 10^2) X (4 X 10^0) X (9 X 10-^{2})X(20X10^{-3})

Write in order from least to greatest.

26. 0.7968; 0.7000; 0.7909 , 7.909, 77.0909, 707,09009, 70.709904 27. 1.058; 1.0058; 10.0058, 10^9, 21X10^8

Round each number to its greatest place.

28. 3,429,099 29. 0.96153301 30. 954,313.8701

Estimate using front-end estimation with adjustments. Then find the sum or difference.

31. 1229.13 + 756 + 3890.88 32. 1,007,291 – 2,364.06 33. 12,008 – 11,909 + 1,009 + 909.09

34. (1 + 2 + 3 + 4 + ... + 10,000) X $(10,001)^{-1}$ X (25,000) = 5^p X 10^q; p = ... ; q = ...;

35. 201 thousands + 201 hundreds + 201 tens + 201 thousandths + 201 tenths = 201 X ....;

36. What least number should be subtracted from the greatest number of seven digits to make the number divisible by 11?

37. A seven digit number is formed by using different digits without using any of them for two times. Find difference of such greatest and smallest numbers.

38. $(\frac{1}{\sqrt{801}} + \frac{1}{\sqrt{801}} + \frac{1}{\sqrt{801}} \dots\dots\dots 800\ times\ X\ \left(\frac{1}{\sqrt{801}}\right)\ X\ 400\ X\ 3{,}200$ = 2^p X 10^q ; p = ...; q = ...;

39. 20% of x = 30% of y = 60% of z ; $\frac{\left(\frac{1}{x}+\frac{1}{y}+\frac{1}{z}\right)(x+y+z)}{xy+yx+zx}\left(\frac{x}{yz}\right)$ = ...

***.

Worksheet 9

I. Multiply

1. 10×77 2. 30×40 3. 10×0.5 4. 10×0.0049

5. 100×13 6. 400×125 7. 100×0.7 8. 100×0.1003

9. 20×51 10. 5000×30 11. $10{,}000 \times 0.02$ 12. $20{,}000 \times 0.02$

13. 3000×50.123 14. 4000×22 15. 100×19.41 16. 1000×12.0006

Find the products. Then write them in order from least to greatest.

17. a. 10×94 b. 100×930 c. 1000×92

18. a. 100×0.05 b. 10×0.7 c. 1000×0.94

19. a. 1000×0.0062 b. 100×0.005 c. 10×0.042

20. a. 100×0.61 b. 100×0.70 c. 1000×0.0010

Find the missing factor.

21. $b \times 45 = 900$ 22. $y \times 96 = 9600$ 23. $300 \times a = 5100$

II. Estimate:

1 . 121X 101 2. 235 X 2001 3. 2009 X 309 4. 38.09 X 11,001

5. 335×129 6. 824×617 7. 925×376 8. 5847×219 9. 7932×324

10. $44.25 × 142 11. $53.38 × 319 12. $847.69 × 293 13. $795.20 × 498

14. 10.6×23 15. 5.52×1.78 16. 0.9×13.6 17. 137×2.85

18. 6235×3.7 19. 2.8×31.89 20. 3.2×14.79 21. 0.7×103.95

22. $10.7 \times 2.9 \times 28.04$ 23. $1.5 \times 2.8 \times 12.1$ 24. $4.3 \times 18.07 \times 1.79$

25. $3.54 \times 13.9 \times 428$ 26. $19.45 \times 24 \times 2.3$ 27. $7.81 \times 67.19 \times 112$

Estimate to compare. Write <, =, or >.

28. 679×325 __?__ 679×425 29. 7976×853 __?__ 7976×753

30. 225×1125 ? 425×1300 31. 9651×438 ? 438×9651

III. Write the decimal point in each product.

1. 5.9 × 3 = 1 7 7

2. 0.2 3 5 × 7 = 1 6 4 5

3. 9.2 7 × 1.5 = 1 3 9 0 5

4. 0.4 6 3 × 0.2 2 6 = 0 1 0 4 6 3 8

5. 1 2.9 2 × 0.7 = 9 0 4 4

Multiply. Round to the nearest cent when necessary.

6. 0.9 × 22
7. 0.7 × 79
8. 0.59 × 43
9. 0.47 × 21
10. 0.32 × 73
11. 0.43 × 0.19
12. 0.61 × 0.93
13. 0.163 × 0.03
14. 0.911 × 9.11
15. 0.414 × 0.72
16. 13.5 × 9.2
17. 0.20 × 9.1
18. $8.05 × 1.9
19. $9.20 × 4.5
20. $10.50 × 8
21. $59.50 × 2.4
22. 8.5 × 0.6
23. 4.12 × 1.8
24. 8.74 × 3.15
25. 9 × $56.95
26. 1.5 × 8.00
27. 6.2 × 9.5
28. 4.75 × $85
29. 11X 22,022
30. 1.01 X 16,000
31. 10.008 X 201
32. 2.002 X 22.022

IV. Write in Scientific Notation:

1. 10 × 45
   100 × 45
   1000 × 45
2. 25 × 2
   25 × 20
   25 × 200
   25 × 2000
3. 10 × 0.3
   100 × 0.3
   1000 × 0.3
   10,000 × 0.3

Use rounding to estimate the product.

4. 62 × 19
5. 874 × 26
6. 54.2 × 1.78
7. 431 × 156
8. 5.49 × 62.83
9. 177.08 × 2684

Round to estimate. Then find each product.

10. 709 × 333
11. 0.26 × 9.3
12. 382 × 1101
13. $58.79 × 209
14. 8009 × 3206
15. $13.50 × 42

Write the standard form for each.

16. 2^4
17. 3^4
18. 9^1
19. 5^3
20. 30^2

***.

Worksheet 10

I: Divide

1. $3\overline{)81,993}$ 2. $6\overline{)84,174}$ 3. $5\overline{)490,135}$ 4. $7\overline{)315,714}$

5. 688,932 ÷ 4 6. 912,848 ÷ 8 7. 2,496,598 ÷ 2 8. 6,975,687 ÷ 3

Predict if the quotient has a remainder. Explain why or why not. Then divide to check your prediction.

9. $5\overline{)509,845}$ 10. $3\overline{)68,734}$ 11. $2\overline{)149,568}$ 12. $3\overline{)710,625}$

Find each quotient by short division. Use R to write remainders.
Check by multiplying the divisor and the quotient and then adding the remainder.

13. $4\overline{)137,973}$ 14. $9\overline{)836,138}$ 15. $5\overline{)139,864}$ 16. $7\overline{)180,523}$

17. \$8157.75 ÷ 5 18. \$644.68 ÷ 4 19. 36,570 ÷ 7 20. 19,580 ÷ 6

Write the divisor. Use divisibility rules to help you.

21. $\begin{array}{r} 2891 \\ ?\overline{)5782} \end{array}$ 22. $\begin{array}{r} 1966 \\ ?\overline{)5898} \end{array}$ 23. $\begin{array}{r} 7{,}489 \text{ R3} \\ ?\overline{)67{,}404} \end{array}$ 24. $\begin{array}{r} 7{,}915 \text{ R7} \\ ?\overline{)63{,}327} \end{array}$

25. What least number should be subtracted from six digit greatest number to make the value divisible by 3, 6 and 9 leaving remainder 2 in each case?

26. (1 + 2 + ... + 1,000) ÷ (1,001) = ...

II. Estimate the quotient. Use compatible numbers.

1. 2164 ÷ 43 2. 5838 ÷ 28 3. 7842 ÷ 37
4. 3984 ÷ 19 5. 82,461 ÷ 41 6. \$51,206 ÷ 53
7. 13,642 ÷ 206 8. 85,136 ÷ 409 9. \$485,725 ÷ 520
10. 672,385 ÷ 710 11. 879,500 ÷ 425 12. \$972,360 ÷ 325

Choose the best estimate.

13. $32\overline{)2940} \approx$? a. 1 b. 10 c. 100 d. 1000
14. $19\overline{)6248} \approx$? a. 3 b. 30 c. 300 d. 3000
15. $210\overline{)380,493} \approx$? a. 2 b. 20 c. 200 d. 2000
16. $389\overline{)792,432} \approx$? a. 2 b. 20 c. 200 d. 2000

III. Divide..

1. $52\overline{)6638}$
2. $34\overline{)5777}$
3. $15\overline{)1634}$
4. $40\overline{)2060}$
5. $36{,}389 \div 82$
6. $30{,}139 \div 93$
7. $25{,}297 \div 84$
8. $72{,}072 \div 72$
9. $86{,}129 \div 43$
10. $36{,}408 \div 912$
11. $2710 \div 759$
12. $88{,}408 \div 514$

Find the value of the variable.

13. $n = 28{,}671 \div 57$
14. $d = 14{,}558 \div 29$
15. $504{,}144 \div 36 = m$
16. $696{,}024 \div 24 = a$
17. $c = 400{,}458 \div 186$
18. $b = 681{,}042 \div 223$

Use the table to find the number of carats in each gem. (1 carat = 20 centigrams)

19. Cut diamond
20. Ruby
21. Emerald
22. Sapphire
23. Opal

Gem	Mass (in centigrams)
Cut diamond	10 600
Ruby	170 000
Emerald (single crystal)	140 500
Sapphire (carved)	46 040
Opal	527 000

IV. Divide and check.

1. $67.2 \div 6$
2. $7.5 \div 3$
3. $49.32 \div 9$
4. $0.95 \div 5$
5. $21.60 \div 15$
6. $13.2 \div 22$
7. $0.784 \div 7$
8. $8.792 \div 4$
9. $62.1 \div 3$
10. $9.520 \div 7$
11. $\$77.20 \div 8$
12. $0.732 \div 6$
13. $5\overline{)99.5}$
14. $6\overline{)135.6}$
15. $7\overline{)\$17.85}$
16. $8\overline{)41.52}$
17. $12\overline{)\$34.80}$
18. $42\overline{)349.44}$
19. $4\overline{)0.8644}$
20. $5\overline{)0.8325}$
21. $2\overline{)0.9314}$
22. $5\overline{)\$50.25}$
23. $3\overline{)0.732}$
24. $4\overline{)\$24.12}$
25. $6\overline{)14.10}$
26. $3\overline{)0.1077}$
27. $8\overline{)0.016}$
28. $6\overline{)7.836}$

Compare. Write <, =, or >.

29. $0.57 \div 30$ __?__ $0.57 \div 3$
30. $92.4 \div 6$ __?__ $9.24 \div 6$
31. $4\overline{)48}$ __?__ $4\overline{)4.8}$
32. $5\overline{)0.015}$ __?__ $5\overline{)0.15}$

33. $\left(\frac{1}{\sqrt{10001}} + \frac{2}{\sqrt{10001}} + \frac{2}{\sqrt{10001}} + \ldots\ldots\ldots\ldots + \frac{10{,}000}{\sqrt{10001}}\right) X \left(25{,}000X\frac{12}{\sqrt{10001}}\right)$ = ...

34. Nandanwar finished a work in 66 days while working 10 hours per day. She wanted to finish her work earlier by increasing her daily engagement by 1 hour. Find the number of days saved by Nandanwar.

V. **Estimate to place the decimal point in the quotient.**

1. 29.52 ÷ 7.2 = ... **2.** 18.7 ÷ 5.5 = ... **3.** 49.6 ÷ 8 = ...

4. 38.13 ÷ 15.5 = ... **5.** 40.18 ÷ 19.6 = ... **6.** 225.15 ÷ 7.5 = ...

7. 396.5 ÷ 12.2 = ... **8.** 9.21 ÷ 7.5 = ... **9.** $37.75 ÷ 5 = ...

Estimate each quotient. Use compatible numbers.

10. 41.9 ÷ 8.6 **11.** 54.3 ÷ 9.3 **12.** 47.17 ÷ 6.88

13. 358.8 ÷ 5.99 **14.** 225.741 ÷ 6.8 **15.** 182.827 ÷ 3.5

16. 505.905 ÷ 52.7 **17.** 798.238 ÷ 68.4 **18.** 328 ÷ 15.9

19. 885 ÷ 30.9 **20.** $63.28 ÷ 4.4 **21.** $596.78 ÷ $9.50

Compare. Write $<$, $=$, or $>$.

22. 8 ÷ 9 __?__ 1 **23.** 27.6 ÷ 7.4 __?__ 1 **24.** 14.9 ÷ 8.7 __?__ 1

25. 6.8 ÷ 18.9 __?__ 1 **26.** 1 __?__ 0.7 ÷ 5.88 **27.** 1 __?__ 41.1 ÷ 0.999

28. 1 __?__ 1.28 ÷ 3.01 **29.** 1 __?__ 12.1 ÷ 0.894 **30.** 1 ÷ 0.1 __?__ 1

VI. Place decimal in quotients

1. $\begin{array}{r} 281 \\ 2.3\overline{)6.463} \end{array}$ **2.** $\begin{array}{r} 092 \\ 0.19\overline{)0.1748} \end{array}$ **3.** $\begin{array}{r} 311 \\ 0.92\overline{)2.8612} \end{array}$

4. $\begin{array}{r} 603 \\ 0.8\overline{)4.824} \end{array}$ **5.** $\begin{array}{r} 85 \\ 0.011\overline{)0.0935} \end{array}$ **6.** $\begin{array}{r} 012 \\ 0.012\overline{)0.00144} \end{array}$

7. $\begin{array}{r} 0003 \\ 1.5\overline{)0.0045} \end{array}$ **8.** $\begin{array}{r} 02 \\ 0.18\overline{)0.036} \end{array}$ **9.** $\begin{array}{r} 006 \\ 0.024\overline{)0.00144} \end{array}$

Divide and check.

10. $0.5\overline{)7.55}$ **11.** $0.6\overline{)9.66}$ **12.** $0.4\overline{)0.76}$ **13.** $0.7\overline{)8.61}$

14. 92.4 ÷ 0.4 **15.** 6.3 ÷ 0.3 **16.** 257.2 ÷ 0.4 **17.** 0.96 ÷ 0.8

18. 2.214 ÷ 0.9 **19.** 0.084 ÷ 0.3 **20.** 555.6 ÷ 0.6 **21.** 391.2 ÷ 0.4

22. $0.28\overline{)4.396}$ **23.** $0.75\overline{)0.7725}$ **24.** $0.07\overline{)3.5028}$ **25.** $0.08\overline{)1.9216}$

26. 6.9 ÷ 2.3 **27.** 8.93 ÷ 4.7 **28.** 0.78 ÷ 0.26 **29.** 0.014 ÷ 0.07

31. Half of a quarter of certain number is equal to 8,072.064. Find fifth multiple of that number.

32. 201 hundreds + 402 thousands + 603 tens + 2.01 + 0.0201 = 201 X ....

33. By selling 20 breads a shopkeeper gained an amount equal to selling price of 2 breads. Find percentage gain of that vendor.

VII. **Write the value of each variable.**

1. $\frac{9}{13} \div \frac{3}{5} = \frac{9}{13} \times \frac{5}{3} = a$
2. $\frac{12}{25} \div \frac{3}{10} = \frac{12}{25} \times \frac{10}{3} = b$
3. $\frac{3}{7} \div \frac{1}{14} = \frac{3}{7} \times \frac{x}{y} = z$
4. $\frac{1}{8} \div \frac{1}{16} = \frac{p}{r} \times \frac{16}{1} = s$

Solve for n. Draw a diagram to help you.

5. $\frac{1}{2} \div \frac{1}{4} = n$
6. $\frac{2}{5} \div \frac{1}{10} = n$
7. $\frac{1}{4} \div \frac{1}{16} = n$
8. $\frac{1}{2} \div \frac{1}{10} = n$
9. $n = \frac{7}{8} \div \frac{1}{8}$
10. $n = \frac{5}{6} \div \frac{1}{6}$
11. $n = \frac{6}{8} \div \frac{3}{8}$
12. $n = \frac{6}{16} \div \frac{2}{16}$

Find the quotient.

13. $\frac{5}{8} \div \frac{5}{8}$
14. $\frac{2}{5} \div \frac{2}{5}$
15. $\frac{5}{24} \div \frac{5}{12}$
16. $\frac{6}{13} \div \frac{3}{26}$
17. $\frac{2}{9} \div \frac{1}{3}$
18. $\frac{1}{8} \div \frac{1}{5}$
19. $\frac{16}{25} \div \frac{3}{5}$
20. $\frac{9}{28} \div \frac{3}{7}$
21. $\frac{14}{15} \div \frac{8}{9}$
22. $\frac{9}{10} \div \frac{6}{7}$
23. $\frac{1}{6} \div \frac{1}{11}$
24. $\frac{1}{11} \div \frac{1}{6}$

VIII. **Compare the dividend and the divisor to determine whether the quotient *is less than 1* or *is greater than 1*. Write < or >. Then find the quotient.**

1. $\frac{6}{7} \div \frac{3}{7}$ ___?___ 1
2. $\frac{2}{5} \div \frac{4}{5}$ ___?___ 1
3. $\frac{1}{3} \div \frac{1}{10}$ ___?___ 1
4. $\frac{1}{15} \div \frac{1}{12}$ ___?___ 1
5. $\frac{3}{7} \div \frac{3}{11}$ ___?___ 1
6. $\frac{4}{5} \div \frac{4}{9}$ ___?___ 1
7. $\frac{2}{3} \div \frac{3}{4}$ ___?___ 1
8. $\frac{7}{8} \div \frac{5}{6}$ ___?___ 1
9. $\frac{5}{9} \div \frac{7}{18}$ ___?___ 1
10. $\frac{17}{36} \div \frac{5}{12}$ ___?___ 1
11. $\frac{11}{12} \div \frac{3}{7}$ ___?___ 1
12. $\frac{4}{9} \div \frac{9}{10}$ ___?___ 1
13. $\frac{1}{8} \div \frac{3}{7}$ ___?___ 1
14. $\frac{3}{10} \div \frac{9}{11}$ ___?___ 1
15. $\frac{5}{6} \div \frac{4}{5}$ ___?___ 1
16. $\frac{3}{8} \div \frac{5}{7}$ ___?___ 1

Estimate. Round each mixed number to the nearest compatible whole number.

17. $8\frac{1}{3} \div 1\frac{5}{6}$
18. $9\frac{3}{4} \div 4\frac{3}{4}$
19. $11 \div 1\frac{7}{8}$
20. $17 \div 2\frac{1}{4}$
21. $6\frac{1}{8} \div 9\frac{2}{5}$
22. $3\frac{8}{9} \div 12\frac{1}{9}$
23. $11\frac{1}{2} \div \frac{11}{12}$
24. $\frac{7}{8} \div 9\frac{1}{2}$

Solution / Hints 2:

1. Square
2. Twice
3. $2n$ or $2n - 1$
4. 0.000049
5. 4
6. 5
7. Less
8. Yes
9. No
10. Two
11. Yes
12. 5
13. Yes
14. x^3, cube
15. m^3
16. 3
17. True
18. 8, 2 and 7, 3
19. Two
20. 1
21. 4 or 5 or 6
22. Even, odd
23. $\frac{3}{2}$
24. 0.7
25. $a^2 \times b^3$
26. -5
27. 6
28. $\sqrt[3]{n}$
29. 1.4
30. $-m^2$

Solution/Hints 3:

1. biquadratic
2. 15
3. False
4. $x^2 + 10x + 1$
5. $a^3 + b^3 + c^3 = 3abc$
6. $(x - y)(x + y)(x^2 + y^2 - xy)(x^2 + y^2 + xy)$
7. $\sqrt{8}x^7y^2$
8. any real number
9. $x + \frac{1}{x}$
10. $4x^2 - \frac{7}{2}x + \frac{5}{2}$
11. -288.
12. $(2x - 1)(3x + 2)$
13. The LCM of given polynomials $= 3 \times 5 \times x^3 \times y^3 \times z^3 = 15x^3y^3z^3$

    The HCF of given polynomials $= 3x^2yz^2$
14. $f(2) = 2^{15}$
15. $f\left(\frac{1}{2}\right) = \frac{101}{32}$
16. $\sqrt{a} - \sqrt{b}$
17. symmetric
18. $a^{\frac{m^2}{2}} \cdot b^{\frac{n^2}{2}}$
19. 20
20. $ab(a^2 + b^2)(a + b)(a - b)$
21. 49
22. $4x^5 + x^4 - x^3$
23. $m^4(m + 1)(m^2 - m + 1)$
24. $\frac{1}{6}(a - 2)(a - 4)$
25. $a = \pm\frac{3}{4}$
26. $(a + b + c)(a^2 + b^2 + c^2 - ab - bc - ca)$
27. $(a^2 + 1)(a + 11)$
28. -461700
29. $-8x^2 + 6x - 14$
30. 8

***.

4. Assignments

Mathematics is a science which deals with time and space..

- *Author*

Assignments 1

Divide. When needed, write zeros as placeholders in the dividend.

1. $0.4\overline{)0.2}$ **2.** $0.5\overline{)0.7}$ **3.** $0.8\overline{)0.5}$ **4.** $1.5\overline{)0.3}$

5. $0.8\overline{)1}$ **6.** $0.4\overline{)9}$ **7.** $2.5\overline{)6}$ **8.** $1.2\overline{)3}$

9. $0.05\overline{)0.7}$ **10.** $0.32\overline{)0.4}$ **11.** $0.08\overline{)0.7}$ **12.** $0.08\overline{)16}$

13. $6\overline{)3}$ **14.** $8\overline{)4}$ **15.** $0.2\overline{)0.03}$ **16.** $2.4\overline{)0.6}$

17. $0.7 \div 1.4$ **18.** $0.3 \div 2$ **19.** $0.03 \div 0.025$ **20.** $0.8 \div 0.032$

Divide. Write zeros in the quotient as needed.

21. $5\overline{)0.15}$ **22.** $4\overline{)0.36}$ **23.** $8\overline{)0.168}$ **24.** $80\overline{)0.8}$

25. $2.1\overline{)0.861}$ **26.** $6.2\overline{)0.372}$ **27.** $2.1\overline{)0.063}$ **28.** $0.6\overline{)0.036}$

29. $7\overline{)0.035}$ **30.** $9\overline{)0.414}$ **31.** $2\overline{)1.802}$ **32.** $9\overline{)0.099}$

33. $9.8\overline{)0.0196}$ **34.** $0.8\overline{)0.0328}$ **35.** $3.1\overline{)0.0279}$ **36.** $0.71\overline{)0.0142}$

37. What percent of all the numbers starting from 1 to 25,000 are multiples of 250?
38. Write greatest and smallest numbers of four digits by using following digits 4, 9 , 3 and 0. Also write sum total of both the numbers.
39. $(x^3 - y^3) \div (x - y) =$ ……………………; Evaluate this value for x = 6 and y = 5.
40. Three equilateral triangles are arranged side by side to form a polygon. Find the number of sides of that polygon. Also find sum total of all the interior angles of that polygon.
41. How many diagonals are there in a pentagon?
42. Supplementary angle of complementary angle of a definite angle is 133^0 . Find measure of the given angle.
43. Two equal sides of a triangle are of 5 cm each. Base of that triangle is equal to 6 cm. Find area of that triangle.
44. Product of three consecutive multiple of 5 is equal to 750. Find sum total of all the three multiples of 5.
45. Mohanlal painted a wall in 20 days while working 6 hours a day. He can paint two such walls in …….. days while working 8 hours a day.

Assignments 2

I. Divide the following:

1. $6\overline{)8}$ **2.** $17\overline{)6}$ **3.** $9.2\overline{)20}$ **4.** $6.5\overline{)15}$

5. $2.3\overline{)0.4}$ **6.** $0.9\overline{)2.1}$ **7.** $3.1\overline{)6.5}$ **8.** $0.3\overline{)0.8}$

9. $0.4\overline{)0.85}$ **10.** $0.4\overline{)1.23}$ **11.** $0.03\overline{)0.11}$ **12.** $0.09\overline{)0.61}$

Divide. Round to the nearest hundredth or nearest cent.

13. $6\overline{)5}$ **14.** $3\overline{)22}$ **15.** $7\overline{)9.2}$ **16.** $4\overline{)1.5}$

17. $1.1\overline{)4.5}$ **18.** $1.5\overline{)0.4}$ **19.** $3.3\overline{)8.1}$ **20.** $0.7\overline{)4.5}$

21. $0.06\overline{)7.1}$ **22.** $0.07\overline{)9.3}$ **23.** $0.7\overline{)0.58}$ **24.** $0.3\overline{)0.71}$

25. $8\overline{)\$1.24}$ **26.** $6\overline{)\$8.23}$ **27.** $2\overline{)\$1.11}$ **28.** $3\overline{)\$5.19}$

Divide. Round to the nearest thousandth.

29. $6\overline{)0.4}$ **30.** $8\overline{)2.73}$ **31.** $3\overline{)7.055}$ **32.** $27\overline{)0.578}$

33. $\left(\frac{1}{\sqrt{6001}}+\frac{2}{\sqrt{6001}}+\frac{3}{\sqrt{6001}}\dots\dots\dots+\frac{6,000}{\sqrt{6001}}\right)X\frac{1}{\sqrt{6001}}\div\frac{1}{3,000}=3^p\ X\ 10^q$; Find value of $\left(\frac{p+q}{p-Q}\right)$

34. A shopkeeper gains an amount equal to cost price of 5 cakes by selling 25 cakes. Find out the gain percentage.

35. $\left(\frac{1}{a}+\frac{1}{b}+\frac{1}{c}\right)=9; find\ \ the\ value\ of\ 3(ab+bc+ac)-27\ abc.$

36. It is observed that sum total of a natural number and two times its reciprocal is equal to 8.25. Find sum total of square and cube root of that number.

37. A passenger train crosses a person standing on 1.5 km long platform in 45 seconds while moving at an average speed of 36 km/h. This train will cross the platform in ....m ....s while moving with same average speed of 36 km/h.

38. A wall mount clock strikes 6 bells at 6 O'Clock in 12 seconds. Find the time taken by this clock to strike 11 bells at 11 a.m.

39. (1 + 2 + ... + 10,000) ÷ 10,001 X 25,000 = $5^x\ 10^y$; find the value of $\left(\frac{x+y}{x-y}\right)-4xy$

***.

Assignments 3

Estimate each quotient. Use compatible numbers.

1. $3041 \div 82$ **2.** $300{,}864 \div 66$ **3.** $736 \div 4.2$ **4.** $37.26 \div 7.1$

Write in scientific notation.

5. 0.000056 **6.** 0.00158 **7.** 0.00012 **8.** 0.00000235

Find the quotient.

9. $0.83 \div 1000$ **10.** $9\overline{)189{,}567}$ **11.** $4\overline{)\$14.24}$ **12.** $0.7\overline{)7.91}$

13. $0.558 \div 6.2$ **14.** $0.032\overline{)0.288}$ **15.** $4.26\overline{)17{,}615.1}$ **16.** $0.25\overline{)7.625}$

Write each mathematical expression as a word phrase.

17. $98m$ **18.** $62.5 \div q$ **19.** $45 \cdot 25$

Find the value of each algebraic expression for $c = 0.3$ and $d = 2340$.

20. $d \div 6 \times 30$ **21.** $c \times d \div 1000$ **22.** $36 \div c \times d$

23. What fraction of all the numbers starting from 1 to 1000 are multiples of 121?

24. Mohanlal planted saplings at a uniform interval of 20 m alongside a stretch of 2 km 40 m long road. Find the number of saplings used by Mohanlal for this purpose.

25. Sum total of three consecutive number is equal to 3,0003. Find all the numbers.

26. Speed of a boat while moving against river stream is 2 m/s. That boat moves along stream at an average speed of 18 m/s. Speed of stream is less than the stream of the boat. Calculate the actual seed of that boat.

27. Is there any pair of number having LCM 1331 and HCF 169?

28. Is there any pair of natural having HCF 121 and LCM 1331?

29. Sum total of five consecutive multiple of 5 is equal to 250. Find product of second and fourth multiple of the numbers included in this series.

30. $(\frac{1}{\sqrt{3}+\sqrt{2}} X \frac{1}{\sqrt{3}-\sqrt{2}}$ = p; find the value of $(p-1)(p^2+p+1)$

31. One of the interior angle of a regular polygon is equal to 108^0. How many sides are there in that polygon? How many diagonals can be drawn in that polygon?

***.

Assignments 4

Tell which operation is to be done first. Then compute.

1. $3 \times 9 + 8$ **2.** $16 \div 4 + 2$ **3.** $15 - 6 \div 3$

4. $\frac{7 + 11}{9} \times 3$ **5.** $21 - \frac{9 + 11}{10}$ **6.** $27 \div \frac{9 \times 3}{5 + 4}$

7. $(14 \div 2) + 6^2$ **8.** $2^2 \times [15 - 3]$ **9.** $64 \div (8 \times 8)$

Use the order of operations to compute. Justify each step in the process.

10. $4 \times 8 \times 3 - 2$ **11.** $18 \div 6 \div 3 - 1$

12. $9 + 3 \times 2 + 4^2$ **13.** $12 - 3 \times 1 + 2^3$

14. $(40 \div 4) + 5 - 3 + [0.6 \times 40]$ **15.** $5 + (34 - 2) \div 8 + (1.7 + 2)$

16. $10 \times 3 + (48 \div 6)^2 \times 0.4$ **17.** $(50 \div 10)^3 \times 2 + 6 \times 0.6$

18. $\frac{7 + 3}{2^2 + 1} - [5 \div 5 \times 2]$ **19.** $(24 + \frac{1 \times 7}{3^2 - 2^3} - 6) \div 5^2$

Insert parentheses to make each number sentence true.

20. $48 \div 3^2 - 1 + 7 = 13$ **21.** $5 \times 10^2 \div 41 - 4^2 = 20$

II. **Match each exercise to its estimated sum or difference in the box.**

1. $\frac{1}{5} + \frac{8}{9}$ **2.** $\frac{6}{7} + \frac{11}{12}$

3. $\frac{9}{10} - \frac{5}{8}$ **4.** $\frac{6}{13} - \frac{8}{18}$

a. $1 + 1 = 2$	**b.** $1 - \frac{1}{2} = \frac{1}{2}$
c. $\frac{1}{2} - \frac{1}{2} = 0$	**d.** $0 + 1 = 1$

Estimate the sum or difference.

5. $\frac{1}{11} + \frac{4}{9}$ **6.** $\frac{15}{16} - \frac{1}{10}$ **7.** $\frac{2}{9} + \frac{5}{6}$ **8.** $\frac{11}{12} + \frac{12}{14}$

9. $\frac{7}{15} - \frac{1}{10}$ **10.** $\frac{18}{20} - \frac{13}{24}$ **11.** $\frac{3}{11} - \frac{1}{6}$ **12.** $\frac{1}{9} + \frac{4}{10}$

13. $\frac{9}{10} + \frac{1}{6} + \frac{3}{8}$ **14.** $\frac{1}{9} + \frac{1}{7} + \frac{1}{2}$ **15.** $\frac{15}{16} + \frac{5}{8} + \frac{4}{9} + \frac{3}{25}$

26. $\left(\frac{1}{139} + \frac{2}{139} + \cdots \ldots \ldots \ldots + \frac{138}{139}\right) X \frac{1}{69} X\ 125\ X\ 8$ = 10^p ; find the value of $(p^2 + 1)(p^2 - 1)$ -4pq.

Assignments 5

Solve and check.

1. $x + 2597 = 6233$ **2.** $y + 13.84 = 20.29$ **3.** $0.793 = n + 0.65$

4. $119 + 246 + f = 893$ **5.** $1.1 + 1.83 + g = 6.25$ **6.** $0 + m = 2.3$

7. $4.263 = 4.263 + k$ **8.** $0.52 = 0.13 + 0.15 + r$ **9.** $3.415 = 1.626 + s$

10. $z + \$3.95 = \$9.20$ **11.** $\$8.31 = \$3.22 + w$ **12.** $\$75.40 = \$25.40 + b$

13. $p + 1.93 + 1.17 = 9$ **14.** $5 + r + 1.435 = 8.435$ **15.** $4 = s + 0.367 + 2.033$

16. $9.25 + x + 1.5 = 12$ **17.** $a + 286 = 123 + 459$ **18.** $798 + m = 89.5 + 943$

Write and solve an equation.

19. A number *y* increased by 3.7 is equal to 9.372.

20. The sum of a number *w* and 85 is equal to one hundred eight.

21. Twenty-three hundredths more than a number *x* is equal to six tenths.

22. When 245 is added to the sum of 130 and a number *y*, the result is 506.

23. $(x - 2)(x + 2)(x^2 + 4)(x^4 + 16) = 0$; find the value of $(x - 1)(x^2 + x + 1)$ = ...

24. Somalwar's father is 44 years old. If he is 5 years older than thrice Somalwar's age, which of these equations gives, the age of his father?
(A) 3x + 5 = 44 (B) 44 + 5x = 3x (C) 44-3y = 5+3y (D) 3x-5 = 44

25. The present age of A is twice that of B. 30 years from now, age of A will be 1 ½ times that of B. Find the present ages (in years) of A and B respectively.

26. Ramesh got 15 marks more than Sonu in a test. If the total marks secured by them are 645, how many marks did Ramesh get?

27. In a math test, the highest marks obtained by a student in the class is 7 added to twice the lowest marks. If the highest score is 87, what is the lowest score?

28. The lengths of the sides of a triangle are (2a + 1) cm, (3a + 2) cm and (4a -1) cm. For what value of 'a' is the perimeter of the triangle 92 cm?

29. A father is 26 years older than his son. In 3 years' time, the son's age will be one third his father's age. What is the present age of the son?

30. Snehal has 196 marbles and Pinki has 163 marbles. How many marbles should Pinki give Snehal so that Snehal will have twice as many marbles as Pinki?

Assignments 6

Solve and check.

1. $x - 1456 = 234$
2. $t - 13.27 = 6.041$
3. $c - \$3.48 = \$0.23$
4. $\$57.69 - z = \$28.35$
5. $17.82 - b = 17.82$
6. $3317 = f - 52{,}000$
7. $n - (451 + 513) = 630$
8. $p - (183 + 8462) = 135$
9. $s - (9.2 + 9.8) = 2.5$
10. $8.7 = e - (107 + 14.3)$
11. $446 = q - (235 + 925)$
12. $27.2 = d - (6.5 + 4.15)$

Write and solve an equation.

13. If Kerry decreases a number y by 9.2, the result is 7.239.
14. The difference between a number w and 87 is equal to three hundred one.
15. Thirty-four hundredths less than a number x is equal to nine tenths.
16. If Li subtracts the sum of 279 and 38 from a number y, the result is 126.

II. **Solve and check.**

1. $\frac{7}{9} - y = \frac{2}{9}$
2. $\frac{5}{8} + k = 3\frac{1}{8}$
3. $2\frac{3}{10} - g = 1\frac{1}{5}$
4. $d - \frac{3}{5} = \frac{4}{5}$
5. $h - 1\frac{5}{8} = 3\frac{1}{8}$
6. $x - \frac{4}{7} = \frac{5}{14}$
7. $t + 2\frac{1}{6} = 7\frac{11}{12}$
8. $10\frac{1}{2} - u = 8\frac{3}{8}$
9. $p + 1\frac{3}{5} = 3\frac{3}{10}$
10. $w - 2\frac{1}{4} = 4\frac{5}{12}$
11. $10\frac{5}{6} = s + 3\frac{5}{8}$
12. $2\frac{1}{6} = v - 7\frac{4}{9}$

III. **Add or subtract. Estimate to help you.**

1. $\frac{7}{12} + \frac{13}{24}$
2. $\frac{5}{6} - \frac{1}{5}$
3. $2\frac{1}{5} + 4\frac{3}{5}$
4. $9\frac{5}{7} - 8\frac{2}{7}$
5. $8\frac{3}{5} + 6\frac{1}{3}$
6. $5\frac{5}{7} + 4$
7. $4\frac{3}{8} - 1\frac{1}{7}$
8. $1\frac{1}{2} + 2\frac{1}{3} + 1\frac{5}{6}$
9. $12 - 1\frac{1}{8}$
10. $15\frac{9}{10} - 14\frac{1}{3}$

Compute. Use the addition properties when possible.

11. $2\frac{4}{5} + (1\frac{1}{3} - 1\frac{1}{3})$
12. $(\frac{1}{4} + 5\frac{3}{8}) + 3\frac{3}{4}$
13. $2\frac{1}{2} + 4 + 1\frac{1}{4}$

***.

Assignments 7

Evaluate....

1. $12 + 7 \times 9^2$ 2. $6 \times (7 - 4)^2 + 13$ 3. $14 \times (6 + 79) \div 7$

4. $19^4 - 100 + (85 - 4 \times 2)$ 5. $156 \div 3 \times 7^3 + 19$ 6. $(19 \times 6)^4 + 214 \div 2$

Evaluate. Use a calculator to check your work.

7. $12 + 7 \times 9^2$ 8. $6 \times (7 - 4)^3 + 13$ 9. $10^4 \times (6 + 78) \div 7$

10. $19^2 - 100 + (85 - 4 \times 2)$ 11. $156 \div 3 \times 7^2 + 19$ 12. $(20 \times 6)^2 + 214 \div 2$

13. $(4 \times 7 + 5)^2 \div 11 + 1$ 14. $87 - 54 + 12 \times 5^3$ 15. $3^3 \times (15 + 19 - 10) \div 9$

16. $(9^2 - 19) + 42 \div 6 \times 2^3$ 17. $51 + 5^2 \times 31 + 18^2 - 9 \times 7$

Compare. Write <, =, or >.

18. $16^2 \times 5 - 90$? $90 \times 5 - 16^2$ 19. $(64 + 192) \div 8^2$? $64 + 192 \div 8^2$

20. $195 \div 5 \cdot 9^2$? $195 \div (5 \cdot 9)^2$ 21. $17(3)^2 \cdot (18 - 3)$? $17 \cdot 3^2 \cdot (18 - 3)$

II. **Multiply. Use the GCF to simplify whenever possible.**

1. $\frac{7}{18} \times \frac{3}{5}$ 2. $\frac{12}{20} \times \frac{5}{6}$ 3. $\frac{5}{9} \times \frac{2}{3}$ 4. $\frac{3}{4} \times \frac{2}{9}$ 5. $\frac{7}{12} \times \frac{1}{7}$

6. $\frac{9}{16} \times \frac{4}{5}$ 7. $\frac{4}{21} \times \frac{1}{8}$ 8. $\frac{14}{18} \times \frac{2}{3}$ 9. $\frac{24}{50} \times \frac{10}{12}$ 10. $\frac{1}{9} \times \frac{1}{10}$

11. $\frac{9}{10} \times \frac{1}{2} \times \frac{2}{9}$ 12. $\frac{5}{8} \times \frac{2}{3} \times \frac{7}{10}$ 13. $\frac{3}{4} \times \frac{1}{6} \times \frac{2}{5}$

14. $\frac{5}{12} \times \frac{4}{5} \times \frac{2}{3}$ 15. $\frac{4}{5} \times \frac{1}{2} \times \frac{3}{8}$ 16. $\frac{3}{5} \times \frac{5}{7} \times \frac{7}{9} \times \frac{9}{11}$

Draw a diagram to illustrate each product. Then write a multiplication sentence. Explain your diagram.

17. $\frac{3}{4} \times \frac{1}{5}$ 18. $\frac{5}{8} \times \frac{1}{3}$ 19. $\frac{3}{7} \times \frac{5}{6}$ 20. $\frac{8}{10} \times \frac{1}{2}$ 21. $\frac{7}{8} \times \frac{3}{4}$

22. $\frac{3P+2}{5} - \frac{4P-3}{7} + \frac{P-1}{35} = 4$, find the value of $P^2 + 7p - 14$;

23. If one-fourth of one sixth of a number decreased by 48 is 24,000, what is the number?

24. Sum total of five consecutive multiple of 8 is 400 , what is the third number?

Assignments 8

Simplify:

1. (5 – 5 + 5 – 5 + 5 – 5 + 5 – 5 + ------- 12,987 times) = ...; 2. $(-1.01)^3$ = ...
3. (1.01) X (-1.001) = ... 4. $(1.1)^2$ X $(-1.1)^3$ 5. (0.3) $(-0.3)^3$ 6. 5 X 5^{-1} X $(-5)^3$ X $(-5)^{-}$

Identify the point that corresponds to the integer on the number line.

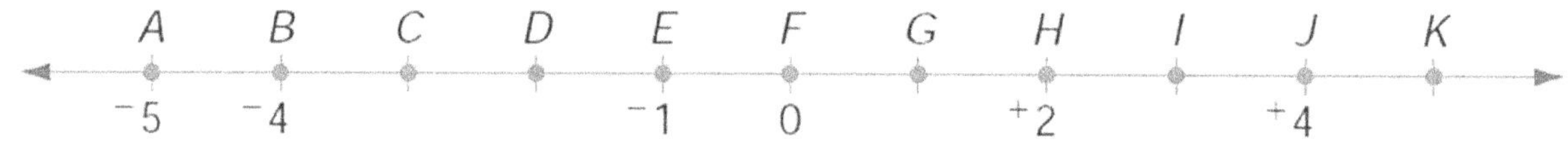

7. $^{-}5$ 8. $^{+}4$ 9. $^{-}1$ 10. *C* 11. *I* 12. *K*

Write the integer that is just before and just after each given number on a number line.

13. $^{+}7$ 14. $^{-}2$ 15. $^{+}1$ 16. $^{-}10$ 17. $^{-}99$ 18. $^{-}14$

Write the opposite of each integer.

19. $^{-}9$ 20. $^{+}20$ 21. $^{+}16$ 22. $^{-}15$ 23. $^{+}13$ 24. $^{-}10$

Write the absolute value of the integer.

25. $|^{-}8|$ 26. $|^{+}17|$ 27. $|^{-}56|$ 28. $|293|$ 29. $^{-}|^{-}701|$

Name each integer on a horizontal number line.

30. five to the right of negative five 31. seven to the right of negative eight

32. Sixteen more than the sixteenth multiple of – 1.001 added to – 14 .
33. (15 + 15 – 15 +15– 15 + ... 12,056 times) X 6 X 5 = $(p)^2$; $P^2 + p + 1$ = ...
34. Seventeenth multiple of – 17 less than 180.0017

35. Rohini can finish her project activity in 36 days and her friend Nikita can finish the same project in 54 days while working 8 hours a day. In how many days the project will be finished if they continue working together for 9 hours a day?

36. If 0.12(2x -1)- 0.25(3x - 1) = 0.46, what is the value of 'x'?.

37. $\frac{3x-1}{5} - \frac{1+x}{2} = 3 - \frac{x-1}{2}$; find the value of $\left(x+\frac{1}{x}\right)\left(x-\frac{1}{x}\right)\left(x^2+\frac{1}{x^2}\right)$

38. 4 is added to a number and the sum is multiplied by 5. If 20 is subtracted from the product and the difference is divided by 8, the result is equal to 10. Find the number.

39. In which of the following cases does an equality NOT hold?
(A) Adding the same number on both the sides. (B) Not performing the same operation on both the sides.
(C) Subtracting the same number from both the sides.
(D) Multiplying both the sides by the same non-zero number.

Assignments 9

Compare...

1. $^{+}7, ^{+}10$
2. $^{-}9, ^{-}3$
3. $^{+}3, ^{-}5$
4. $^{-}7, ^{+}6$
5. $0, ^{-}9$
6. $^{+}8, 0$
7. $^{-}12, ^{-}25$
8. $^{+}20, ^{-}20$

Compare. Write <, =, or >.

9. $^{-}10$ _?_ $^{+}6$
10. $^{+}4$ _?_ $^{+}8$
11. 3 _?_ $^{-}6$
12. $^{-}3$ _?_ $^{+}4$
13. $^{+}7$ _?_ 0
14. $^{-}4$ _?_ $^{+}4$
15. 0 _?_ $^{-}3$
16. $^{-}2$ _?_ $^{-}5$
17. $|^{-}8|$ _?_ $|^{+}7|$
18. 0 _?_ $^{-}|8|$
19. $|^{-}6|$ _?_ $^{-}(6)$
20. $^{-}(^{-}7)$ _?_ $^{-}(^{+}4)$
21. $^{-}|11|$ _?_ $^{-}13$
22. $^{-}(^{+}13)$ _?_ 0
23. $|^{+}12|$ _?_ $|^{-}12|$
24. $^{-}(^{-}10)$ _?_ $^{-}|^{-}20|$

Arrange in order from least to greatest.

25. $^{+}6, ^{+}8, ^{+}7$
26. $^{-}10, ^{-}8, ^{-}6$
27. $^{-}6, 0, ^{-}3$
28. $^{+}9, 0, ^{+}3$
29. $^{-}5, ^{-}6, ^{-}3, ^{-}7$
30. $^{+}4, ^{-}2, ^{+}5, ^{-}4$

Arrange in order from greatest to least.

31. $^{-}6, ^{+}3, ^{-}4$
32. $^{-}2, ^{-}10, ^{+}5$
33. $0, ^{-}7, ^{-}12$

II. Evaluate the following....

1. $5\frac{1}{2} + n$, when $n = 3\frac{1}{4}$
2. $7\frac{1}{8} - y$, when $y = 0$
3. $1\frac{1}{6} + r + 1\frac{2}{5}$, when $r = 1\frac{3}{4}$
4. $k - 10\frac{1}{10} + 0$, when $k = 14\frac{2}{3}$
5. $9\frac{1}{6} + \frac{5}{6} - m$, when $m = \frac{1}{2}$
6. $1\frac{1}{2} + s + 6\frac{3}{4}$, when $s = 1\frac{3}{8}$
7. $f - 1\frac{3}{5} + g$, when $f = 2\frac{1}{4}$ and $g = 5\frac{1}{2}$
8. $5 + 3\frac{3}{8} + d + 2\frac{5}{8}$, when $d = 6\frac{1}{6}$

Simplify each expression. Use mental math and the properties of addition.

9. $5\frac{2}{5} + 3\frac{3}{5} + 6\frac{1}{4}$
10. $8\frac{1}{8} + 4\frac{1}{4} + 5\frac{7}{8}$
11. $0 + 11\frac{2}{5}$
12. $9\frac{1}{6} + 0$
13. $7\frac{1}{2} + 6 + 4\frac{1}{4}$
14. $3\frac{3}{4} + 2\frac{1}{2} + 11$
15. $12\frac{1}{4} + 5\frac{1}{8} + 2\frac{1}{2}$
16. $9\frac{1}{2} + 4\frac{3}{7} + 1\frac{1}{4}$
17. $(\frac{1}{2} + 2\frac{3}{5}) + 1\frac{1}{2}$
18. $8\frac{1}{4} + (4\frac{1}{9} + \frac{3}{4})$

Assignments 10

1. (12.5 – 12.5 +12.5 – 12.5 + 12.5 – 12.5 + ... 12,654 times) = ...
2. (12.5 – 12.5 +12.5 – 12.5 + 12.5 – 12.5 + ... 12,6575times) = ...

Add. Use a number line to help.

3. $^{+}2 + {}^{+}1$ 4. $^{-}4 + {}^{-}3$ 5. $^{-}1 + {}^{-}4$ 6. $^{+}6 + {}^{+}1$

7. $^{-}6 + {}^{+}4$ 8. $^{+}7 + {}^{-}5$ 9. $^{-}5 + {}^{-}6$ 10. $^{+}4 + {}^{+}4$

11. $^{-}4 + {}^{+}8$ 12. $^{-}8 + {}^{+}5$ 13. $^{+}6 + 0$ 14. $0 + {}^{-}8$

15. $^{+}4 + {}^{-}5 + {}^{-}6$ 16. $^{-}6 + {}^{-}2 + {}^{+}4$ 17. $^{-}3 + {}^{-}3 + {}^{-}3$

18. $^{-}2 + {}^{-}2 + {}^{-}2$ 19. $^{+}7 + {}^{-}5 + {}^{-}2$ 20. $^{-}8 + {}^{+}6 + {}^{+}9$

Find the value of the variable.

21. $^{+}7 + a = {}^{+}16$ 22. $^{-}5 + b = {}^{+}3$ 23. $^{+}11 + c = {}^{+}9$

24. $d + {}^{+}7 = {}^{-}7$ 25. $e + {}^{-}8 = {}^{-}13$ 26. $f + {}^{-}15 = {}^{-}12$

27. $^{+}9 + k = 0$ 28. $h + 7 = {}^{-}6$ 29. $^{-}13 + i = {}^{-}15$

II. **Compute mentally.** Find the whole-number part and then the fraction part.

1. $8\frac{2}{3} - 5\frac{1}{3}$ 2. $6\frac{7}{8} - 2\frac{5}{8}$ 3. $10\frac{1}{12} + 1\frac{7}{12}$

4. $12\frac{1}{16} + 8\frac{7}{16}$ 5. $10\frac{3}{8} - 4\frac{1}{8} + 2$ 6. $9\frac{7}{15} - 3\frac{2}{15} - 4$

Compute mentally. Look for sums of 1.

7. $6\frac{1}{3} + 8\frac{2}{3} + 7$ 8. $2\frac{3}{8} + 1\frac{5}{8}$ 9. $5\frac{1}{4} + 1\frac{1}{4} + \frac{1}{2}$

10. $1\frac{1}{16} + 5\frac{1}{2} + 2\frac{3}{16} + 2\frac{1}{4}$ 11. $3\frac{1}{12} + 7\frac{7}{12} + 8\frac{1}{3}$

12. $3\frac{1}{3} + 6\frac{4}{5} + 10\frac{2}{3} + 3\frac{1}{5}$ 13. $9\frac{3}{4} + 5\frac{6}{11} + 6\frac{1}{4}$

***.

Assignments 11

Write subtraction sentence:

1.

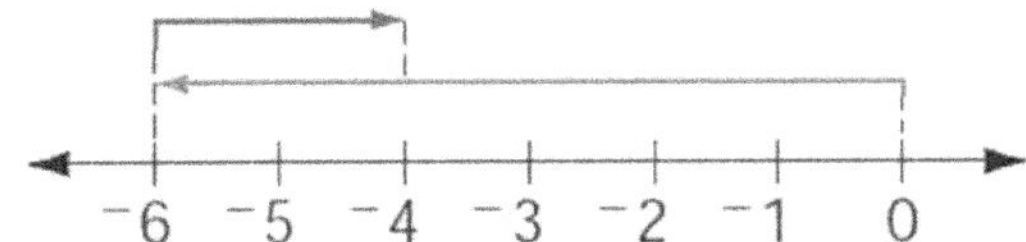

2.

−4 −3 −2 −1 0 +1 +2

Subtract. Use a number line to help.

3. $^{+}8 - ^{+}4$	**4.** $^{+}5 - ^{+}8$	**5.** $^{-}4 - ^{+}5$	**6.** $^{-}6 - ^{+}2$
7. $^{-}3 - ^{-}7$	**8.** $^{+}9 - ^{+}7$	**9.** $^{+}7 - ^{-}4$	**10.** $^{-}5 - ^{+}8$
11. $^{+}8 - ^{+}10$	**12.** $^{+}3 - ^{-}2$	**13.** $^{-}8 - ^{-}10$	**14.** $^{-}3 - ^{+}5$
15. $^{-}7 - ^{+}2$	**16.** $^{+}9 - ^{+}11$	**17.** $^{-}5 - ^{-}3$	**18.** $^{+}7 - ^{-}9$
19. $^{+}5 - ^{-}10$	**20.** $^{-}6 - ^{-}7$	**21.** $^{+}6 - 0$	**22.** $^{-}12 - 0$
23. $^{+}9 - ^{+}4$	**24.** $^{+}2 - ^{-}3$	**25.** $0 - ^{-}8$	**26.** $0 - ^{+}4$

Find the value of the variable.

27. $^{-}9 - a = ^{-}15$ **28.** $^{+}14 - b = ^{-}13$ **29.** $^{-}8 - c = ^{+}4$

30. $(x-1)(x+1)x = 750$ **31.** $(21x)(3x)(7x) = 210 \times 2100 \times 8$; **32.** $8x^3 \times 125 \times x^3 = 10^{12}$

33. $(1 + 2 + 3 + \ldots\ldots\ldots\ldots + 10{,}000) \times (10{,}001)^{-1} \times 25{,}000 = \ldots\ldots \times 10^6$;

II. **Estimate and then subtract.** Write each answer in simplest form.

1. $6\frac{4}{9} - 4\frac{1}{9}$ **2.** $7\frac{5}{8} - 3\frac{3}{8}$ **3.** $5\frac{3}{4} - 1\frac{3}{4}$ **4.** $2\frac{9}{10} - 2\frac{9}{10}$ **5.** $9\frac{1}{8} - 3\frac{5}{8}$ **6.** $11\frac{5}{7} - 9\frac{6}{7}$

7. $9\frac{1}{3} - 1\frac{5}{6}$ **8.** $13\frac{1}{6} - 9\frac{3}{4}$ **9.** $10\frac{2}{5} - 3\frac{7}{10}$ **10.** $11\frac{1}{4} - 6\frac{2}{3}$

11. $8\frac{1}{6} - 3\frac{3}{4} + 2\frac{1}{2}$ **12.** $9\frac{1}{12} - 5\frac{3}{8} - 1\frac{3}{4}$ **13.** $6\frac{1}{2} + 7\frac{1}{3} - 8\frac{1}{4}$

14. What fraction of all the numbers from 100 to 200 are multiples of 5?

15. Half of a quarter of 8,048 + quarter of one sixth of 24,144 + one third of one seventh of 21,126 = ...

16. 131.05 -100.001 – 12.003 – 11.011 = ...

***.

Assignments 12

Simplify:

1. $^-62 - {}^+84 \div {}^-4 + {}^+33$

2. $^-92 \times (^-91 + {}^+93) \div {}^-23$

3. $^+71 + {}^-175 - {}^+56 \div {}^-8$

4. $^+3 \times {}^-16 - (^+36)^2 \div {}^-12$

5. $^-4[6 + (8 - 5)^2]$

6. $^+4 \times [(^+6 - {}^-4)^2 \times 15] + {}^-5$

Compute. Watch the order of operations.

7. $^+16 - {}^-279 \div {}^+31$

8. $^-226 - {}^+190 \div {}^+10 + {}^-28$

9. $^+80 \div (^+93 + {}^-77) + {}^-304$

10. $^+67 + (^+68 - {}^+80)^2 \times {}^-30$

11. $7 - (^-9 - 5) \times 2^2$

12. $^-16 - {}^+4 \div (^+1 + {}^+1)^2$

13. $^-87 - {}^+60 \div {}^+15 + (^-40 + {}^+36)^2$

14. $^+24(^+45 + {}^-36) - {}^-21 - {}^+38 \times {}^+3$

15. $(^-24 \div {}^-3)(^-20 \div {}^+4) \div {}^+2$

16. $^-16 - {}^-14 + {}^-14 - {}^-16 + {}^-8 + {}^+3$

iI. Complete the following....

1. $4\frac{1}{6} = 4\frac{?}{24}$; $+3\frac{1}{4} = 3\frac{?}{24}$; $7\frac{?}{24} = 7\frac{?}{12}$

2. $8\frac{4}{5}$; $+\ 9\frac{1}{5}$; $17\frac{?}{?} = \underline{?}$

3. $7\frac{7}{20} = 7\frac{?}{?}$; $+4\frac{4}{5} = 4\frac{16}{?}$; $11\frac{?}{20} = 12\frac{?}{20}$

Add. Estimate to help.

4. $6\frac{2}{9} + 3\frac{2}{9}$

5. $6\frac{1}{7} + 8\frac{3}{7}$

6. $4\frac{1}{6} + 2\frac{3}{8}$

7. $1\frac{5}{6} + 2\frac{1}{3}$

8. $2\frac{2}{5} + 3\frac{1}{10}$

9. $6\frac{2}{3} + 7\frac{2}{5}$

10. $14 + 7\frac{5}{9}$

11. $9\frac{3}{8} + 4$

12. $8\frac{7}{12} + \frac{5}{12}$

13. $16\frac{1}{8} + 7\frac{7}{8}$

14. $12\frac{7}{10} + 23\frac{7}{30}$

15. $25\frac{7}{18} + 15\frac{1}{6}$

16. $3\frac{7}{8} + 3\frac{1}{2}$

17. $8\frac{3}{4} + 6\frac{1}{3}$

18. $6\frac{11}{16} + 12\frac{3}{4}$

19. $18\frac{3}{4} + 20\frac{2}{3}$

20. $10\frac{9}{20} + 8\frac{3}{4}$

21. $15\frac{5}{6} + 12\frac{7}{9}$

Assignments 13

I. Evaluate each expression when $a = {}^{+}5$, $b = {}^{-}4$, $c = {}^{-}2$, and $d = 0$.

1. $b \div c$
2. $a - b$
3. $a + b \cdot c$
4. $(b - d) \div c$
5. $\frac{ab}{2c}$
6. $a - \frac{b}{c}$
7. $cd - a$
8. $\frac{bd}{{}^{-}3c}$
9. $(a + b)^3 + c$
10. $bd - a^2$
11. $a^2 + bc$
12. $b \div (c \cdot d)$

Solve each equation. Use the replacement set $\{{}^{+}5, {}^{-}5, 0, {}^{+}25, {}^{-}25\}$.

13. $n - {}^{+}10 = {}^{-}15$
14. $n + {}^{+}10 = {}^{-}15$
15. $n + {}^{-}5 = {}^{+}20$
16. $n - {}^{+}5 = 0$
17. ${}^{+}25 = n + 0$
18. $n - {}^{-}25 = {}^{+}5$

Solve and check.

19. $b + {}^{-}4 = {}^{-}6$
20. $x - {}^{+}3 = {}^{+}11$
21. ${}^{+}5 + h = {}^{-}13$
22. ${}^{+}8t = {}^{-}104$
23. $\frac{y}{{}^{-}6} = {}^{+}9$
24. ${}^{+}15z = 0$
25. $\frac{d}{{}^{-}10} = 0$
26. ${}^{+}14 - g = {}^{-}1$
27. ${}^{-}9 + f = {}^{-}20$
28. ${}^{+}15 = \frac{v}{{}^{+}3}$
29. ${}^{-}33 = {}^{+}11r$
30. ${}^{-}243 = {}^{-}9p$

II. Write each as an integer.

1. a gain of 5 lb
2. 11 m backward
3. 17 floors down

Find the absolute value of the integer.

4. $|{}^{-}18|$
5. $|{}^{+}19|$
6. $|{}^{-}73|$
7. $|502|$
8. $|{}^{-}643|$

Arrange in order from least to greatest.

9. ${}^{+}9, {}^{-}9, 0$
10. ${}^{-}9, {}^{+}6, {}^{-}2$
11. ${}^{-}60, {}^{+}30, 0, {}^{-}70$

Compute.

12. ${}^{-}11 + {}^{-}7$
13. ${}^{-}8 + {}^{+}4$
14. ${}^{+}366 \div {}^{+}6$
15. ${}^{+}2448 \div {}^{-}24$

Evaluate each expression when $a = {}^{+}7$, $b = {}^{-}2$, $c = {}^{-}3$, and $d = 0$.

16. $b \times (c + a)$
17. $ad \div c$
18. $a + b \cdot c$
19. $(a - b)^2 \div c$

Solve and check.

20. $y \div {}^{-}6 = {}^{+}7$
21. ${}^{+}15z = 0$
22. ${}^{-}9 + f = {}^{-}25$
23. ${}^{+}17 - g = {}^{-}1$

24. 144 beads were shared equally among some children. If there were 3 children fewer, each child would have 16 beads each. How many children were there?

Assignments 14

I. Check divisibility ...

1. 333 **2.** 128 **3.** 225 **4.** 7535 **5.** 8289

6. 9410 **7.** 99,483 **8.** 67,704 **9.** 67,713 **10.** 67,722

11. 23,918 **12.** 35,932 **13.** 85,446 **14.** 40,620 **15.** 90,990

16. 17,934 **17.** 49,708 **18.** 77,075 **19.** 13,104 **20.** 486,890

21. 207,984 **22.** 352,860 **23.** 607,712 **24.** 581,889 **25.** 270,228

Find the missing digit or digits that would make each number divisible by the given number.

26. 3,95□; by 10

Think
The last digit must be **0** to be divisible by 10.

27. 17,84□; by 3 **28.** 243,05□; by 9 **29.** 698,39□; by 3 and by 9

30. 17,39□; by 5 **31.** 14,5□2; by 8 **32.** 13,□12; by 8 and by 3

33. 27,1□8; by 6 **34.** 20,71□; by 4 **35.** 502,7□5; by 3 and by 5

II. Write missing factor: 1. 1331 x = 121; 2. 12321 x = 111

Write the missing term to complete the equivalent fraction.

3. $\frac{3}{4} = \frac{n}{12}$ **4.** $\frac{1}{11} = \frac{a}{88}$ **5.** $\frac{2}{9} = \frac{c}{81}$ **6.** $\frac{2}{3} = \frac{q}{12}$ **7.** $\frac{5}{7} = \frac{40}{f}$

8. $\frac{1}{8} = \frac{6}{b}$ **9.** $\frac{1}{10} = \frac{3}{q}$ **10.** $\frac{3}{11} = \frac{6}{s}$ **11.** $\frac{9}{10} = \frac{r}{100}$ **12.** $\frac{1}{25} = \frac{4}{d}$

13. $\frac{9}{30} = \frac{m}{10}$ **14.** $\frac{4}{12} = \frac{t}{3}$ **15.** $\frac{21}{28} = \frac{z}{4}$ **16.** $\frac{40}{45} = \frac{x}{9}$ **17.** $\frac{2}{6} = \frac{1}{h}$

18. $\frac{4}{k} = \frac{20}{25}$ **19.** $\frac{6}{13} = \frac{24}{m}$ **20.** $\frac{49}{e} = \frac{7}{8}$ **21.** $\frac{x}{15} = \frac{36}{45}$ **22.** $\frac{9}{16} = \frac{y}{144}$

Write two equivalent fractions for each fraction.

23. $\frac{5}{9}$ **24.** $\frac{3}{5}$ **25.** $\frac{1}{4}$ **26.** $\frac{5}{10}$ **27.** $\frac{6}{8}$

28. $\frac{3}{7}$ **29.** $\frac{11}{15}$ **30.** $\frac{9}{12}$ **31.** $\frac{25}{75}$ **32.** $\frac{8}{12}$

***.

Assignments 15

I: Write all the common factors for each set of numbers.

1. 8 and 24 2. 10 and 30 3. 15 and 35 4. 12 and 18
5. 16 and 20 6. 12 and 24 7. 30 and 18 8. 45 and 20
9. 4, 6, and 8 10. 6, 9, and 12 11. 5, 12, and 14 12. 6, 14, and 22

Find the GCF and the GCD of each set of numbers.

13. 6 and 12 14. 12 and 36 15. 8 and 10 16. 6 and 14
17. 9 and 30 18. 8 and 36 19. 24 and 42 20. 7 and 40
21. 8, 24, 32 22. 5, 30, and 35 23. 15, 30, and 45

Find the GCF. Use prime factorization.

24. 48 and 56 25. 64 and 96 26. 36 and 72 27. 80 and 100
28. 45 and 75 29. 39 and 104 30. 48 and 84 31. 100 and 125
32. 14, 49, 70 33. 48, 80, and 112 34. 18, 54, 72 and 90

II. Evaluate ....

1. $4^4 \times 4^{-2}$ 2. $(3^2)(3^{-5})$ 3. $(6^2)^0$ 4. $\frac{3^4}{3^9}$

5. $(v^6)^{-3}$ 6. $\frac{b^8}{b^{-2}}$ 7. $(k^{-10})(k^{-2})$ 8. $(5^{-3})^{-1}$

9. $\frac{2^{-6}\times 2^3}{2^{-5}}$ 10. $(j^3)^{-2} \times j^6$ 11. $\frac{(m^{-3})^5}{m^5}$ 12. $\frac{4^6}{4^{-2}} \times 4^{-6}$

Determine if the following equations are true. Justify your answer.

13. $8^{-5} \times 8^6 = 8^0 \times 8$ 14. $(j^2)^{-5} = \frac{j^{10}}{j^2}$

15. $\frac{m^3 \times m^{-5}}{m^2} = \frac{m^4}{m^0}$ 16. $(4^{-5})^4 = (4^{10})^{-2}$

Determine the appropriate exponent to make the equation true.

17. $\frac{p^5}{p^{-5}} = (p^2)^{?}$ 18. $2^{-10} \times 2^2 = 2^{-4} \times 2^{?}$

19. 10% of a = 40% of b = 60% of c; Find the value of $(a+b+c)\left(\frac{1}{a}+\frac{1}{b}+\frac{1}{c}\right)$ = ...

20. $(1a^0 + 2a^1 + 3a^2 + \ldots\ldots\ \ldots\ldots\ 10{,}000\ a^{9{,}999}) = \left(1 - \frac{1}{10{,}001}\right) X\ 125{,}000 = 5^p \text{ X } 10^q$; p = ...; q = ...;

21. What least number should be subtracted from six digit greatest number to make the value divisible by 6,12,18 and 36 leaving remainder 5 in each case.

Assignments 16

Convert into lowest term:

1: $\frac{1}{121} X \frac{11}{169} X \frac{13}{225} X \frac{143}{1000} X \frac{15}{49} X \frac{105}{1000}$ 2: 1/12th of 1/4th of 48,048 3: (1.001 X 10.01 X 100.1)X 10^4

4: $\left(\frac{1}{16} X \frac{3}{32} X \frac{7}{64} X 2^{12} X \frac{1}{1000}\right)$ 5. $(3^4 X \frac{1}{27} X \frac{1}{9} X \frac{1}{225} X 15$ 6. $\frac{15 X 1.005 X 100.5 X 1005 X 10}{1005^3}$

Is the fraction in lowest terms? Write *Yes* or *No*. If no, rename the fraction in simplest form.

7. $\frac{2}{3}$ **8.** $\frac{1}{8}$ **9.** $\frac{4}{8}$ **10.** $\frac{5}{10}$ **11.** $\frac{3}{10}$ **12.** $\frac{1}{12}$

13. $\frac{7}{21}$ **14.** $\frac{12}{25}$ **15.** $\frac{10}{18}$ **16.** $\frac{6}{21}$ **17.** $\frac{12}{18}$ **18.** $\frac{5}{24}$

19. $\frac{16}{27}$ **20.** $\frac{9}{12}$ **21.** $\frac{14}{35}$ **22.** $\frac{24}{34}$ **23.** $\frac{17}{36}$ **24.** $\frac{18}{72}$

Rename each as a fraction in simplest form.

25. $\frac{18}{36}$ **26.** $\frac{15}{40}$ **27.** $\frac{16}{48}$ **28.** $\frac{3}{18}$ **29.** $\frac{16}{20}$ **30.** $\frac{9}{45}$

31. $\frac{5}{55}$ **32.** $\frac{12}{16}$ **33.** $\frac{20}{50}$ **34.** $\frac{21}{49}$ **35.** $\frac{12}{24}$ **36.** $\frac{12}{30}$

37. $\frac{12}{44}$ **38.** $\frac{30}{55}$ **39.** $\frac{14}{42}$ **40.** $\frac{14}{18}$ **41.** $\frac{5}{35}$ **42.** $\frac{20}{32}$

43. $\frac{14}{20}$ **44.** $\frac{16}{24}$ **45.** $\frac{20}{32}$ **46.** $\frac{9}{36}$ **47.** $\frac{6}{27}$ **48.** $\frac{16}{28}$

II. Answer the following:

Multiply.

1. $4 \times \frac{3}{4}$ **2.** $10 \times \frac{3}{5}$ **3.** $18 \times \frac{1}{3}$ **4.** $24 \times \frac{1}{12}$

5. $25 \times \frac{4}{5}$ **6.** $20 \times \frac{3}{10}$ **7.** $9 \times \frac{3}{4}$ **8.** $27 \times \frac{1}{2}$

9. $\frac{5}{6} \times 18$ **10.** $\frac{7}{9} \times 45$ **11.** $\frac{4}{5} \times 12$ **12.** $\frac{3}{7} \times 9$

III. **Find the value of *n*.** Use the properties of multiplication.

1. $\frac{1}{5} \times \frac{3}{4} = \frac{3}{4} \times n$ **2.** $\frac{3}{8} \times n = \frac{3}{8}$ **3.** $n \times \frac{5}{6} = \frac{5}{6}$

4. $\frac{1}{2} \times n = 0$ **5.** $\frac{1}{3} \times 0 = n \times \frac{1}{3}$ **6.** $\frac{7}{10} \times n = \frac{2}{3} \times \frac{7}{10}$

7. $\frac{1}{4} \times (\frac{1}{5} \times \frac{1}{6}) = (\frac{1}{4} \times n) \times \frac{1}{6}$ **8.** $n \times (4 + \frac{1}{3}) = (\frac{1}{2} \times 4) + (\frac{1}{2} \times \frac{1}{3})$

13. $\left(\frac{1}{2899} + \frac{1}{2899} + \cdots \ldots\ldots\ldots\ldots 2898\ times\right) X\ 161\ X\ 3^2$ = $(p X q X r)^2$; p =…….; q = …….; r = ……….;

Assignments 17

Find the LCM of each set of numbers.

1. 3, 4	2. 3, 6	3. 2, 5	4. 8, 24	5. 12, 15
6. 4, 10	7. 1, 9	8. 6, 5	9. 12, 10	10. 40, 16
11. 3, 4, 6	12. 1, 6, 7	13. 4, 5, 10	14. 4, 6, 8	
15. 5, 6, 12	16. 3, 9, 12	17. 8, 12, 36	18. 10, 18, 72	
19. 4, 6, 9	20. 5, 10, 15	21. 3, 5, 9	22. 8, 9, 10	

Find the LCM of each set of numbers. Use prime factorization.

23. 3, 7	24. 2, 3	25. 7, 21	26. 3, 9	27. 12, 4	28. 10, 5
29. 7, 2	30. 11, 5	31. 3, 15	32. 16, 32	33. 1, 9	34. 12, 1
35. 7, 8, 56	36. 8, 10, 40	37. 12, 48,72	38. 8, 13, 52		
39. 5, 9, 27	40. 9, 14, 16	41. 9, 15, 25	42. 4, 14, 49		

II. **Compare. Write <, =, or >. You can use a number line to help.**

1. $\frac{7}{8} \underline{?} \frac{5}{8}$ **2.** $\frac{9}{20} \underline{?} \frac{9}{20}$ **3.** $\frac{14}{30} \underline{?} \frac{26}{30}$ **4.** $\frac{17}{21} \underline{?} \frac{10}{21}$

5. $\frac{12}{7} \underline{?} \frac{16}{7}$ **6.** $\frac{9}{8} \underline{?} \frac{8}{8}$ **7.** $\frac{22}{6} \underline{?} \frac{32}{6}$ **8.** $\frac{19}{19} \underline{?} \frac{20}{19}$

Rename each pair of fractions using the LCD as their denominator.

9. $\frac{3}{5}$ and $\frac{1}{4}$ **10.** $\frac{3}{4}$ and $\frac{1}{10}$ **11.** $\frac{7}{8}$ and $\frac{5}{6}$ **12.** $\frac{1}{2}$ and $\frac{2}{3}$

13. $\frac{1}{12}$ and $\frac{3}{24}$ **14.** $\frac{1}{3}$ and $\frac{4}{9}$ **15.** $\frac{5}{7}$ and $\frac{12}{49}$ **16.** $\frac{2}{5}$ and $\frac{4}{7}$

Compare. Write <, =, or >. You can use a number line to help.

17. $\frac{1}{4} \underline{?} \frac{7}{16}$ **18.** $\frac{7}{10} \underline{?} \frac{3}{5}$ **19.** $\frac{4}{21} \underline{?} \frac{1}{7}$ **20.** $\frac{6}{14} \underline{?} \frac{2}{7}$

21. $\frac{3}{5} \underline{?} \frac{5}{8}$ **22.** $\frac{4}{7} \underline{?} \frac{6}{9}$ **23.** $\frac{7}{12} \underline{?} \frac{9}{15}$ **24.** $\frac{10}{25} \underline{?} \frac{7}{10}$

25. When two line segments meet at a point forming right angles, what type of segments are they called?
(A) Parallel segments (B) Perpendicular segments (C) Equal segments (D) Bisecting segments

26. What are the lines which lie on the same plane and do not intersect at any point called?
(A) Perpendicular lines (B) Intersecting lines (C) Parallel lines (D) Collinear lines

27. Ratio of three interior angles of a triangle is 1:2:3. Find measure of each of the angles.

28. Two identical and regular pentagons are joined side by side to form another polygon. How many sides will be there in newly formed pentagon? What will be the sum total of all the interior angles of that polygon?

Assignments 18

Write in order from least to greatest.

1. $\frac{4}{5}, \frac{7}{10}, \frac{3}{4}$
2. $\frac{5}{12}, \frac{3}{8}, \frac{5}{6}$
3. $9\frac{3}{5}, 9\frac{5}{8}, 9\frac{7}{10}$
4. $7\frac{2}{9}, 7\frac{1}{3}, 7\frac{3}{4}$

Write in order from greatest to least.

5. $\frac{7}{12}, \frac{1}{2}, \frac{2}{3}$
6. $\frac{1}{4}, \frac{1}{3}, \frac{1}{5}$
7. $\frac{2}{5}, \frac{7}{10}, \frac{1}{3}$
8. $\frac{7}{12}, \frac{4}{5}, \frac{9}{10}$
9. $5\frac{4}{5}, 5\frac{3}{4}, 5\frac{7}{8}$
10. $2\frac{2}{3}, 3\frac{3}{4}, 2\frac{4}{5}$
11. $\frac{17}{18}, \frac{7}{9}, \frac{2}{3}$
12. $\frac{3}{7}, \frac{1}{2}, \frac{3}{14}$
13. $\frac{21}{9}, \frac{12}{9}, \frac{9}{12}$
14. $\frac{7}{6}, \frac{14}{5}, \frac{31}{10}$
15. $1\frac{2}{15}, \frac{18}{15}, 1\frac{4}{15}$
16. $\frac{21}{9}, 1\frac{5}{9}, \frac{8}{3}$

17. $\left(\frac{1}{1009} + \frac{2}{1009} + \dots\dots + \frac{1007}{1009}\right) + \left(1 - \frac{1}{1,009}\right) \times \frac{1}{504}$ = ...

18. $\frac{11}{31}, \frac{13}{310}, \frac{139}{260}, \frac{128}{930}$ ... arrange these fractions in ascending order.

Choose the equivalent decimal or fraction.

1. $\frac{7}{100}$ a. 0.700 b. 0.07 c. 0.007 d. 700.7
2. $13\frac{28}{100}$ a. 13.28 b. 13.028 c. 13.0028 d. 0.1328
3. $\frac{109}{1000}$ a. 100.9 b. 0.0109 c. 0.109 d. 109.001
4. 8.09 a. $8\frac{9}{10}$ b. $8\frac{9}{100}$ c. $8\frac{9}{1000}$ d. $\frac{89}{100}$
5. 12.37 a. $12\frac{37}{1000}$ b. $123\frac{7}{10}$ c. $1\frac{237}{1000}$ d. $12\frac{37}{100}$

6. (1.001 X 20.02 X 300.03 X 4.004 X 0.5005) = 1,001 X ....

7. $[1\times(1,001)^{-1} + 2\times(1,001)^{-1} + 3\times(1,001)^{-1} + \dots\dots 1,000\times(1,001)^{-1}] \times 125,000,000$ = ...

[Express your answer in exponential form.]

8. If the angles $(2a - 10)^0$ and $(a - 11)^0$ are complementary, what is the value of 'a'?

Assignments 19

Write each decimal as a fraction in simplest form.

10. 0.9 **11.** 0.07 **12.** 0.43 **13.** 0.77 **14.** 0.003

15. 0.127 **16.** 0.45 **17.** 0.36 **18.** 0.675 **19.** 0.325

20. 0.0033 **21.** 0.0009 **22.** 0.441 **23.** 0.101 **24.** 0.0500

Write each decimal as a mixed number in simplest form.

25. 1.09 **26.** 5.7 **27.** 11.31 **28.** 12.1 **29.** 2.5

30. 8.4 **31.** 9.16 **32.** 6.35 **33.** 1.055 **34.** 3.004

35. 6.0005 **36.** 8.0010 **37.** 3.375 **38.** 2.95 **39.** 20.0750

Rename each decimal as a fraction or mixed number in simplest form.

40. A tortoise travels 0.7 mile per hour.

41. An elephant can run at a speed of 24.5 miles per hour.

42. The height of a zebra may be 1.55 meters.

43. The height of a flower may be 0.44 meter.

II. Write the following in the form of simplest decimal form:

1. 0.66666 . . . **2.** 0.11111 . . . **3.** 0.45454 . . . **4.** 0.09090 . . .

5. 0.83333 . . . **6.** 0.26666 . . . **7.** 2.384848 . . . **8.** 5.13232 . . .

Write each repeating decimal showing eight decimal places.

9. $0.\overline{1}$ **10.** $0.\overline{12}$ **11.** $0.1\overline{4}$ **12.** $0.2\overline{8}$

13. $5.\overline{3}$ **14.** $12.\overline{06}$ **15.** $7.2\overline{7}$ **16.** $13.2\overline{17}$

Rename each fraction as a terminating or repeating decimal.

17. $\frac{1}{8}$ **18.** $\frac{13}{20}$ **19.** $\frac{5}{11}$ **20.** $\frac{1}{3}$ **21.** $\frac{3}{4}$

22. $\frac{2}{9}$ **23.** $\frac{7}{16}$ **24.** $\frac{5}{12}$ **25.** $\frac{11}{18}$ **26.** $\frac{1}{16}$

Rename each mixed number as a terminating or repeating decimal.

27. $4\frac{2}{5}$ **28.** $6\frac{1}{4}$ **29.** $12\frac{2}{3}$ **30.** $15\frac{2}{3}$ **31.** $1\frac{3}{8}$

***.

Assignments 20

Compare and write comparative signs

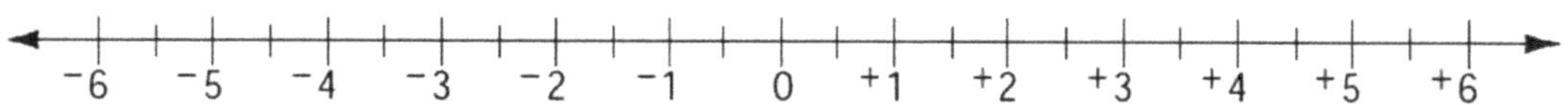

1. $\frac{^{-}1}{2}\ \underline{\ ?\ }\ \frac{^{-}3}{4}$ **2.** $^{-}0.5\ \underline{\ ?\ }\ ^{+}0.75$ **3.** $^{-}3.5\ \underline{\ ?\ }\ ^{-}4.25$ **4.** $^{+}3\frac{1}{4}\ \underline{\ ?\ }\ ^{+}3\frac{1}{8}$

5. $^{-}4\ \underline{\ ?\ }\ \frac{^{-}6}{3}$ **6.** $^{+}2.5\ \underline{\ ?\ }\ ^{-}3\frac{1}{2}$ **7.** $^{-}5\frac{1}{8}\ \underline{\ ?\ }\ ^{+}4$ **8.** $^{-}6\ \underline{\ ?\ }\ ^{-}5.75$

9. $0\ \underline{\ ?\ }\ ^{-}3.25$ **10.** $\frac{^{+}3}{4}\ \underline{\ ?\ }\ 0$ **11.** $\frac{^{-}8}{2}\ \underline{\ ?\ }\ ^{-}4$ **12.** $\frac{^{-}1}{8}\ \underline{\ ?\ }\ ^{-}0.125$

Write in order from least to greatest. Use the number line above to help.

13. $^{-}3,\ ^{-}4\frac{1}{2},\ 2$ **14.** $0,\ \frac{^{-}1}{2},\ 2\frac{1}{4}$ **15.** $5,\ 0,\ \frac{2}{1}$ **16.** $^{-}4,\ 3\frac{1}{4},\ ^{-}1.5$

17. $^{-}2.25,\ ^{+}0.25,\ ^{-}1.5$ **18.** $^{-}2\frac{1}{2},\ 2.5,\ ^{-}1\frac{1}{4}$ **19.** $\frac{1}{4},\ \frac{^{-}1}{4},\ 0$ **20.** $5\frac{1}{4},\ ^{-}1,\ ^{-}2\frac{3}{4}$

21. $\frac{6}{3},\ \frac{^{-}3}{4},\ ^{-}4$ **22.** $\frac{^{-}3}{4},\ \frac{2}{1},\ 1\frac{1}{4}$ **23.** $\frac{3}{2},\ ^{-}2\frac{1}{2},\ 3$ **24.** $\frac{^{-}4}{2},\ ^{-}1.5,\ ^{-}2\frac{1}{2}$

II. Answer the following:

Find the prime factorization and write in exponential form.

1. 28 **2.** 30 **3.** 75 **4.** 84

Write the missing number to complete the equivalent fraction.

5. $\frac{2}{3} = \frac{x}{9}$ **6.** $\frac{3}{4} = \frac{9}{y}$ **7.** $\frac{20}{90} = \frac{z}{9}$ **8.** $\frac{15}{45} = \frac{p}{3}$

9. $\frac{10}{13} = \frac{x}{65}$ **10.** $\frac{38}{44} = \frac{19}{t}$ **11.** $\frac{23}{69} = \frac{w}{3}$ **12.** $\frac{7}{11} = \frac{49}{s}$

Find the GCF of each pair of numbers.

13. 3 and 27 **14.** 12 and 48 **15.** 21 and 35

16. 10, 14, and 34 **17.** 22, 33, and 55 **18.** 27, 63, and 81

Find the LCM of each pair of numbers.

19. 3 and 5 **20.** 6 and 18 **21.** 4 and 15

22. 4, 7, and 8 **23.** 9, 12, and 15 **24.** 8, 24, and 36

5. Worksheets Level 3

Following worksheets and assignments are related to additional mathematical processing.

Assignments 1

I: **Simplify each mathematical expression.**

1. $6 \times \frac{1}{2} \div (\frac{1}{4})^2$ **2.** $9 \times \frac{1}{3} \div (\frac{1}{2})^3$ **3.** $\frac{5}{6} + \frac{1}{6} - 0.5$

4. $\frac{4}{9} - \frac{1}{9} + \frac{2}{3}$ **5.** $\frac{1}{8} + 0.5 \times 16$ **6.** $1\frac{2}{3} - 6 \times (\frac{1}{6})^2$

Simplify. Check with a calculator.

7. $(1\frac{1}{4} \times 4) - (\frac{1}{3})^2$ **8.** $(8 \div 1\frac{1}{3}) + 6^2$ **9.** $(1\frac{2}{3} \times 1\frac{1}{2}) \div 5$

10. $(10 \div 1\frac{2}{3}) \times \frac{7}{8}$ **11.** $(\frac{2}{3})^2 \times (1\frac{1}{2} + 1\frac{3}{4})$ **12.** $1\frac{1}{3} \times (2\frac{1}{2} - 1\frac{1}{4})^2$

Simplify using the Distributive Property.

13. $\frac{1}{8} \times (8 - \frac{8}{11})$ **14.** $\frac{1}{6} \times (12 - \frac{3}{5})$ **15.** $\frac{1}{3} \times (15 - \frac{3}{8})$

16. $\frac{3}{4} \times (4 - \frac{1}{3})$ **17.** $\frac{8}{9} \times (18 - \frac{1}{4})$ **18.** $\frac{3}{7} \times (14 - \frac{1}{9})$

II. **Compute.** Round to the nearest cent when necessary.

1. $\frac{1}{2}$ of \$46 **2.** $\frac{1}{5}$ of \$85 **3.** $\frac{1}{3}$ of \$6.09 **4.** $\frac{1}{4}$ of \$8.32

5. $\frac{3}{4}$ of \$70 **6.** $\frac{2}{5}$ of \$86 **7.** $\frac{2}{3}$ of \$21.50 **8.** $\frac{3}{8}$ of \$16.50

9. $\$3.50 \div 3\frac{1}{2}$ **10.** $\$5.50 \div 1\frac{2}{3}$ **11.** $\$36.75 \div 3\frac{3}{4}$ **12.** $\$11.20 \div 1\frac{1}{3}$

13. $\$14.90 \div 2\frac{1}{2}$ **14.** $\$11.40 \div 1\frac{1}{5}$ **15.** $\$6.65 \div 1\frac{3}{4}$ **16.** $\$56 \div \frac{7}{8}$

17. Age of Fontana is 5 years less than Snehal. Five years back difference of their age was 10 years. Find sum total of their ages after five years.
18. Ratio of angles of a quadrilateral is 2:3:4:6. Find magnitude of all the angles.
19. What least number should be subtracted from seven digit greatest number to make the value divisible by 22?

Assignments 2

I. Evaluate each expression.

1. $\frac{3}{5}z$, when $z = \frac{3}{8}$
2. $c \div \frac{7}{12}$, when $c = \frac{7}{9}$
3. $2\frac{3}{4}t$, when $t = \frac{8}{11}$
4. $m \div \frac{9}{10}$, when $m = 5\frac{2}{5}$
5. $7h$, when $h = \frac{10}{21}$
6. $x \div \frac{8}{9}$, when $x = 14$
7. $6\frac{7}{8}y$, when $y = \frac{8}{15}$
8. $3\frac{2}{3} \div z$, when $z = 2\frac{4}{9}$
9. $7\frac{1}{8}b$, when $b = 1\frac{13}{19}$
10. $(a + b) \div \frac{1}{6}a$, when $a = \frac{2}{3}$ and $b = \frac{1}{12}$
11. $c + \frac{1}{2}d$, when $c = 2\frac{1}{6}$ and $d = \frac{2}{3}$
12. $(x - y)z \div y$, when $x = \frac{3}{4}$, $y = \frac{3}{8}$, and $z = \frac{3}{10}$
13. $m + (p + s) \div s$, for $m = 1\frac{1}{2}$, $p = \frac{3}{5}$, and $s = \frac{2}{3}$

II. Solve for *x*.

1. $\frac{5}{8}x = 95$
2. $20x = \frac{10}{13}$
3. $x \div \frac{8}{9} = 21$
4. $x \div 9 = 9\frac{2}{3}$
5. $x \div 11\frac{7}{9} = 18$
6. $5x = 5\frac{5}{8}$
7. $2\frac{7}{10}x = 21$
8. $x \div \frac{2}{3} = \frac{6}{7}$
9. $\frac{4}{5}x = \frac{2}{3}$
10. $x \div \frac{7}{12} = 3\frac{3}{7}$
11. $10\frac{4}{5}x = \frac{9}{10}$
12. $x \div 6\frac{7}{8} = 1\frac{5}{11}$
13. $\frac{8}{15}x = 1\frac{1}{9}$
14. $x \div 7\frac{1}{2} = 13\frac{1}{4}$
15. $8\frac{4}{9}x = 1\frac{1}{3}$
16. $2x + \frac{1}{2}x = 25$

III. Multiply. Simplify using the GCF whenever possible.

1. $\frac{5}{6} \times \frac{3}{4}$
2. $18 \times \frac{2}{3}$
3. $\frac{2}{9}$ of 3
4. $\frac{6}{11} \times \frac{33}{42}$
5. $\frac{4}{5} \times \frac{3}{7}$

Find the value of *n*. Name the property of multiplication used.

6. $\frac{5}{6} \times \frac{6}{5} = n$
7. $n \times (8 \times \frac{2}{3}) = (\frac{1}{4} \times 8) \times \frac{2}{3}$
8. $n \times \frac{3}{5} = \frac{3}{5}$
9. $\frac{2}{11} \times (5 + \frac{11}{14}) = (\frac{2}{11} \times n) + (\frac{2}{11} \times \frac{11}{14})$

Estimate. Then multiply or divide.

10. $4\frac{1}{5} \times 2\frac{2}{3}$
11. $2\frac{4}{7} \times 3\frac{1}{2}$
12. $8 \div 3\frac{1}{5}$
13. $10\frac{2}{5} \div 2\frac{1}{6}$

Compute.

14. $\frac{1}{3}$ of \$48
15. $\frac{3}{5}$ of \$12.75
16. \$36.40 $\div 1\frac{1}{7}$
17. \$8 $\div \frac{4}{5}$

Evaluate.

18. $(m + n) \div \frac{2}{5}n$, when $m = \frac{3}{10}$ and $n = \frac{1}{5}$
19. $x + \frac{1}{2}y$, when $x = \frac{1}{6}$ and $y = \frac{2}{3}$

***.

Assignments 3

Simplify each complex fraction.

1. $\dfrac{\frac{2}{3}}{8}$ 2. $\dfrac{8}{\frac{2}{5}}$ 3. $\dfrac{\frac{3}{7}}{\frac{9}{10}}$ 4. $\dfrac{^{-}21}{\frac{7}{8}}$ 5. $\dfrac{\frac{5}{9}}{^{-}3}$ 6. $\dfrac{\frac{^{-}7}{10}}{\frac{^{-}5}{12}}$

7. $\dfrac{\frac{1}{12}+\frac{1}{3}}{\frac{3}{8}+\frac{5}{24}}$ 8. $\dfrac{\frac{1}{5}-\frac{1}{25}}{\frac{1}{2}-\frac{2}{5}}$ 9. $\dfrac{\frac{5}{6}-\frac{7}{8}}{\frac{2}{9}+\frac{7}{12}}$

10. $\left(\frac{11}{12}\ X\frac{12}{13}\ X\frac{13}{14}X\ \ldots\ldots\ldots\frac{999}{1000}\right)X\frac{1}{121}\ X\frac{154}{1000}\ X\ 10^6$ = ...

II. Simplify:

1. $\frac{7}{8}\times\frac{6}{35}\times\frac{5}{9}$ 2. $5\frac{2}{5}\times 3\frac{1}{3}$ 3. $6\frac{2}{3}\times 1\frac{1}{5}$ 4. $\frac{7}{10}$ of \$20

5. $\frac{7}{8}\div\frac{5}{16}$ 6. $7\frac{5}{7}\div\frac{9}{14}$ 7. $7\frac{1}{2}\div 3\frac{3}{4}$ 8. $\$9\div 1\frac{1}{3}$

Evaluate.

9. $(c+d)\div\frac{1}{6}c$, when $c=\frac{1}{2}$ and $d=\frac{1}{12}$ 10. $x\div\frac{1}{2}y$, when $x=2\frac{1}{6}$ and $y=\frac{2}{3}$

Solve and check.

11. $\frac{3}{8}x=15$ 12. $5x=\frac{10}{13}$ 13. $x\div\frac{5}{9}=20$ 14. $x\div 14=3\frac{2}{7}$

Convert the temperature to °C or to °F. Watch for the degree unit.

15. 5°C = 16. 50°C = 17. 23°F = 18. $^{-}49$°F =

19. Find area of the following shapes.

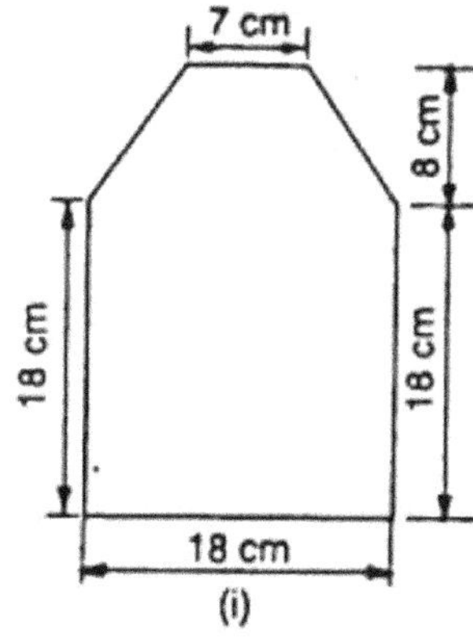

(i)

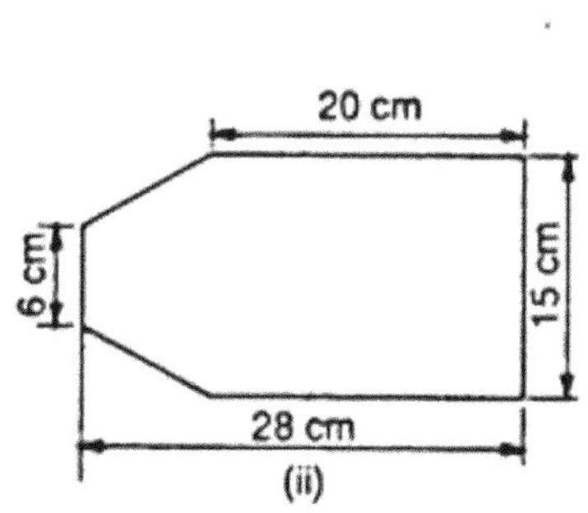

(ii)

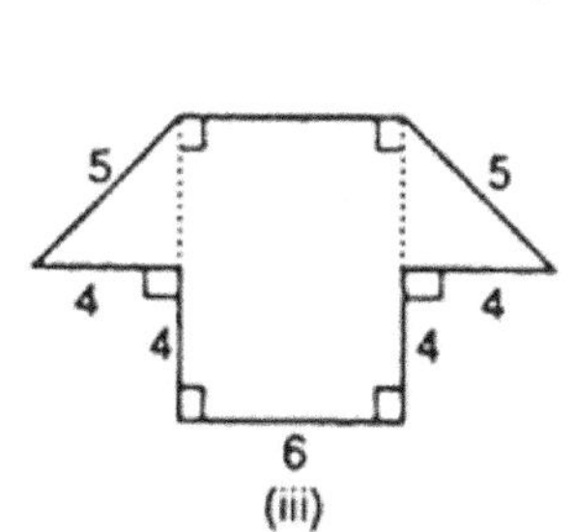

(iii)

***.

Assignments 4

Solve for the variable.

1. 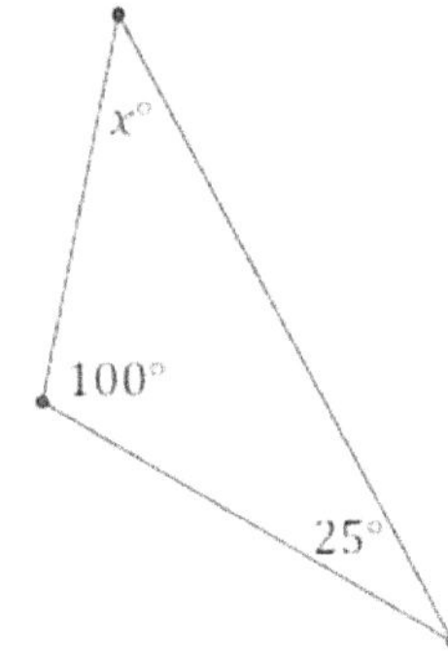

2. 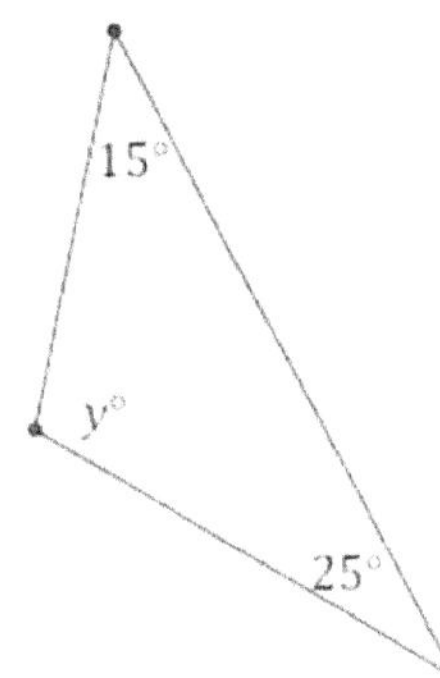

3. 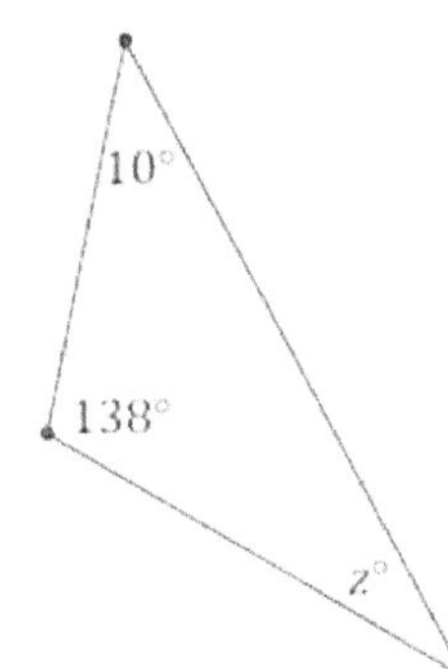

4. 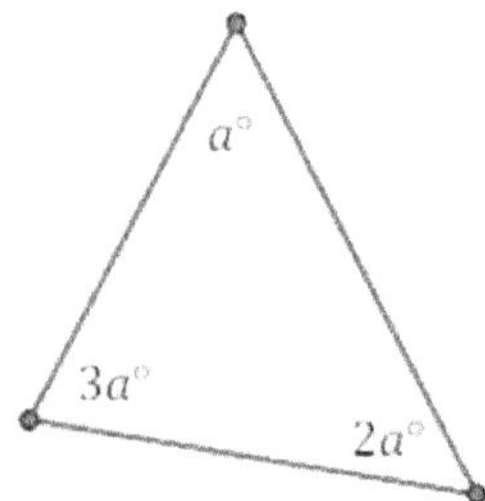

5. 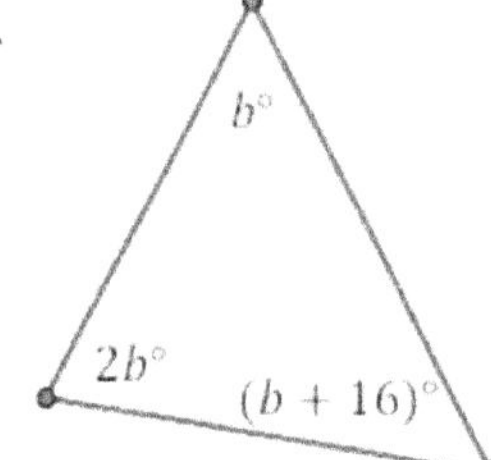

6. 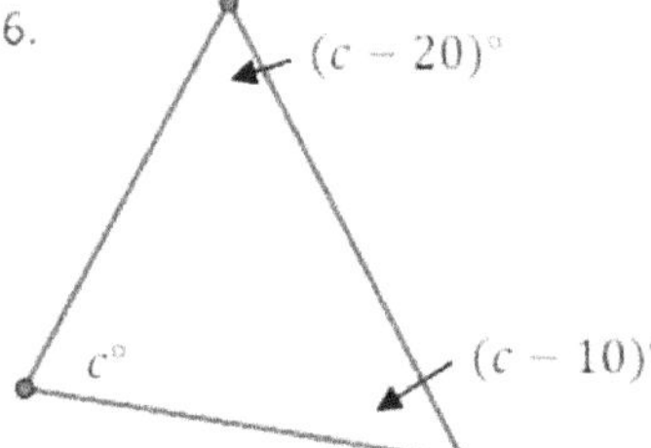

7. 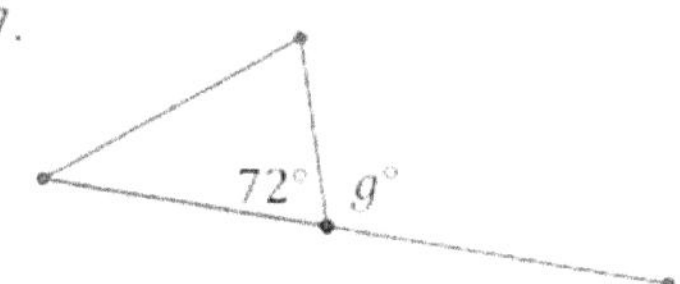

8. 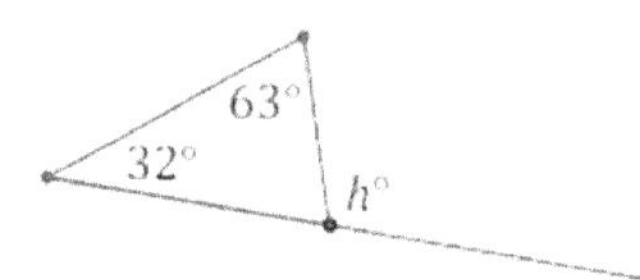

9. 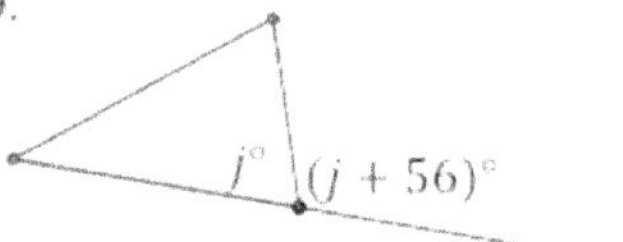

10. 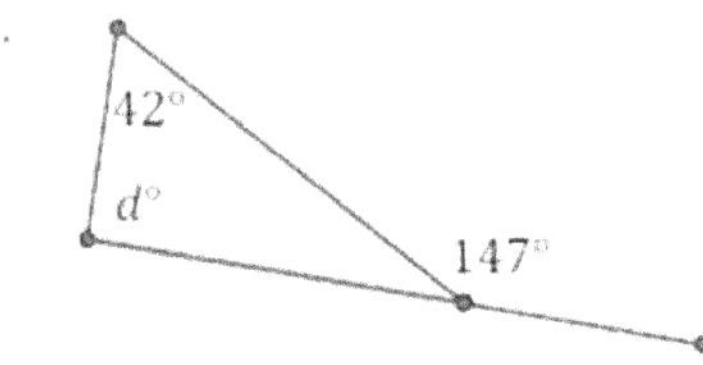

11. 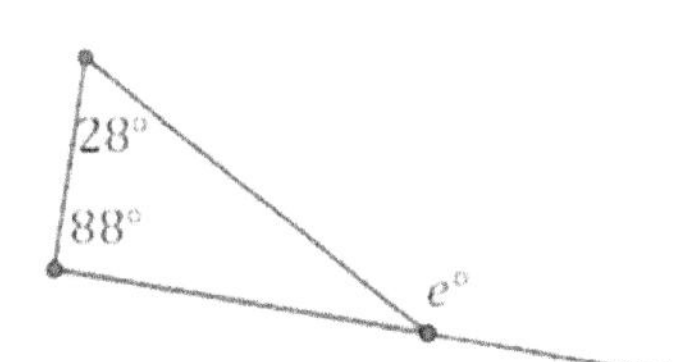

12. 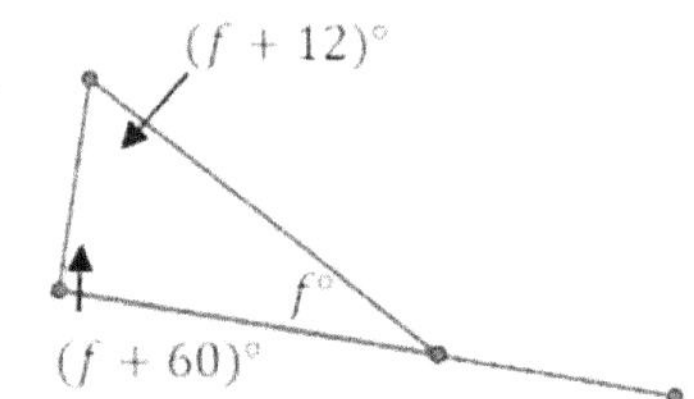

***.

Assignments 5

1: Observe the figure given below and answer questions as follows.

Use the following picture to answer the questions.

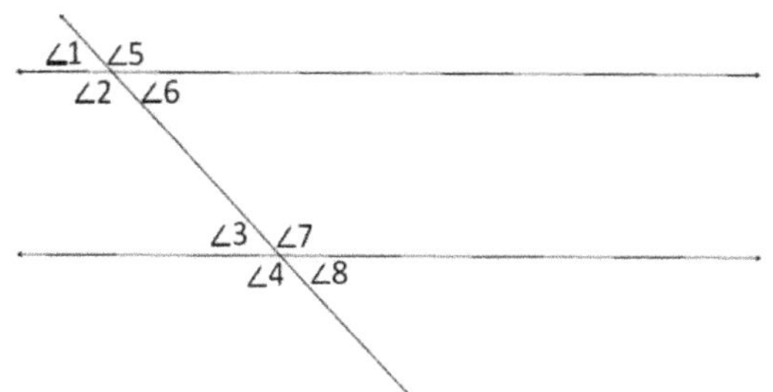

1. Name a pair of vertically opposite angles.
2. Name a pair of interior opposite angles.
3. Name a pair of corresponding angles.
4. If angle 7 = 130^0 then find angles 1,3,5, and 8.
5. Establish relationship between angles 1 and 8.
6. Which angle is adjacent to angle 7.
7. Name three linear pairs.

2. Write names of specific transformation as displayed in the following figures...

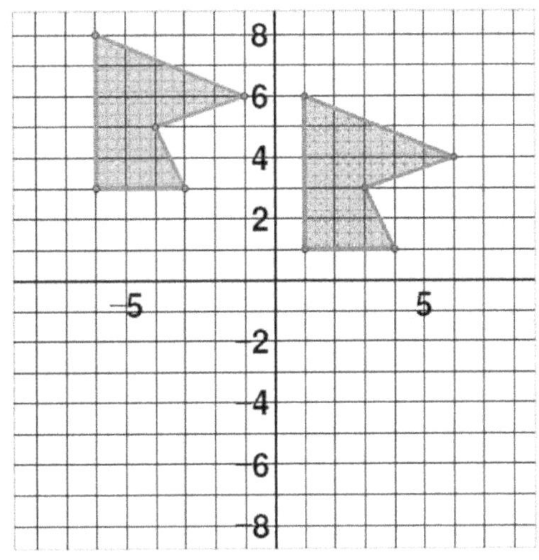

A: .... B: ....

3. Three speed –time graphs are displayed ..

A. 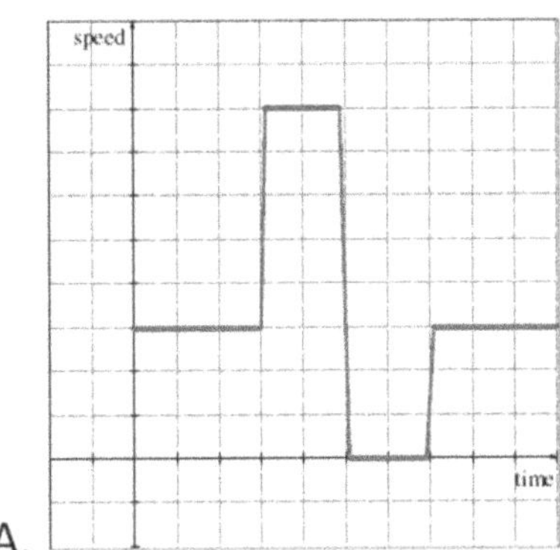

B. 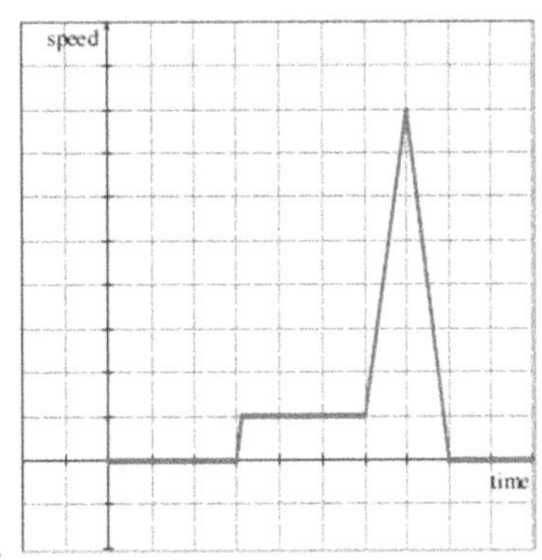

C. 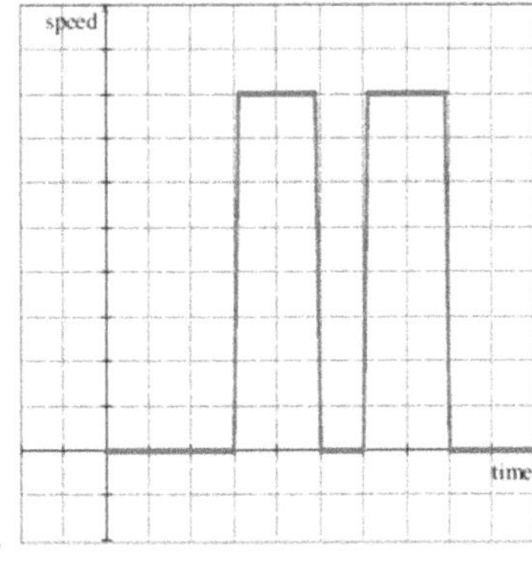

During which phase of motion initial and final speed of the reference object was identical?

4. A train was moving from city P to city Q with a uniform speed of 75 km/h. During return journey speed of the train was 100 km/h. What was the average speed of that train during the entire journey?

[Ans: 85.6 km /h (estimated up to two decimal)]

***.

Assignments 6

1. Observe the figure and answer the question as follows.

A
7.5 cm
6.5 cm
D
E
B
C
F
7 cm

Find height of DF.
Conditions:

a) Area of triangle ABC is equal to area of parallelogram DBCE.
b) Triangle ABC is a scalene triangle.

2. Find the variables.

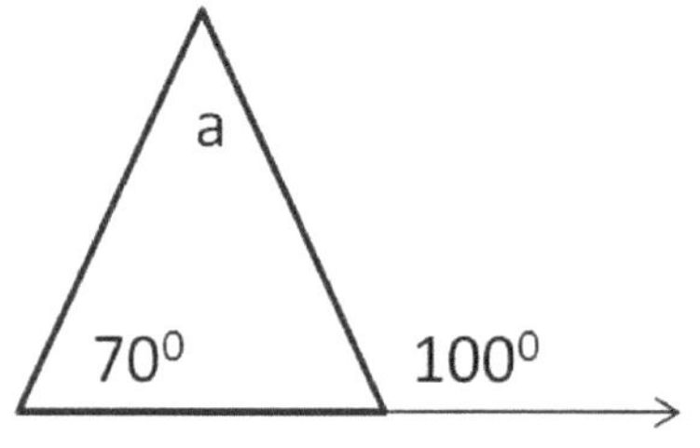

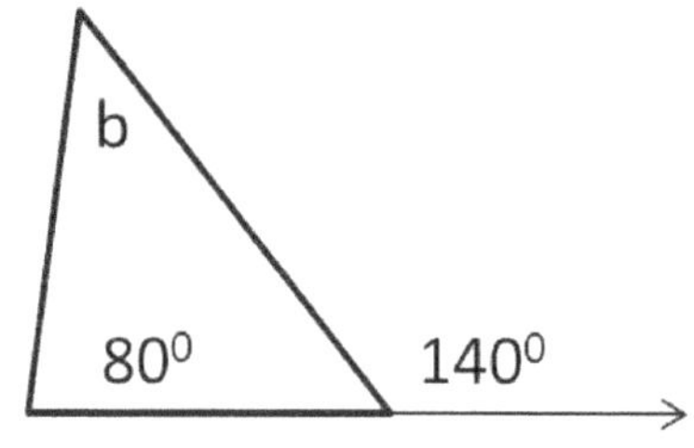

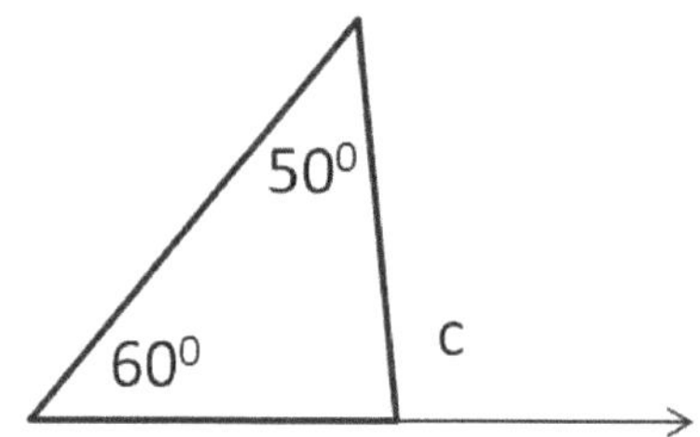

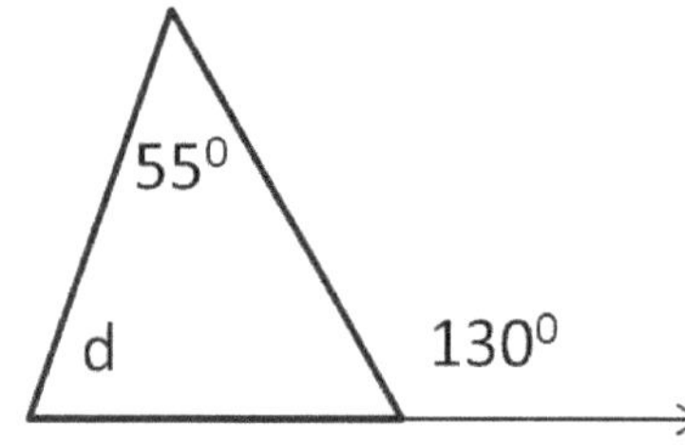

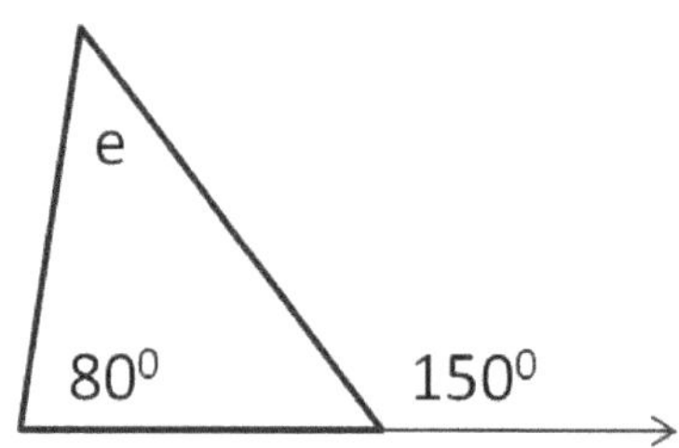

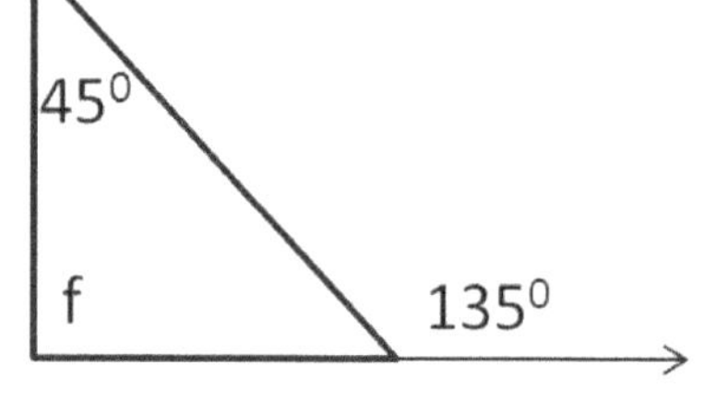

3. Find the greatest possible and smallest possible outer boundary which can be obtained by arranging 16 different squares of side 10 cm each.

4. Ratio of three different interior angles of a triangle are in the ratio of 2x + 3, 3x + 4 and 4x + 5. Find the value of x. Also find magnitude of different angles.

5. Three squares each of area 144 sq. cm. are used to make a rectangle by arranging all the three squares side by side. Find outer boundary of that rectangle.

Assignments 7

I: Find volume of each of the given shapes.

1.

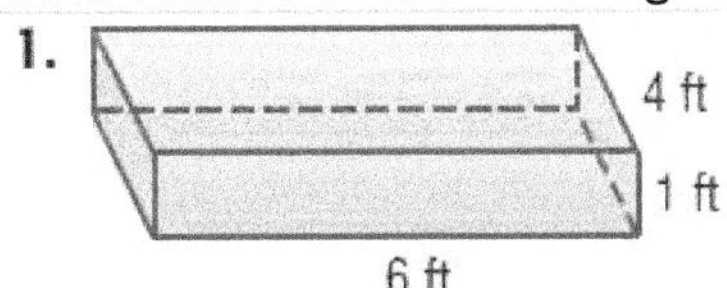

2. 8.5 cm, 2 cm, 2 cm

3. $12\frac{1}{2}$ mm, 3 mm, 4 mm

4.

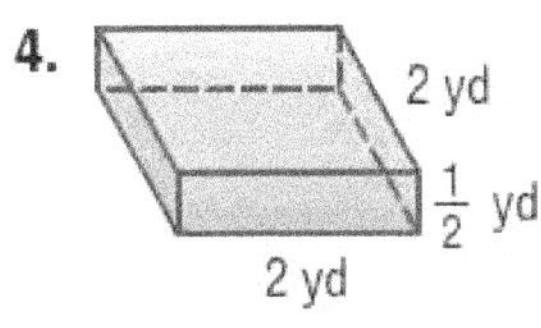

5.

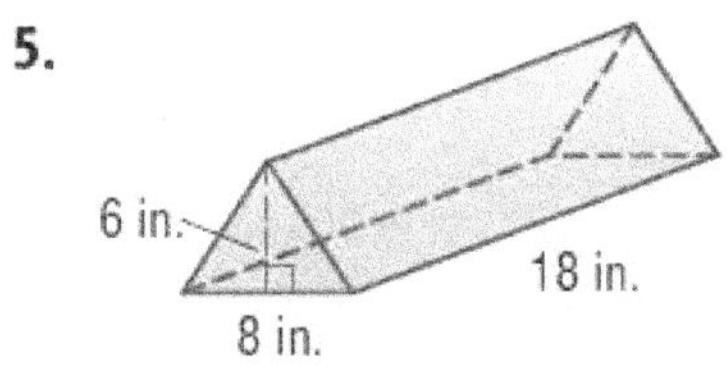

6.

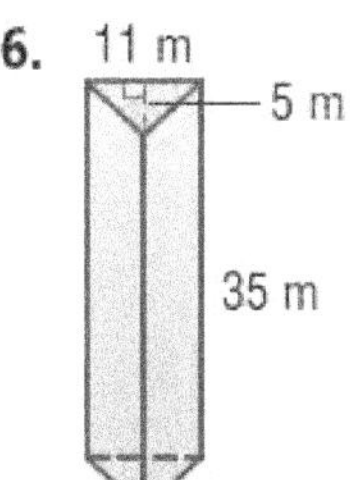

7.

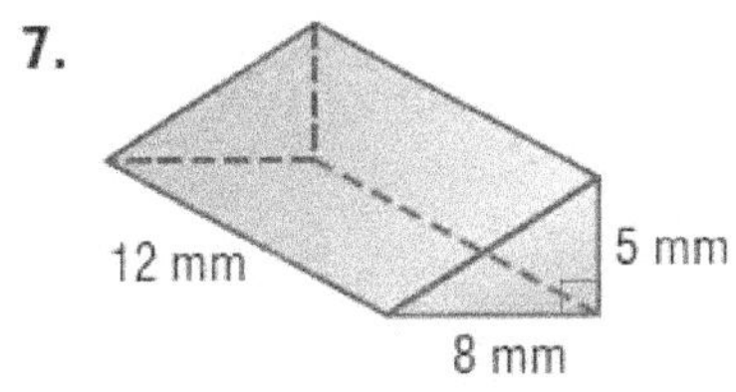

8.

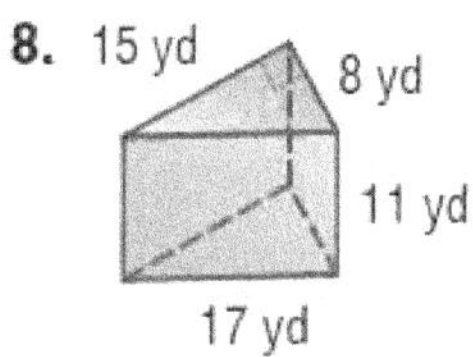

9.

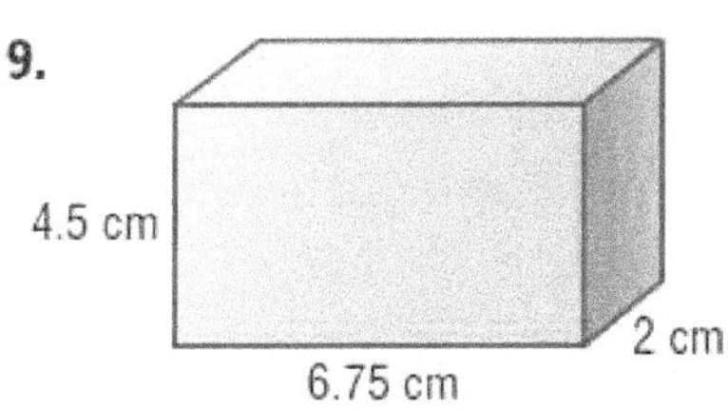

II. Find the surface area of each cylinder. Round to the nearest tenth if necessary.

1.

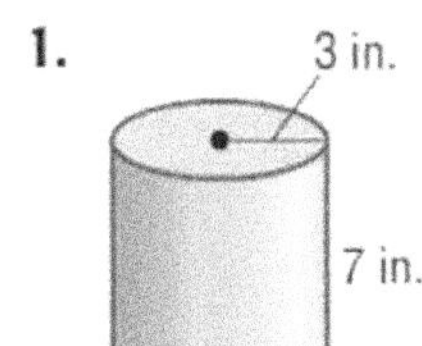

2.

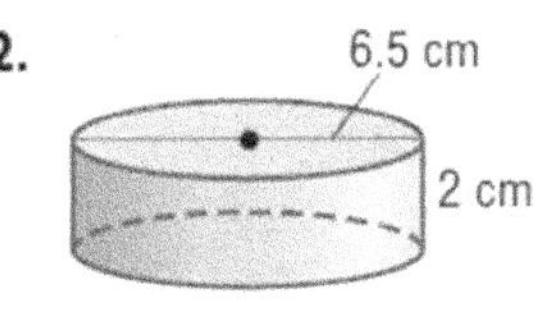

3.

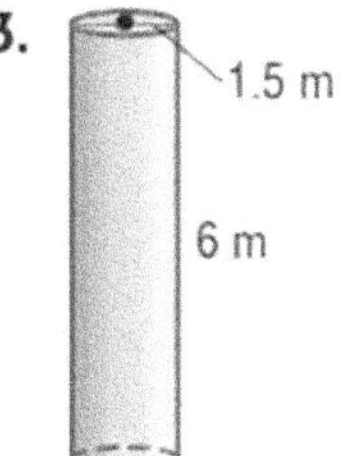

4.

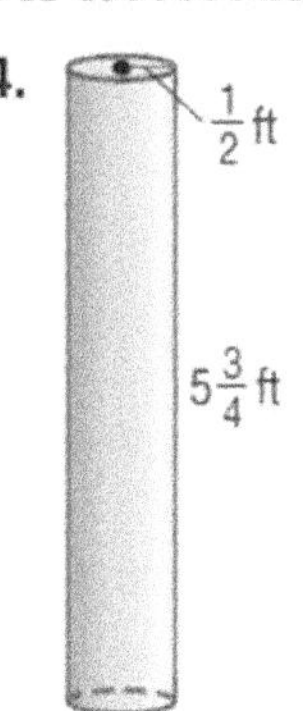

5. height = 6 cm
radius = 3.5 cm

6. height = 16.5 mm
diameter = 18 mm

7. height = 22 yd
radius = 10.5 yd

8. height = 10.2 mi
diameter = 4 mi

9. height = 8.6 cm
diameter = 8.2 cm

10. height = 32.7 m
radius = 21.5 m

11. height = $2\frac{2}{3}$ yd
diameter = 6 yd

12. height = $12\frac{3}{4}$ ft
radius = $7\frac{1}{4}$ ft

13. height = $5\frac{1}{2}$ in.
diameter = 3 in.

***.

Assignments 8

I: Complete.

1. 400 mm = cm	2. 4 km = m	3. 660 cm = m
4. 0.3 km = m	5. 30 mm = cm	6. 84.5 m = km
7. m = 54 cm	8. 18 km = cm	9. mm = 45 cm
10. 4 kg = g	11. 632 mg = g	12. 4,497 g = kg
13. mg = 0.51 kg	14. 0.63 kg = g	15. kg = 563 g
16. 662 m = km	17. 5,283 mL = L	18. 0.24 cm = mm
19. 380 kL = L	20. 10.8 g = mg	21. 83,000 mL = L

II. **Find the surface area of each rectangular prism. Round to the nearest tenth if necessary.**

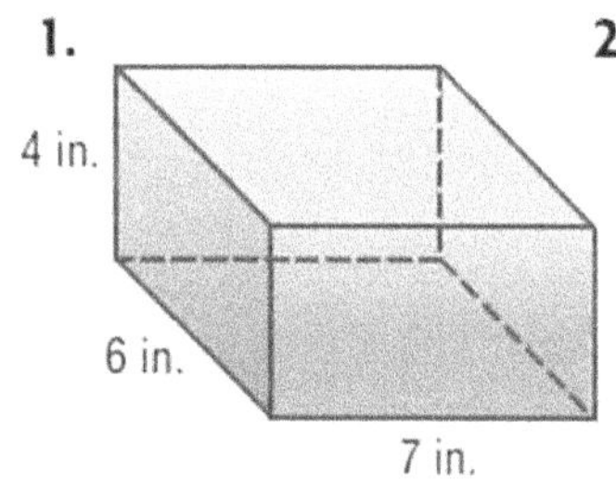

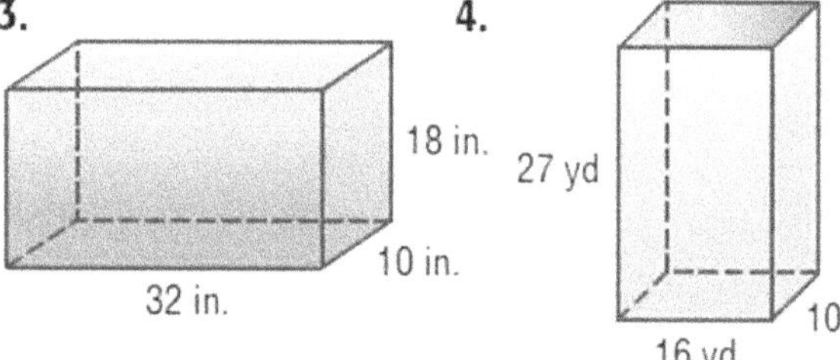

5. length = 10 m
width = 6 m
height = 7 m

6. length = 20 mm
width = 15 mm
height = 25 mm

7. length = 8 ft
width = 6.5 ft
height = 7 ft

8. length = 20.4 cm
width = 15.5 cm
height = 8.8 cm

9. length = 8.5 mi
width = 3 mi
height = 5.8 mi

10. length = $7\frac{1}{4}$ ft
width = 5 ft
height = $6\frac{1}{2}$ ft

11. length = $15\frac{2}{3}$ yd
width = $7\frac{1}{3}$ yd
height = 9 yd

12. length = $4\frac{1}{2}$ in.
width = 10 in.
height = $8\frac{3}{4}$ in.

13. length = 12.2 mm
width = 7.4 mm
height = 7.4 mm

14. Mid points of four sides of a quadrilateral are joined serially and a square is obtained. The kind of quadrilateral must be ....

15. A swimming pool can be filled at the rate of 205 litres per minute using ten special pumps. About how many hours will it take to fill a pool that holds 410,000 gallons of water?

16. In a 9-room house, 6 rooms are tiled, 2 rooms are painted, and 1 room is both tiled and painted. How many rooms are not tiled or painted?

17. Rate of rain was 1.03 inches per hour. Speed of rain was doubled after three hours and again came down to 90 cm per minute after 7th hour. Calculate the total rainfall of that place in 10 hours.

***.

Assignments 9

1: Which of the following distance –time graph shows a heavy loaded truck is moving with non-uniform motion?

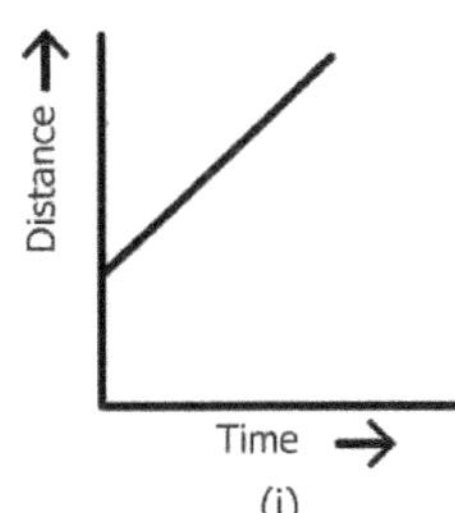

(i)

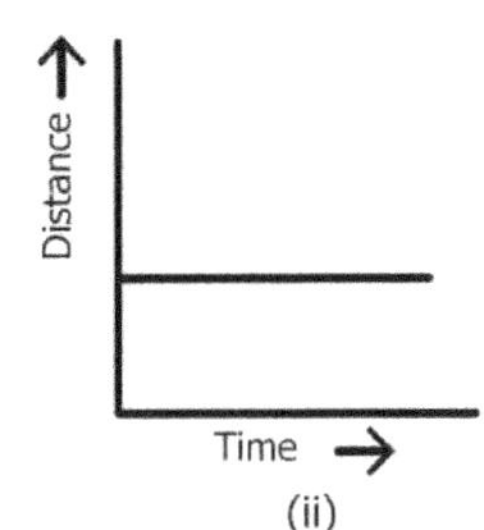

(ii)

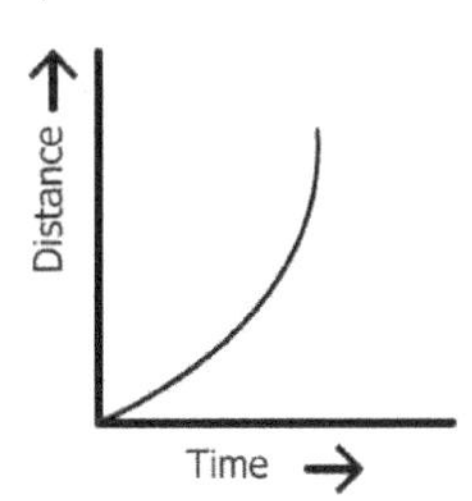

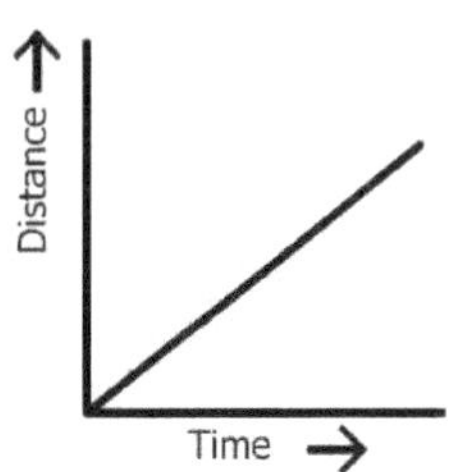

2. A Data sheet is provided which records repeated counting of digits at various instances. Use this data sheet to work out a frequency chart to display occurrence of digits at different instances.

2	2	2	2	2	2	2	2	2	2
3	3	3	3	3	3	3	3	3	3
3	3	3	3	3	3	3	3	3	3
4	5	5	6	6	6	9	9	9	9
4	5	5	6	6	6	9	9	9	9
4	5	5	7	7	7	7	7	1	1
4	5	5	7	7	7	7	7	1	1
4	5	5	7	7	7	7	7	1	1
4	5	5	8	8	8	8	8	8	8

Digits	Tally Mark	Frequency
1		
2		
3		
4		
5		
6		
7		
8		
9		

3. Calculate average rainfall from January to September on the basis of the data provided.

Months	Jan	Feb	March	Apr	May	Jun	July	Aug	Sept
Rainfall in mm	101	87	98	54	121	343	376	376	243

4. The .... of a triangle is the point of concurrence of its medians.
5. The .... of a triangle are the line segments joining the vertices of the triangle to the midpoints of the opposite sides.
6. ....of triangle are the perpendiculars drawn from the vertices of a triangle to the opposite sides.
7. The .... is the point of concurrence of the altitudes of a triangle.
8. The ....of a right angled triangle is the vertex containing the right angle.

9. The .... drawn on equal sides of an isosceles triangle are equal.
10. The .... bisects the base of an isosceles triangle.
11. The .... of an equilateral triangle are equal.
12. The .... of an equilateral triangle coincides with its orthocentre.
13. What is the length of the hypotenuse of a right angled triangle whose two legs measure 12 cm and 0.15 m?
14. If the two legs of a right angled triangle are equal and the square of the hypotenuse is 800 sq. units, what is the length of each leg?
15. If in a Δ. ABC, ∠ A = 60° and AB = AC, of what type is Δ. ABC?

(A) An isosceles triangle. (B) A right angled triangle.
(C) An isosceles right angled triangle . (D) An equilateral triangle.

16. Answer the following:

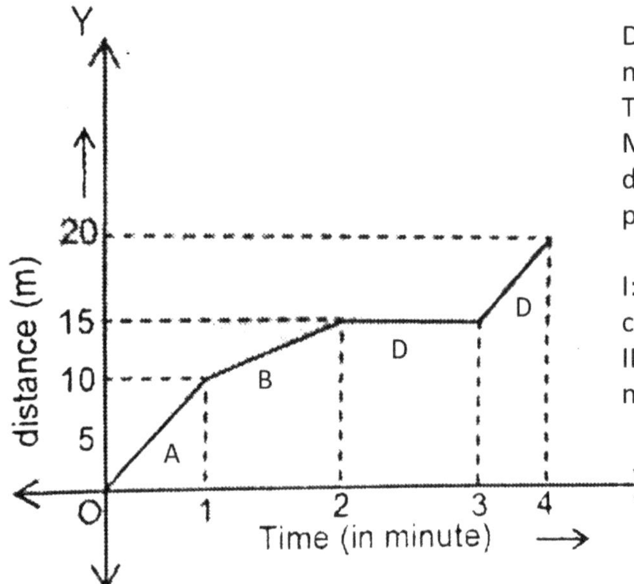

Distance – Time Graph is plotted to record movement of a car along a road having heavy Traffic.
Motion of the car through entire journey is divided into four distinct phases. In one of the phase

I: Find out the phase of movement at which the car remained stationary.
II: Find out the place at which the car gained maximum seed.

17. Which of the following basic shapes have measure of exterior angle equal to 72^0 . How many sides are there in that polygon?

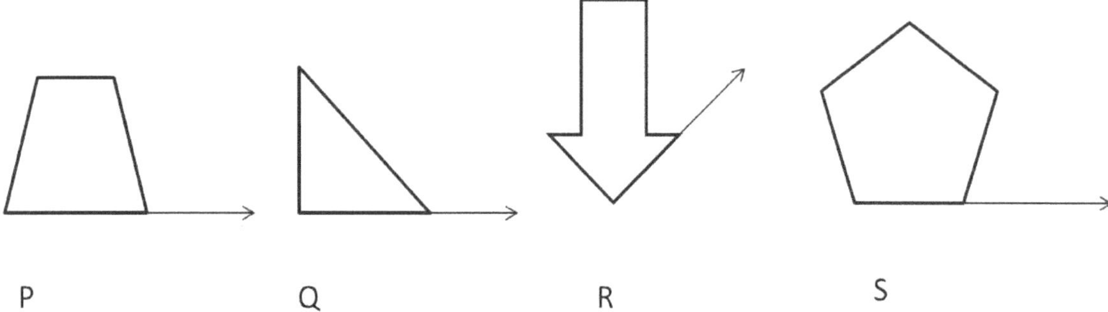

18. Find a greatest numbers of seven digits which can be divided by 3, 6, 9 , 18 and 36 leaving remainder 2 in each case.

{key: 4 = centroid; 5 = medians; 6 = Altitudes ; 7 = orthocentre; 8 = orthocentre; 9 = altitudes; 10= altitude; 11 =altitudes; 12 = centroid; 17 = S; 18:]

Assignments 10

1. Determine which of the following polynomials has $(x+1)$ a factor :

(i) x^3+x^2+x+1 (ii) $x^4+x^3+x^2+x+1$

(iii) $x^4+3x^3+3x^2+x+1$ (iv) $x^3-x^2-\left(2+\sqrt{2}\right)x+\sqrt{2}$

2. Use the Factor Theorem to determine whether $g(x)$ is a factor of $p(x)$ in each of the following cases:

(i) $p(x)=2x^3+x^2-2x-1,\ g(x)=x+1$

(ii) $p(x)=x^3+3x^2+3x+1,\ g(x)=x+2$

(iii) $p(x)=x^3-4x^2+x+6,\ g(x)=x-3$

3. Find the value of k, if $x-1$ is a factor of $p(x)$ in each of the following cases:

(i) $p(x)=x^2+x+k$ (ii) $p(x)=2x^2+kx+\sqrt{2}$

(iii) $p(x)=kx^2-\sqrt{2}x+1$ (iv) $p(x)=kx^2-3x+k$

4. Factorise :

(i) $12x^2-7x+1$ (ii) $2x^2+7x+3$

(iii) $6x^2+5x-6$ (iv) $3x^2-x-4$

5. Factorise :

(i) x^3-2x^2-x+2 (ii) x^3-3x^2-9x-5

(iii) $x^3+13x^2+32x+20$ (iv) $2y^3+y^2-2y-1$

6. Sum total of a natural number, its cube root and value of reciprocal is equal to 10.125. Find the number.

7. $(x-1)(x+1)(x^2+1)(x^4+1)=127$. What is the value of $(x+1)(x^2-x+1)$?

8. $\left(\sqrt{16+\sqrt{16+16+\sqrt{16}+16+\sqrt{16}\ldots\ldots\ldots\propto}}\right) X \left(\sqrt{\frac{1}{32}+\sqrt{\frac{1}{32}+\sqrt{\frac{1}{32}+\ldots\ldots\ldots\propto}}}\right) = \ldots\ldots$

9. During a thunder storm the top of a broken tree touches the ground at a distance of 15 m from its base. If the tree is broken at a height of 8 m from the ground, what was the actual height of the tree?

10. Factorise: (i) $49a^2+70ab+25b^2$ (ii) $\left(\sqrt{10+4\sqrt{3}}\right)\left(\sqrt{2-4\sqrt{3}}\right)$ (iii) $81x^2-121y^2-27x-33y$

11. Calculate HCF: $(x^{16}-1)$, (x^8-1), (x^4-1), (x^2-1), $(x+1)$,

***.

6. Word Problems

Selected Assignments for solving Word Problems are included in this section.

Word Problems 1

1. What least number should be subtracted from six digit greatest numbers to make the value divisible by 2, 4 and 8 leaving remainder 1 in each case?
2. Which of the following statements is true?
   (A) The mean height of the mountains is greater than their median height.
   (B) The mean height of the mountains is less than their mode.
   (C) The median height of the mountains is less than their mode.
   (D) The median height of the mountains is greater than their mean height.

3. A comet passed by the Earth in the year 1835. It passes by the Earth every 60 years. Based on this information, in which of the following years can the comet be expected to pass by the Earth?

4. Somerfield can finish a project work in 16 days and his counterpart takes 24 days to finish the same project work. If they start working together then the project work can be finished in .... Days.

5. Relationship of Celsius and Fahrenheit temperature scale is given by an equation on the basis of the fundamental intervals. Fundamental interval in Celsius scale is 1 and in Fahrenheit scale is 1.8.
(i) If the temperature is 86°F, what is the temperature in Celsius?
(ii) If the temperature is 35°C, what is the temperature in Fahrenheit?
(iii) If the temperature is 0°C what is the temperature in Fahrenheit and if the temperature is 0°F, what is the temperature in Celsius?
(iv) What is the numerical value of the temperature which is same in both the scales?

6. How many multiples of 22 located in between 100 and 200 are also multiples of 33?

7. Find out a greatest possible number of six digits which can be divided by 18, 36, 54 and 72 leaving remainder 17 in each case.

8. A wall mount clock strikes 5 bells at 5 O'Clock in 10 seconds. Calculate the time taken by this clock to strike 9 bells at 9 a.m.

9. What fraction of all the numbers from 1 to 100 are multiples of 11?

10. Simplify: (3.333.... + 4.44444.... + 5.5555.....) – (12.101010......) + $\frac{1}{3} + \frac{1}{5} + \frac{1}{9}$

11. $\left(p + \frac{1}{p}\right) = 2; find\ the\ value\ of\ \left(p^2 - \frac{1}{p^2}\right)\left(p^2 + \frac{1}{p^2}\right)\left(p^4 + \frac{1}{p^4}\right)$

12. There is an increase of 36^0 F of temperature during day time in a city. Find the corresponding increase recorded in ^{0}C.

***.

Word Problems 2

1. What least number should be subtracted from seven digit greatest number to make the value divisible by 4, 8 and 16 leaving remainder 3 in each case?
2. Read the following passage related to Terminating and Non-terminating decimals:

   I. What fraction of all the natural number from 1 to 200 are multiples of 9?

   II: Statements related to terminating and non-terminating decimals are as follows:

   Terminating decimals : In terminating decimals, the finite numbers of digits are in the right side of a decimal points. For example, 0.12,1.023,7.832,54.67,.......... etc. are terminating decimals.

   Recurring decimals : In recurring decimals, the digits or the part of the digits in the right side of the decimal points will occar repeatedly. For example, 3.333......, 2.454545......, 5.12765765.......... etc. are recurring decimals.

   Non-terminating decimals : In non-terminating decimals, the digits in the right side of a decimal point never terminate, i.e., the number of digits in the right side of decimal point will not be finite neither will the part occur repeatedly. For example. 1.4142135......, 2.8284271....... etc. are non-terminating decimals.

   Terminating decimals and recurring decimals are rational numbers and non-terminating decimals are irrational numbers. The value of an irrational number can be determined upto the required number after the decimal point. If the numerator and denominator of a fraction can be expressed in natural numbers, that fraction is a rational number.

   Classify the decimals stating reasons:

   a. 5.2333... b. 0.0025 c. 0.105105 ...... d. 0.450123

   d. $\sqrt{0.0625}$ e. 2.1356124 .... f. $\sqrt[3]{0.001331}$ g. 0.121121

   h. $\sqrt[4]{0.0256}$ i. 3.120304 j. $\sqrt[5]{0.03125}$ k. 121.0121

3. Solve the following:

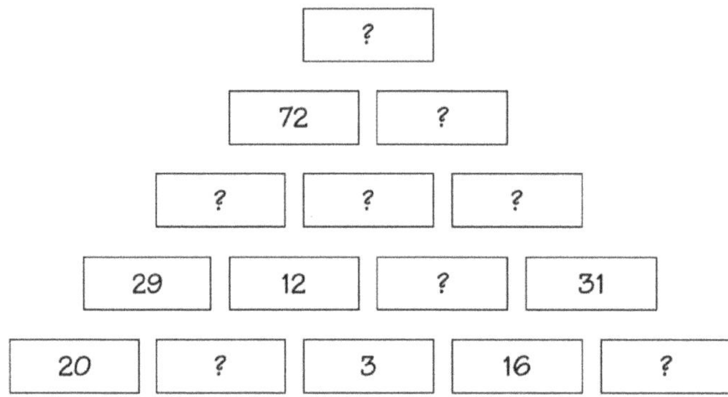

4. What fraction of numbers from 1 to 1,000 are divisible by 5, 25 and 125?

Word Problems 3

1. What least number should be added to seven digit smallest number to make the value divisible by 11, 22 and 33 leaving remainder 8 in each case?
2. Find value of angles in each case...

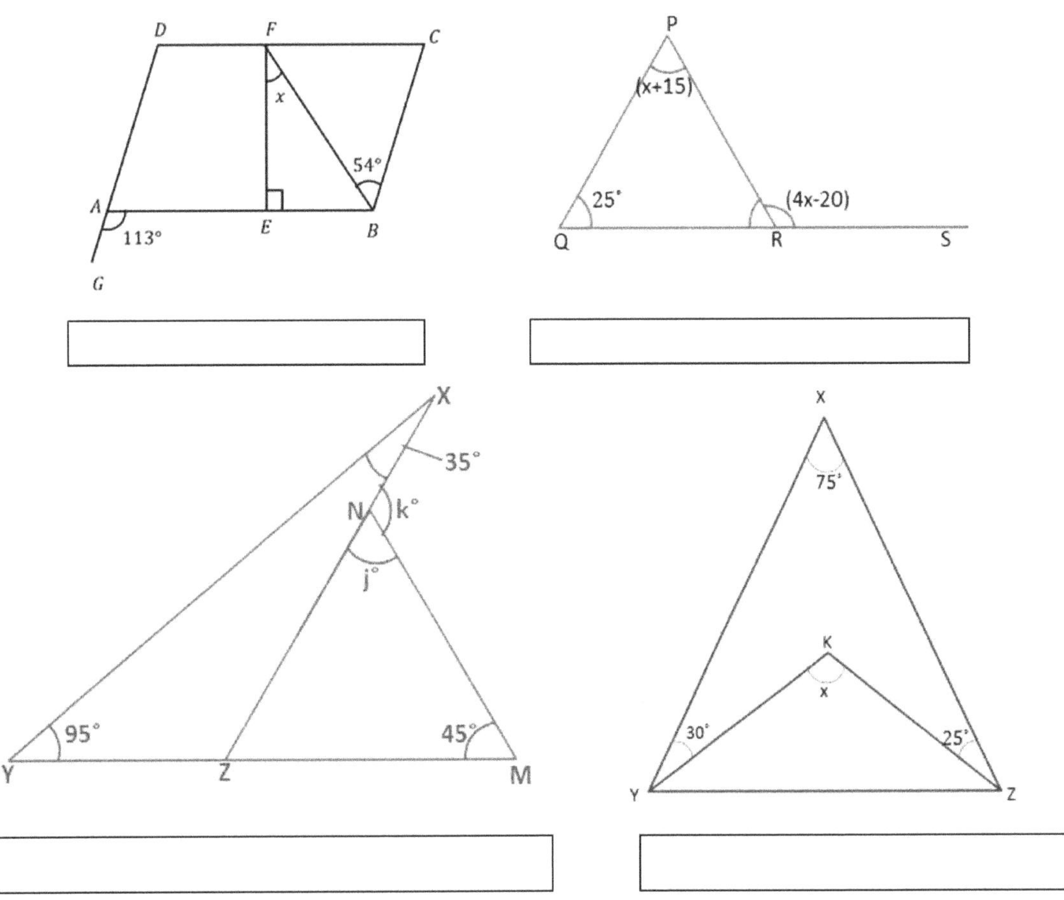

3. 20% of 30% of 21,042 = ... X 1,002
4. A shopkeeper gained an amount equal to selling price of 2 breads by selling 20 breads. What is the gain percentage made by the shopkeeper?
5. Three bells toll at an interval of 20 s, 30 s and 40s respectively. Find the time interval after which all these three bells toll together.
6. A farmer can finish farm activities in 7 days while working 8 hours a day. Find in how many days he can finish farm activities while working 7 hours a day.
7. Rijuana observed that a train is taking 1.5 hours to reach another station. During return journey it took 1 h 20 m in covering up the same speed. Find average speed of that train.
8. Sum total of five consecutive multiples of 9 is equal to 135. Find product of third and fourth multiples if we arrange them all in ascending order.
9. (1 + 2 + 3 + ... + 10,000) X $\left(\frac{1}{10,001} + \frac{1}{10001} + \cdots \ldots \ldots \ldots + 10,000\ times\right)$ = ...

II. Solve the following.....

Add or subtract. Write in simplest form.

1. $\frac{3}{4}+\left(-\frac{1}{6}\right)$
2. $-\frac{5}{8}+\frac{1}{2}$
3. $-\frac{4}{9}+\left(-\frac{2}{3}\right)$
4. $\frac{7}{8}-\frac{3}{4}$
5. $\frac{7}{13}-\frac{2}{9}$
6. $\frac{14}{15}-\left(-\frac{12}{21}\right)$
7. $-3\frac{2}{5}+1\frac{5}{6}$
8. $3\frac{5}{8}-1\frac{1}{3}$
9. $-4\frac{7}{12}-\left(-3\frac{7}{72}\right)$
10. $\left(1-\frac{1}{2}\right)\left(1-\frac{1}{3}\right)\ldots\ldots\left(1-\frac{1}{1000}\right) X\ 101{,}101\ X\frac{1}{101}$ = ...

Add or subtract. Write in simplest form.

11. $\frac{1}{4}+\left(-\frac{7}{12}\right)$
12. $-\frac{3}{8}+\frac{5}{6}$
13. $-\frac{6}{7}+\left(-\frac{1}{2}\right)$
14. $-\frac{5}{9}+\left(-\frac{3}{8}\right)$
15. $\frac{1}{3}-\frac{7}{8}$
16. $\frac{4}{5}-\left(-\frac{2}{15}\right)$
17. $-\frac{2}{9}-\left(-\frac{3}{11}\right)$
18. $-\frac{7}{15}-\left(-\frac{12}{25}\right)$
19. $3\frac{1}{5}+\left(-8\frac{1}{2}\right)$
20. $1\frac{1}{6}+\left(-6\frac{2}{3}\right)$
21. $8\frac{3}{7}-\left(-6\frac{1}{2}\right)$
22. $7\frac{3}{4}-\left(-1\frac{1}{8}\right)$
23. $-4\frac{3}{4}-5\frac{5}{8}$
24. $-8\frac{1}{3}-4\frac{5}{6}$
25. $-15\frac{5}{8}+11\frac{2}{3}$
26. $-22\frac{2}{5}+15\frac{5}{6}$

III. What fraction of all the shapes displayed below are polygons?

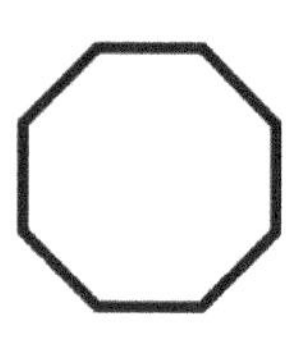

Rectangle Circle Square Rhombus Octagon Hexagon

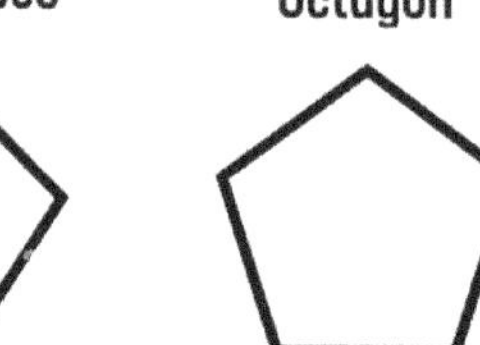

Parallelogram Ellipse Triangle Kite Pentagon Trapezoid

***.

7. Test Papers

Evaluate your skills.

Test Paper I

I. **Find the simple interest earned to the nearest cent for each principal, interest rate, and time.**

1. \$2,000, 8%, 5 years **2.** \$500, 10%, 8 months **3.** \$750, 5%, 1 year

4. \$175.50, $6\frac{1}{2}$%, 18 months **5.** \$236.20, 9%, 16 months **6.** \$89, $7\frac{1}{2}$%, 6 months

7. \$800, 5.75%, 3 years **8.** \$225, $1\frac{1}{2}$%, 2 years **9.** \$12,000, $4\frac{1}{2}$%, 40 months

Find the simple interest paid to the nearest cent for each loan, interest rate, and time.

10. \$750, 18%, 2 years **11.** \$1,500, 19%, 16 months **12.** \$300, 9%, 1 year

13. \$4,750, 19.5%, 30 months **14.** \$2,345, 17%, 9 months **15.** \$689, 12%, 2 years

16. \$390, 18.75%, 15 months **17.** \$1,250, 22%, 8 months **18.** \$3,240, 18%, 14 months

II. **Use the spinner at the right to find each probability. Write as a fraction in simplest form.**

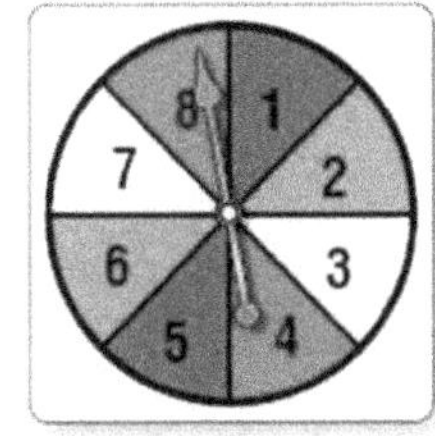

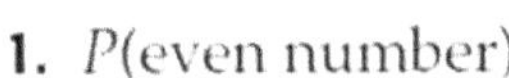

1. *P*(even number) **2.** *P*(prime number)

3. *P*(factor of 12) **4.** *P*(composite number)

5. *P*(greater than 10) **6.** *P*(neither prime nor composite)

A package of balloons contains 5 green, 3 yellow, 4 red, and 8 pink balloons. Suppose you reach in the package and choose one balloon at random. Find the probability of each event. Write as a fraction in simplest form.

7. *P*(red balloon) **8.** *P*(yellow balloon) **9.** *P*(pink balloon)

10. *P*(orange balloon) **11.** *P*(red or yellow balloon) **12.** *P*(*not* green balloon)

13. 30% of a = 50% of b = 70% of c; find the value of $\frac{a3 + b3 + c3}{abc}$ and $\frac{a^2 + b^2 + c^2}{ab+bc+ac}$

14. Two rectangles of dimension 3 cm X 4 cm and 6cm X 8 cm are arranged in such a way that their diagonals lie on the same line. Find total length of the line segment made up of two diagonals.

15. $\left(\sqrt{101} + \sqrt{101} + \cdots \ 10{,}000\ times\right)\left(1 + \frac{1}{10{,}000}\right) X \sqrt{1 + \frac{1}{100}}\ X\ 10^{-5}$ = ...

***.

Test Paper II

1. The least 4 digit number which is a perfect square is ______.

(a) 1024 (b) 1016

(c) 1036 (d) 1044

2. An odd number when multiplied by itself gives 2401. Find the number.

(a) 41 (b) 39

(c) 49 (d) 51

3. If the units digit of a perfect square is 4, then the units digit of its square root can be ______.

(A) 2 (B) 8

(a) Only (A) (b) Only (B)

(c) Either (A) or (B) (d) Neither (A) nor (B)

4. What will be the units digit of the squares of the following numbers?

(A) 71 (B) 669

(C) 2533 (D) 30,827

(a) 1 (b) 9

(c) Both (a) and (b) (d) 8

5. Which of the following is not a perfect square?

(a) 12,544 (b) 3136

(c) 23,832 (d) 1296

6. The smallest number with which 120 should be multiplied, so that the product is a perfect square is ______.

(a) 120 (b) 60

(c) 30 (d) 15

7. The greatest 3-digit number which is a perfect square is ______.

(a) 729 (b) 927

(c) 961 (d) 972

8. If p and q are perfect squares, then $\sqrt{\frac{p}{q}}$ is always a rational number. Is the statement true?

(a) Yes (b) No

(c) Cannot be determined (d) None of these

9. $\sqrt[3]{\frac{-a^6 \times b^3 \times c^{21}}{c^9 \times a^{12}}}$ = ______.

(a) $\frac{-bc^3}{a^2}$ (b) $\frac{bc^4}{a^2}$

(c) $\frac{-ab^4}{c^2}$ (d) $\frac{-bc^4}{a^2}$

10. If $3(x - 2)^2 = 507$, then x can be ______.

(a) 13 (b) 12

(c) 15 (d) 14

11. The value of $\sqrt{117^2 - 108^2}$ is ______.

(a) 55 (b) 45

(c) 35 (d) 65

12. The square root of $\frac{36}{5}$ when corrected to two decimal places is ______.

(a) 2.68 (b) 2.69

(c) 2.67 (d) 2.66

13. If the product of two equal numbers is 1444, then the numbers are ______.

(a) 48, 48 (b) 38, 38

(c) 32, 32 (d) 42, 42

14. The cube of the number p is 16 times the number. Then find p where $p \neq 0$ and $p \neq -4$.

(a) 4 (b) 3

(c) 8 (d) 2

15. The cube of a number x is nine times of x, then find x, if $x \neq 0$ and $x \neq -3$.

(a) 8 (b) 2

(c) 4 (d) 3

16. The digit in the units place for the cube of a four-digit number of the form $xyz8$ is ______.

(a) 8 (b) 4

(c) 2 (d) Cannot say

17. The digit in the units place for the cube of the number 12,34,568 is ______.

(a) 8 (b) 2

(c) 4 (d) 6

18. Which of the following number becomes a perfect cube when we divide the number by 5?

(a) 25 (b) 125

(c) 625 (d) 3125

19. The least number to be subtracted from 220 so that it becomes a perfect cube is _______.

(a) 4 (b) 10

(d) 16 (d) 20

20. If $x^{y^z} = 2^8$, then find the maximum possible value of $(x)\ (y)\ (z)$ where $x, y, z > 0$.

(a) 16 (b) 12

(c) 256 (d) 24

21. The smallest number which must be subtracted from 3400 to make it a perfect cube is ______.

(a) 35 (b) 25

(c) 65 (d) 15

22. If $a = 2b$ and $b = 4c$, then $\sqrt[3]{\dfrac{a^2}{16bc}}$ = _______.

(a) 1 (b) 2

(c) 3 (d) 4

23. Which of the following is not a perfect square?

(a) 16,384 (b) 23,857

(c) 18,496 (d) 11,025

24. The least number which must be added to 1200, so that the sum is a perfect square is _______.

(a) 52 (b) 25

(c) 35 (d) 45

25. The cube root of 110592 is _______.

(a) 44 (b) 38

(c) 58 (d) 48

26. $\sqrt[3]{\dfrac{3^6 \times 4^3 \times 2^6}{8^9 \times 2^3}}$ = ______

(a) $\dfrac{3}{8}$ (b) $\dfrac{9}{8}$

(c) $\dfrac{3}{64}$ (d) $\dfrac{9}{64}$

27. If n is a perfect cube, then every prime factor of 'n' occurs _______.

(a) One time

(b) Two times

(c) 3 times

(d) 4 times

28. The cube root of the number 10,648 is ______.

(a) 42 (b) 38

(c) 28 (d) 22

29. The cube of a number ending in 3 ends in ______.

(a) 3 (b) 7

(c) 9 (d) 1

30. If n leaves a remainder 1 when divided by 2, then n^3 leaves a remainder of _______, when divided by 2.

(a) 1 (b) 2

(c) 0 (d) 3

31. If $169 = b^2 + 25$, then find the value of b. The following steps are involved in solving the above problem. Arrange them in sequential order from the first to the last.

(A) $b^2 = 144$

(B) $169 = b^2 + 25 \Rightarrow b^2 = 169 - 25$

(C) $b = \pm\sqrt{144} \Rightarrow b = \pm 12$

(a) BAC (b) BCA

(c) CAB (d) ACB

32. Area of a square plot is 6561 m^2. Find the length of a diagonal of the square plot. The following steps are involved in solving the above problem. Arrange them in sequential order.

(A) Area of the square plot = $x^2 = 6561$ (given)

(B) Length of the diagonal = $\sqrt{2} \times x = 81\sqrt{2}$ m

(C) Let the side of the square plot be x cm.

(D) $\therefore$ Side of the square plot, $x = \sqrt{6561} = 81$ m

(a) DCBA (B) BCAD

(c) CADB (d) ABDC

33. The length of a diagonal of a square plot is 24 cm. Find the area of the square plot.

The following steps are involved in solving the above problem. Arrange them in sequential order.

(A) Area of the square plot = $\frac{1}{2} \times (24)^2 = 288$ cm^2

(B) Given that the length of diagonal of a square plot (d) = 24 cm.

(C) Area of a square, when diagonal is given, is $\frac{1}{2}d^2$.

(a) CAB (b) BCA

(c) ABC (d) BAC

34. Find the smallest number by which 2592 should be divided so that the quotient is a perfect cube. The following steps are involved in solving the above problem. Arrange them in sequential order.

(A) On prime factorization, $2592 = 2^5 \times 3^4$.

(B) 2592 should be divided by 12, so that the quotient is a perfect cube.

(C) Now, $2592 = (6)^3 \times 12$.

(a) ACB (b) ABC

(c) CAB (d) CBA

35. Find the smallest number by which 5400 should be multiplied so that the product is a perfect cube. The following steps are involved in solving the above problem. Arrange them in sequential order.

(A) $\Rightarrow 5400 = 2^3 \times 3^3 \times 5^2$

(B) On prime factorization of 5400, we get $5400 = 2 \times 2 \times 2 \times 5 \times 5 \times 3 \times 3 \times 3$.

(C) $\therefore$ 5400 must be multiplied by 5 so that the product is a perfect cube.

(D) In the prime factorization of 5400, we observe that 5 has not appeared n times, where n is a multiple of 3.

(a) BACD (b) BADC

(c) BDAC (d) ABDC

36. The square root of 102 up to three places of decimal is ________.

(a) 10.098 (b) 10.099

(c) 10.097 (d) 10.096

37. A number is multiplied by half of itself and then 32 is added to the product. If the final result is 130, then find the original number.

(a) 4 (b) 7

(c) 5 (d) 14

38. A man purchased a plot which is in the shape of a square. The area of the plot is 12 hectares 3201 m^2. Find the length of each side of the plot (in m).

(a) 349 (b) 351

(c) 359 (d) 361

39. A certain number of men went to a hotel. Each of them spent as many rupees as one-fourth of the men. If the total bill paid was ₹ 20,449, then how many men visited the hotel?

(a) 286 (b) 284

(c) 281 (d) 283

40. Find the divisor, given that the dividend is 2200, remainder is 13, and the divisor is one-third of the quotient.

(a) 25 (b) 27

(c) 24 (d) None of these

41. The least positive integer with which 661.25 should be multiplied so that the product is a perfect square is ________.

(a) 4 (b) 5

(c) 6 (d) 2

42. A number is multiplied by $2\frac{1}{3}$ times itself and then 61 is subtracted from the product obtained. If the final result is 9200, then the number is ________.

(a) 36 (b) 63

(c) 67 (d) 37

43. The units digit of the square of a number and the units digit of the cube of the number are equal to the units digit of the number. How many values are possible for the units digits of such numbers?

(a) 2 (b) 4

(c) 5 (d) 3

44. What should be added to 2714 to make the sum a perfect cube?

(a) 10 (b) 517

(c) 30 (d) 150

45. When 616 is divided by a certain positive number, which is $66\frac{2}{3}$ % of the quotient, it leaves 16 as the remainder. Find the divisor.

(a) 20 (b) 30

(c) 24 (d) 15

46. If a and b are whole numbers such that $a^b = 512$, where $a > b$ and $1 < b < 4$, then $\sqrt[b]{a}$ = _______.

(a) 2 (b) 3

(c) 4 (d) 8

47. Find the value of $\sqrt[3]{6075} \times \sqrt[3]{88935s} \times \sqrt[3]{9625}$.

(a) 17,355 (b) 17,255

(c) 17,315 (d) 17,325

49. The units digit of the square root of a number and the units digit of the cube root of the number is equal to the units digit of the number. How many values are possible for the units digits of such numbers?

(a) 2 (b) 3

(c) 4 (d) 5

50. Find the smallest positive integer that should be added to 3369 so that the sum is a perfect cube.

(a) 5 (b) 4

(c) 6 (d) 7

51. $\sqrt[3]{1+3+5+7+\ldots+53}$ = _____

(a) 11 (b) 13

(c) 7 (d) 9

52. What is the least positive integer that should be subtracted from 2750 so that the difference is a perfect cube?

(a) 15 (b) 14 (c) 9 (d) 6

48. The sides of a triangle are denoted by x, y, and z. Area of the triangle and semiperimeter of the triangle are denoted by P and q, respectively. If $P = \sqrt{q(q-x)(q-y)(q-z)}$ and $x + y - z = y + z - x = z + x - y = 4$, then find P (in square units).

(a) $2\sqrt{3}$ (b) $3\sqrt{3}$

(c) $4\sqrt{3}$ (d) $6\sqrt{3}$

(c) 9 (d) 6

53. If $\sqrt{x} + \frac{58}{\sqrt{x}} = 31$, then which of the following can be the value of x?

(a) 529 (b) 931

(c) 729 (d) 841

54. In an Atlas, a map occupies $\frac{1}{5}$th of a page with dimensions 25 cm and 30 cm, respectively. If the real area of the map is 194400 m^2, then the scale to which the map is drawn is _______.

(a) 1 cm = 36 m (b) 1 cm = 26 m

(c) 1 cm = 33 m (d) 1 cm = 23 m

55. The volume of a spherical ball is given by the formula $V = \frac{4}{3}\pi r^3$, where V is the volume and r is the radius. Find the diameter of the sphere whose volume is $\frac{117128}{21}$ m3.

(a) 22 m (b) 11 m

(c) 33 m (d) 44 m

56. If a is any natural number, then $a^3 - \frac{1}{a^3}$ will always be greater than or equal to _______.

(a) $3\left(a+\frac{1}{a}\right)$ (b) $a+\frac{1}{a}$

(c) $\left(a^3+\frac{1}{a^3}\right)$ (d) $3\left(a-\frac{1}{a}\right)$

57. In a four-digit number $5a3b$, $a > b$ and $a = b^3$. Then the difference of the number and its cube root is _______.

(a) 5850 (b) 5220

(c) 5256 (d) 5814

58. In a school, there are as many children in each room as thrice the number of rooms in the school. For the charity, each child contributed an average amount of Rs $5\frac{1}{3}$. Find total contribution made by all the children was Rs 25,600. How many children were there?

Test Paper III

1. Express $122^{\frac{2}{3}}$ as qth root of x^p using $x^{\frac{p}{q}} = (x^p)^{\frac{1}{q}}$.

   (a) $\sqrt[6]{122}$ (b) $\sqrt[3]{122}$

   (c) $\sqrt[3]{(122)^2}$ (d) $\sqrt{(122)^3}$

2. Evaluate $(16)^{\frac{5}{2}}$.

   (a) 1024 (b) 512

   (c) 256 (d) 128

3. Evaluate a^n.

   (a) 64 (b) 128

   (c) 32 (d) 256

4. $(21^2 - 15^2)^{\frac{4}{3}}$ = ________

   (a) $36\sqrt[3]{6}$ (b) 1296

   (c) $\sqrt[3]{1296}$ (d) $\left(\sqrt[3]{6}\right)^4$

5. $64^{\frac{2}{3}} \times 64^{\frac{1}{3}} \times 64^{\frac{-5}{3}}$ = ________

   (a) $\frac{1}{64}$ (b) $\frac{1}{16}$

   (c) 32 (d) $\frac{1}{32}$

6. Find value of $(61^2 - 11^2)^{\frac{3}{2}}$.

   (a) 50^3 (b) 216,000

   (c) 3600 (d) 60

7. $\sqrt[6]{0.004096}$ = ________

   (a) 0.2 (b) 0.4

   (c) 0.6 (d) 0.8

8. $\left[\frac{169^{-3}}{(196)^{-8}}\right]^{\frac{1}{48}}$ = ________

11. If $4(4x)^7 = 4^{6^2}$, then what is the value of x?

   (a) 5 (b) 25

   (c) 64 (d) 256

12. If $7^n = 2401$, then 7^{n-5} = ________.

   (a) 1 (b) $\frac{1}{7}$

   (c) 7 (d) 49

13. $\sqrt[5]{0.03125}$ = ________

   (a) 0.25 (b) 0.5

   (c) 0.126 (d) 0.15

14. Find the value of $\left(\frac{225}{49}\right)^{\frac{3}{2}}$.

   (a) $\frac{343}{3375}$ (b) $\frac{15}{7}$

   (c) $\frac{3375}{343}$ (d) $\frac{7}{15}$

15. Find the value of $3^{2^{[illegible]}}$.

   (a) 9^{-8} (b) 3^{256}

   (c) 9 (d) 3

16. $4 \times (256)^{\frac{-1}{4}} \div (243)^{\frac{1}{5}}$ = ________

a: $\frac{14^{1/3}}{13^{1/8}}$ b: $\frac{14^{-1/3}}{13^{-1/8}}$ c: $\frac{13^{1/8}}{14^{1/3}}$ d: $\frac{14^{1/8}}{13^{1/3}}$	a: 1/3 b: 4/3 c: ¾ d: 1

9. If $x = \left(8^{\frac{2}{3}} . 32^{-\frac{2}{5}}\right)$, then x^{-5} = ________.

   (a) $\frac{1}{32}$ (b) -1

   (c) 1 (d) -5

10. $81^{\frac{1}{4}} \times 9^{\frac{3}{2}} \times 27^{-\frac{4}{3}}$ = ________

   (a) 1 (b) 3

   (c) 9 (d) $\frac{1}{3}$

Write in Standard form:

17. 31 tenths + 301 thousandths + 21 tens

18: 2.0.1 X 2.001 X 0.2001

19. 8^3 X 0.125^3 X 10^{-9}

20. $[(8^\circ - 7^\circ)(8^\circ + 7^\circ)]^{0^{7^8}}$ = ________.

(a) 1 (b) 0

(c) Not defined (d) 2

21. Value of $\left(\frac{125}{343}\right)^{\frac{2}{3}}$ = ________.

(a) $\frac{5}{7}$ (b) $\frac{7}{5}$

(c) $\frac{25}{49}$ (d) $\frac{49}{25}$

22. If $(81)^x = \frac{1}{(125)^y}$ and x, y are integers, then find the value of $12xy$.

(a) 0 (b) 1

(c) 12 (d) 60

23. If $(6x)^6 = 6^{2^3}$, then find the value of x.

(a) 1 (b) $\sqrt{6}$

(c) $\sqrt[3]{6}$ (d) $\sqrt[6]{6}$

24. Find the value of $(6561)^{(0.125)} + (3125)^{(0.2)}$.

(a) 4 (b) 6

(c) 8 (d) 9

25. Find the value of $(256)^{(0.125)} + (625)^{(0.25)}$.

(a) 2 (b) 7

(c) 11 (d) 14

26. Evaluate the following $\sqrt{\frac{1}{16}} + (0.09)^{\frac{-1}{2}} - (64)^{\frac{5}{6}} \times 7^\circ$.

(a) $\frac{341}{12}$ (b) $\frac{-341}{12}$

(c) $\frac{341}{6}$ (d) $\frac{-341}{6}$

27. If $x^y = 64$, where $y \neq 1$, then find the sum of greatest possible value of $\frac{x}{y}$ and greatest possible value of $\frac{y}{x}$.

(a) $\frac{13}{4}$ (b) 7

(c) 67 (d) 4

28. Which is the greatest among $(81)^{18}$, $(243)^{15}$, $(27)^{21}$, and $(9)^{38}$?

(a) $(243)^{15}$ (b) $(27)^{21}$ (c) $(9)^{38}$ (d) $(81)^{18}$

29. Find the value of $4^{2^{2^{16}}}$.

(a) $(256)^{30}$ (b) $(4)^{120}$

(c) 4^8 (d) 2^8

30. Find the value of $(0.000064)^{\frac{5}{6}} \div (0.00032)^{\frac{6}{5}}$.

(a) 0.2 (b) 0.4

(c) 5 (d) 2.5

Directions for questions 31 to 33: Select the correct answer from the given options.

31. The following steps are involved in solving the problem, if $\left(\frac{32}{243}\right)^n = \frac{8}{27}$, find $\left(\frac{n+0.4}{1024}\right)^{-n}$. Arrange them in sequential order from the first to the last.

(A) $\left(\frac{32}{243}\right)^n = \frac{8}{27} \Rightarrow \left(\left(\frac{2}{5}\right)^5\right)^n = \left(\frac{2}{3}\right)^3$

(B) $\left(2^{-10}\right)^{\frac{-3}{5}} = 2^6 = 64$

(C) $5n = 3 \Rightarrow n = \frac{3}{5}$

(D) $\left(\frac{n+0.4}{1024}\right)^{-n} = \left(\frac{\frac{3}{5}+0.4}{1024}\right)^{\frac{-3}{5}} = \left(\frac{1}{1024}\right)^{\frac{-3}{5}}$

(a) ACDB (b) ACBD (c) CADB (d) CABD

32. Find the value of $\sqrt{18} + \sqrt{12}$, if $\sqrt{2} = 1.414$ and $\sqrt{3} = 1.732$.

The following steps are involved in solving the above problem. Arrange that in sequential order.

(A) $4.242 + 3.464 = 7.706$

(B) $3\sqrt{2} + 2\sqrt{3}$

(C) $\sqrt{18} + \sqrt{12} = \sqrt{3^2 \times 2} + \sqrt{2^2 \times 3}$

(D) $3(1.414) + 2(1.732)$

(a) CBAD (b) CABD

(c) CADB (d) CBDA

33. $(65.61)^{\frac{1}{8}}$ = ________

(a) $\frac{3}{\sqrt[4]{10}}$ (b) 0.3 (c) 0.03 (d) $\frac{3}{\sqrt{10}}$

34. Find the value of $\left[\left[\frac{a}{b}\right]^{\sqrt{99}-\sqrt{97}}\right]^{\sqrt{99}+\sqrt{97}}$.

(a) $\frac{b^2}{a^2}$ (b) $\sqrt{\frac{b}{a}}$

(c) $\sqrt{\frac{b}{a}}$ (d) $\frac{a^2}{b^2}$

35. If $\frac{1}{(243)^x} = (729)^y = 3^3$, then find the value of $5x + 6y$.

(a) 33 (b) 99

(c) 297 (d) 0

36. $\dfrac{\left(\frac{1}{x}+y\right)^{(a+b)}\left(\frac{1}{y}-x\right)^{-(p+q)}}{\left(\frac{1}{x}-y\right)^{-(p+q)}\left(x+\frac{1}{y}\right)^{(a+b)}} =$ ________

(a) $\left(\frac{x}{y}\right)^{(a+b)+(p+q)}$ (b) $\left(\frac{y}{x}\right)^{(a+b)+(p+q)}$

(c) $\left(\frac{y}{x}\right)^{(a+b)-(p+q)}$ (d) $\left(\frac{x}{y}\right)^{(a+b)-(p+q)}$

37. If $7^{(5x-8)} \times 5^{(x+2)} = 30625$, then find x, an integer.

(a) 4 (b) 3

(c) 2 (d) 1

38. If $a^x = b^y = c^z$ and $a^3 = b^2c$, then $\frac{3}{x} - \frac{2}{y} =$ ________.

(a) $\frac{x}{y}$ (b) $\frac{y}{x}$

(c) xyz (d) $\frac{1}{z}$

39. Simplified form of $\dfrac{\left(p+\frac{1}{q}\right)^{(p-q)}\left(p-\frac{1}{q}\right)^{(p+q)}}{\left(q+\frac{1}{p}\right)^{(p-q)}\left(q-\frac{1}{p}\right)^{(p+q)}} =$ ________.

(a) $\left(\frac{p}{q}\right)^{2q}$ (b) $\left(\frac{q}{p}\right)^{2q}$

(c) $\left(\frac{p}{q}\right)^{p}$ (d) $\left(\frac{q}{p}\right)^{q}$

40. If $X = a^1b^2c^3 \ldots z^{26}$ and $Y = z^1y^2x^3 \ldots a^{26}$ where, $abcd \ldots z = \sqrt[54]{64}$, then find XY.

(a) 6 (b) 8

(c) 9 (d) 7

41. If $a^{b^c} = 256$, then find the maximum possible value of abc, where a, b and c are positive integers.

(a) 12 (b) 16

(c) 32 (d) 256

42. If $11^x = 3^y = 99^z$, then $\frac{1}{x} + \frac{1}{y} + \frac{1}{z} =$ ________.

(a) $\frac{2}{z} - \frac{1}{y}$ (b) $\frac{2}{z} + \frac{1}{y}$

(c) $-\frac{1}{y}$ (d) 0

43. If $a^{b^c} = 6561$, then find the least possible value of $(a.b.c)$, where a, b, and c are integers.

(a) 24 (b) 36

(c) 162 (d) 18

44. If $(xy)^{(a-1)} = z$, $(yz)^{(b-1)} = x$, and $(xz)^{(c-1)} = y$, and xyz is not -1, 0 or 1, then which of the following is equal to $ab + bc + ca$?

(a) abc (b) $\frac{abc}{2}$

(c) $2abc$ (d) $3abc$

45. If $x^{200} < 3^{300}$, then the greatest possible integral value of x.

(a) 3 (b) 5

(c) 4 (d) 2

46. If $5^{n-3} = 625$, then 5^{n+3} is ______.

(a) 5^{12} (b) 5^9

(c) 5^{10} (d) 5^{15}

47. Find the value of $(0.00243)^{\frac{3}{5}} + (0.0256)^{\frac{3}{4}}$.

(a) 0.083 (b) 0.073

(c) 0.091 (d) 0.081

48. $\left[\frac{(a^0+b^0)(a^0-b^0)}{a^2-b^2}\right]^{0^{4^5}}$ (where $a \neq 0$ and $b \neq 0$) is ________.

(a) 0 (b) 1
(c) −1 (d) Not defined

49. If $(1331)^{-x} = (225)^y$, where x and y are integers, then find the value of $3xy$.

(a) 0 (b) 1
(c) −3 (d) 3

50. If $\left(\sqrt{3}\right)^{x+y} = 9$ and $\left(\sqrt{2}\right)^{x-y} = 32$, then $2x + y$ is ________.

(a) 1 (b) 0
(c) 17 (d) 11

51. If $6^{x-y} = 36$ and $3^{x+y} = 729$, then find $x^2 - y^2$.

(a) 12 (b) 4
(c) 24 (d) 8

52. If $p^{q^r} = 512$, then find the minimum possible value of $(p)(q)(r)$, where p, q, and r are positive integers.

(a) 18 (b) 12
(c) 24 (d) 512

53. If $2^{x+y} = 128$ and $4^{x-y} = 16$, then find $\frac{x}{y}$.

(a) $\frac{2}{3}$ (b) $\frac{5}{9}$
(c) $\frac{9}{5}$ (d) $\frac{3}{5}$

54. If $x^{400} < 4^{600}$, then find the greatest possible integral value of x.

(a) 6 (b) 5
(c) 7 (d) 4

55. If $2^x = 3^y = 6^z$, then $\frac{1}{x} + \frac{1}{y} + \frac{1}{z} =$ ________.

(a) $\frac{2}{x}$ (b) $\frac{2}{y}$
(c) $\frac{2}{z}$ (d) 1

56. Which of the following is the descending order of $(343)^3$, $(2401)^2$, and $(49)^5$?

(a) $(49)^5$, $(343)^3$, $(2401)^2$
(b) $(2401)^2$, $(343)^3$, $(49)^5$
(c) $(343)^3$, $(49)^5$, $(2401)^2$
(d) $(49)^5$, $(2401)^2$, $(343)^3$

57. If $x^y = y^z = z^x$ and $xz = y^2$, then which of the following is correct?

(a) $z = \frac{2xy}{x+y}$ (b) $y = \frac{x-z}{x+z}$
(c) $x = \frac{y-z}{yz}$ (d) $xyz = \frac{x-z+y}{x+z-y}$

58. If $a = (2^{-2} - 2^{-3})$, $b = (2^{-3} - 2^{-4})$, and $c = (2^{-4} - 2^{-2})$ then find the value of $a^3 + b^3 + c^3$.

(a) $\frac{-9}{1024}$ (b) $\frac{-9}{2048}$
(c) 0 (d) 1

59. Which is the greatest among 2^{156}, 4^{79}, 128^{23}, and 8^{54}?

(a) 4^{79} (b) 128^{23}
(c) 2^{156} (d) 8^{54}

60. Which is the greatest among $(3)^{198}$, $(27)^{64}$, $(9)^{100}$, and $(81)^{49}$?

(a) $(9)^{100}$ (b) $(81)^{49}$
(c) $(27)^{64}$ (d) 3^{198}

Test Paper IV

Write each number in standard form.

1. 4.5×10^3	2. 2×10^4	3. 1.725896×10^6
4. 9.61×10^2	5. 1×10^7	6. 8.256×10^8
7. 5.26×10^4	8. 3.25×10^2	9. 6.79×10^5
10. 3.1×10^{-4}	11. 2.51×10^{-2}	12. 6×10^{-1}
13. 2.15×10^{-3}	14. 3.14×10^{-6}	15. 1×10^{-2}

Write each number in scientific notation.

16. 720	17. 7,560	18. 892
19. 1,400	20. 91,256	21. 51,000
22. 0.012	23. 0.0002	24. 0.054
25. 0.231	26. 0.0000056	27. 0.000123

II. Find each square root.

1. $\sqrt{9}$	2. $\sqrt{81}$	3. $-\sqrt{625}$
4. $\sqrt{36}$	5. $-\sqrt{169}$	6. $\sqrt{144}$
7. $\sqrt{961}$	8. $\sqrt{324}$	9. $-\sqrt{225}$
10. $-\sqrt{4}$	11. $\sqrt{529}$	12. $-\sqrt{484}$
13. $\sqrt{196}$	14. $\sqrt{729}$	15. $\sqrt{289}$
16. $\sqrt{0.04}$	17. $\sqrt{2.25}$	18. $\sqrt{0.01}$
19. $-\sqrt{0.09}$	20. $\sqrt{0.49}$	21. $\sqrt{1.69}$

III. Name all sets of numbers to which each real number belongs.

1. 6.5	2. $\sqrt{25}$	3. $\sqrt{3}$
4. -7.2	5. $-0.\overline{61}$	6. $\frac{1}{2}$
7. $\frac{16}{4}$	8. -102.1	9. $\sqrt{29}$

IV. Estimate each square root to the nearest tenth. Then graph the square root on a number line.

10. $-\sqrt{12}$	11. $\sqrt{23}$	12. $\sqrt{2}$
13. $\sqrt{10}$	14. $-\sqrt{30}$	15. $\sqrt{5}$
16. $\sqrt{21}$	17. $-\sqrt{202}$	18. $-\sqrt{10}$

V. Replace each ● with $<$, $>$, or $=$ to make a true sentence.

19. $\sqrt{7}$ ● 2.8	20. $2\frac{1}{3}$ ● $2.\overline{3}$	21. $\sqrt{121}$ ● 11
22. 5.6 ● $\sqrt{30}$	23. 9.45 ● $9.\overline{4}$	24. $\sqrt{5}$ ● 2.23
25. $\sqrt{6.25}$ ● $2\frac{1}{2}$	26. $5\frac{1}{3}$ ● $\sqrt{30}$	27. $4\frac{2}{3}$ ● $\sqrt{22}$

Test Paper V [Unsolved]

1. If $a + \frac{1}{a} = 3$, then the value of $a^2 + \frac{1}{a^2}$

a) 9 b) 6 c) 7 d) 8

2. If $a^2 + \frac{1}{a^2} = 27$, then the value of $a - \frac{1}{a} = \pm$............

a) 5 b) 6 c) 7 d) 8

3. $(x^2 + 4)(x^2 - 4)(x^4 - 16) =$ ....

4. $\left(\sqrt{36 + \sqrt{36 + \sqrt{36 \ldots \ldots \ldots \propto}}}\right) =$ ....

5. x+ y = 2 and xy = 4; $(x^4 - y^4)(x^3 - y^3) =$ .....

6. Factorise: $P^2 + q^2 - r^2 - 2pq$

7. $\left(\frac{\sqrt{3}+\sqrt{2}}{\sqrt{3}-\sqrt{2}}\right)\left(\frac{\sqrt{(5-2\sqrt{6})}}{\sqrt{5+2\sqrt{6}}}\right)\left(\frac{1}{1001} + \frac{1}{1001} + \cdots \ldots 1{,}000\ times\right) X \left(1 - \frac{1}{2000}\right) X\ 1{,}999 =$ ....

8. $\left(\frac{1}{x} + \frac{1}{y} + \frac{1}{z}\right) = 55,\ \ (x + y + z) = 5,\ \ xy + yz + zx =$ ....

9. $(x - 1)(x^2 + 1)(1 + x)(x^4 - 1) = 255$; Find the value of $\frac{x^2+x+1}{x+1}\ X \left(\frac{1}{\sqrt{x}} + \frac{2}{\sqrt{x}} + \cdots \ldots + \frac{100}{\sqrt{x}}\right) X\ \sqrt[3]{6 + x}$

10. (pq + rs + st) = 256; p + q + r = 625; $p^2 + r^2 + q^2 =$ ....

11. $\left(x + \frac{1}{x}\right) = 11\sqrt{11}$; $x^3 + \frac{1}{x^3} =$ .... ; $x^6 - \frac{1}{x^6} =$ .... ; $x^9 + x^4 - x^{-3} - x^{-9} =$ ....;

12. Factorization of the polynomial $(x - y)^2 a^2 + 2(x - y)(x + y)ab + b^2 (x + y)^2$ gives _________.

13. The polynomial $a^2 - b + ab - a$, on factorization, reduces to _________.

14. $\left(\sqrt{16 + \sqrt{16 + \sqrt{16 + \cdots \ldots \propto}}}\right)\left(\sqrt{81 + \sqrt{81 + \sqrt{81 + \cdots \ldots \propto}}}\right) =$ ....

15. $\left(x^3 + \frac{1}{x^3}\right) = 62$; $\sqrt{x^3} + \frac{1}{\sqrt{x^3}} =$ ....; $\sqrt{x}^3 + \frac{1}{\sqrt{x}^3} =$ ....

16. $\left(\frac{1}{356} + \frac{1}{356} + \frac{1}{356} + \cdots \ldots + 1{,}000\ times\right) X \left(1 + \frac{1}{1000}\right) X\ 1{,}780 =$ ....

17. Simplify: $\left(\sqrt{30 + 2\sqrt{90} + 2\sqrt{110} + 2\sqrt{99}}\right) X \left(\sqrt{33 + 2\sqrt{120} + 2\sqrt{110} + 2\sqrt{132}}\right)$

18. $(1a^0 + 2a^1 + 3a^2 \ldots\ldots\ldots + 1000\ a^{999}) = 1001\ X\ 500$; Find the value of $(a^3 + 3a^2 + 3a + 1)(a - 1)^3$

19. What least number should be added to six digit greatest number to make the value a perfect square number?

20. $(\sqrt{3} + \sqrt{3} + \sqrt{3} + \sqrt{3} + \cdots .\ 2{,}000\ times)\ X\ \frac{1}{\sqrt[3]{14+3\sqrt{3}+)}}\ X\left(1 - \frac{1}{\sqrt{3}}\right) =$ ....

II. 1. Half of a quarter of 8,048 = ...

2. Reciprocal of a n + n = 16.0625. Find ($\sqrt[4]{n} + \sqrt[2]{n}$ + n)

3. The expansion of $(x^2 + 4)(x^2 - 4)(x^4 + 16)$ is ________.

(a) $x^8 - 128$ (b) $x^4 - 16^2$

(c) $x^6 - 256$ (d) $x^8 - 256$

4. If the value of $a^2 + \frac{1}{a^2}$ is 786, then the value of $a - \frac{1}{a}$ is ________.

(a) ±23 (b) ±25

(c) ±17 (d) ±28

5. Which of the following is the factor of $4a^2 + b^2 - 4ab + 2b - 4a + 1$?

(a) $(a - b)$ (b) $(a + b - 2)$

(c) $(a - b + 2)$ (d) $(2a - b - 1)$

6. Expand $\left(\frac{x}{3} - \frac{y}{2}\right)^2$.

(a) $\frac{x^2}{9} + \frac{y^2}{4}$ (b) $\frac{x^2}{9} - \frac{y^2}{4}$

(c) $\frac{x^2}{9} + \frac{y^2}{4} - \frac{xy}{9}$ (d) $\frac{x^2}{9} + \frac{y^2}{4} + \frac{xy}{9}$

7. Simplified form of the expression $\left(\frac{2a}{5} + \frac{3q}{5}\right)^3 - \left(\frac{2a}{5} - \frac{3q}{5}\right)^3$ is ________.

(a) $\frac{1}{125}\left(54q^3 - 72a^2q\right)$

(b) $\frac{1}{125}\left(54q^3 + 72a^2q\right)$

(c) $\frac{1}{125}\left(16q^3 + 108aq^2\right)$

(d) $\frac{1}{125}\left(16a^3 - 108aq^2\right)$

8. Factorise the polynomial $-r^2 + p^2 + q^2 - 2pq$.

(a) $(p - q - r)(p - q + r)$

(b) $(p + q + r)(p - q - r)$

(c) $(p - q)(q - r)$

(a) 12 (b) 13

(c) 14 (d) −14

10. The product of the polynomials $(x^2 - x + 2)$ and $(x - 1)$ is ________.

(a) $x^3 - 2x^2 + 3x - 2$

(b) $x^3 + 3x^2 - 3x + 2$

(c) $x^3 - 2x + 4x^2 - 6$

(d) $x^3 - 2x^2 + 3x + 2$

11. Simplify the equation $\left(\frac{a}{2} - \frac{b}{3}\right)^3 + \left(\frac{a}{2} + \frac{b}{3}\right)^3$.

(a) $\frac{a^3}{4} + ab^2$

(b) $\frac{a^3}{4} + \frac{ab^2}{3}$

(c) $\frac{2b^3}{27} + \frac{a^2b}{2}$

(d) $\frac{2b^3}{27} + a^2b$

12. Expansion of $(x - y)^3 + (y - z)^3 + (z - x)^3$ is ________.

(a) $2x^3 + 2y^3 + 2z^3$

(b) $(x - y)(y - z)(z - x)$

(c) 0

(d) $3(x - y)(y - z)(z - x)$

13. If $x + y = 2$ and $xy = 1$, then find $x^4 + y^4$.

(a) 6 (b) 4

(c) 8 (d) 2

14. The HCF of the polynomials $10(a - 1)(a - 2)^3$, $120(a - 3)(a - 2)^3$, and $135(a + 3)(a - 2)^3$ is ________.

(a) $25(a - 3)(a - 2)$

(b) $5(a - 3)(a + 2)$

(c) $5(a - 2)^3$

(d) $5(a - 3)(a - 2)(a + 3)$

14. The HCF of the polynomials $10(a - 1)(a - 2)^3$, $120(a - 3)(a - 2)^3$, and $135(a + 3)(a - 2)^3$ is ________.

***.

Answer II:

1. (a) 2. (c) 3. (c) 4. (c) 5. (c) 6. (c) 7. (c) 8. (a) 9. (d) 10. (c) 11. (b) 12. (a) 13. (b) 14. (a) 15. (d) 16. (c) 17. (b) 18. (c) 19. (a) 20. (c) 21. (b) 22. (a) 23. (b) 24. (b) 25. (d) 26. (d) 27. (c) 28. (d) 29. (b) 30. (a) 31. (a) 32. (c) 33. (b) 34. (a) 35. (b) 36. (b) 37. (d) 38. (b) 39. (a) 40. (b) 41. (b) 42. (b) 43. (b) 44. (c) 45. (a) 46. (a) 47. (d) 48. (c) 49. (c) 50. (c) 51. (d) 52. (d) 53. (d) 54. (a) 55. (a) 56. (d) 57. (d)

Answer III:

1. (c) 2. (a) 3. (b) 4. (b) 5. (b) 6. (b) 7. (b) 8. (a) 9. (c) 10. (a) 11. (d) 12. (b) 13. (b) 14. (c) 15. (c) 16. (a) 17. (c) 18. (b) 19. (c) 20. (c) 21. (c) 22. (a) 23. (c) 24. (c) 25. (b) 26. (b) 27. (b) 28. (c) 29. (d) 30. (c) 31. (a) 32. (d) 33. (a) 34. (d) 35. (d) 36. (b) 37. (c) 38. (d) 39. (a) 40. (b) 41. (d) 42. (a) 43. (d) 44. (c) 45. (b) 46. (c) 47. (c) 48. (d) 49. (a) 50. (d) 51. (a) 52. (b) 53. (c) 54. (c) 55. (c) 56. (a) 57. (a) 58. (b) 59. (d) 60. (a)

Set of Model Papers

Selected Model Papers

Model Paper I

Complete.

1. 400 mm = ■ cm
2. 4 km = ■ m
3. 660 cm = ■ m
4. 0.3 km = ■ m
5. 30 mm = ■ cm
6. 84.5 m = ■ km
7. ■ m = 54 cm
8. 18 km = ■ cm
9. ■ mm = 45 cm
10. 4 kg = ■ g
11. 632 mg = ■ g
12. 4,497 g = ■ kg
13. ■ mg = 0.51 kg
14. 0.63 kg = ■ g
15. ■ kg = 563 g
16. 662 m = ■ km
17. 5,283 mL = ■ L
18. 0.24 cm = ■ mm
19. 380 kL = ■ L
20. 10.8 g = ■ mg
21. 83,000 mL = ■ L

22. (1ft + 2 ft + ... + 100 ft) = ...

23. 10010 ml = ... L .... Ml

24. (1m 1 cm + 11 m 11mm + 121 m 12 cm 12mm) - .... m .... cm .... mm

Complete. Round to the nearest hundredth if necessary.

1. 2 ft ≈ ■ m
2. 37 cm ≈ ■ in.
3. 2.3 lb ≈ ■ kg
4. 2L ≈ ■ gal
5. 5,280 mi ≈ ■ km
6. 4 yd ≈ ■ m
7. 3.6 lb ≈ ■ g
8. 271 km ≈ ■ mi
9. 500 m ≈ ■ ft
10. 1,200 kg ≈ ■ T
11. 16 in. ≈ ■ cm
12. 2.4 c ≈ ■ mL
13. 108 lb ≈ ■ kg
14. 2,000 mL ≈ ■ qt
15. 100 m ≈ ■ yd
16. 56 in. ≈ ■ cm
17. 32.8 ft ≈ ■ m
18. 609 yd ≈ ■ m
19. 21.78 mi ≈ ■ km
20. 48 lb ≈ ■ g
21. 2.3 T ≈ ■ kg
22. 8.5 c ≈ ■ mL
23. 33 gal ≈ ■ L
24. 1.8 qt ≈ ■ mL

***.

Model Paper II

Find the square of each number.

1. 4 **2.** 19 **3.** 13 **4.** 25

5. 9 **6.** 2 **7.** 14 **8.** 24

9. 40 **10.** 50 **11.** 100 **12.** 250

Find each square root.

13. $\sqrt{324}$ **14.** $\sqrt{900}$ **15.** $\sqrt{2,500}$ **16.** $\sqrt{576}$

17. $\sqrt{8,100}$ **18.** $\sqrt{676}$ **19.** $\sqrt{100}$ **20.** $\sqrt{784}$

21. $\sqrt{1,024}$ **22.** $\sqrt{841}$ **23.** $\sqrt{2,304}$ **24.** $\sqrt{3,025}$

25. $\sqrt[2]{21 + 2\sqrt{42} + 2\sqrt[2]{56} + 2\sqrt[2]{48}} - \sqrt[2]{27 + 2\sqrt{72} + 2\sqrt[3]{90\sqrt{90}} + 2\sqrt[3]{80\sqrt{80}}}$

Estimate each square root to the nearest whole number.

1. $\sqrt{27}$ **2.** $\sqrt{112}$ **3.** $\sqrt{249}$

4. $\sqrt{88}$ **5.** $\sqrt{1,500}$ **6.** $\sqrt{612}$

7. $\sqrt{340}$ **8.** $\sqrt{495}$ **9.** $\sqrt{264}$

10. $\sqrt{350}$ **11.** $\sqrt{834}$ **12.** $\sqrt{3,700}$

Graph each square root on a number line.

13. $\sqrt{58}$ **14.** $\sqrt{750}$ **15.** $\sqrt{1,200}$

16. $\sqrt{1,000}$ **17.** $\sqrt{5,900}$ **18.** $\sqrt{999}$

19. $\sqrt{374}$ **20.** $\sqrt{512}$ **21.** $\sqrt{3,750}$

22. $\sqrt{255}$ **23.** $\sqrt{83}$ **24.** $\sqrt{845}$

25. Simplify the following:

a) $\sqrt{6 + \sqrt{6 + \sqrt{6 + \cdots \ldots\ldots \propto}}} + \sqrt{\frac{36}{81} + \sqrt{\frac{36}{81} + \sqrt{\frac{36}{81} + \cdots \ldots\ldots \propto}}}$ = ...

b) Product of three consecutive number a, b and c is equal to 3,000 . Find the value of $b^3 - b^2 + 1$

c) Simplify: $\left(\frac{1}{\sqrt{109}} + \frac{1}{\sqrt{109}} + \frac{1}{\sqrt{109}} \ldots\ldots 13{,}000\ times\right) X \left(1 + \frac{1}{13{,}000}\right) X \left(1 + \frac{1}{108}\right) x \frac{1}{6{,}500}$ = ...

d) . $\left(1 + \frac{1}{10}\right)\left(1 + \frac{1}{11}\right) \ldots\ldots\ldots X \left(1 + \frac{1}{10{,}000}\right) X \left(1 - \frac{10{,}000}{10{,}001}\right) X\ 0.1021$ = ...

e) . $\frac{121}{169} X\ 1\frac{2}{11}\ X \frac{144}{196}\ X \left(1 + \frac{1}{12}\right) X \left(1 + \frac{2}{11}\right)$ = ...

***.

Model Paper III

Write the ordered pair for each point graphed at the right. Then name the quadrant or axis on which each point is located.

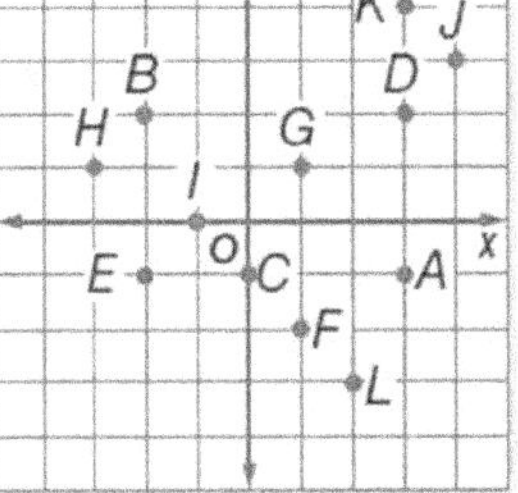

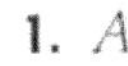

1. A	**2.** B	**3.** C
4. D	**5.** E	**6.** F
7. G	**8.** H	**9.** I
10. J	**11.** K	**12.** L

Graph and label each point on a coordinate plane.

13. $N(-4, 3)$	**14.** $K(2, 5)$	**15.** $W(-6, -2)$	**16.** $X(5, 0)$
17. $Y(4, -4)$	**18.** $M(0, -3)$	**19.** $Z(-2, 0.5)$	**20.** $S(-1, -3)$
21. $A(0, 2)$	**22.** $C(-2, -2)$	**23.** $E(0, 1)$	**24.** $G(1, -1)$

Subtract.

1. $3 - 7$	**2.** $-5 - 4$	**3.** $-6 - 2$
4. $8 - 13$	**5.** $6 - (-4)$	**6.** $12 - 9$
7. $-2 - 23$	**8.** $63 - 78$	**9.** $0 - (-14)$
10. $15 - 6$	**11.** $18 - 20$	**12.** $-5 - 8$

ALGEBRA Evaluate each expression if $k = -3$, $p = 6$, $n = 1$, and $d = -8$.

13. $55 - k$	**14.** $p - 7$	**15.** $d - 15$
16. $n - 12$	**17.** $-51 - d$	**18.** $k - 21$
19. $n - k$	**20.** $-99 - k$	**21.** $p - k$
22. $d - (-1)$	**23.** $k - d$	**24.** $n - d$

25. Solve the following:

1. $8^{\frac{2}{3}} = \left(8^{\frac{1}{3}}\right)^n = 4$

2. $4^{\frac{1}{2}} \times 4^{\frac{1}{2}} \times 4^{\frac{1}{2}} = 4^n = 8$

3. $27^{\frac{1}{3}} \times 27^{\frac{1}{3}} \times 27^n = 27^1 = 27$

4. $10^{\frac{1}{2}} \times 10^n = 10^1 = 10$

5. $25^n = \frac{1}{25^{\frac{1}{2}}} = \frac{1}{\sqrt{25}} = \frac{1}{5}$

6. $\left(3^{\frac{1}{2}}\right)^2 = 3^n = 3$

7. $\left(8^{-\frac{1}{2}}\right)^n = 8^{-2} = \frac{1}{64}$

8. $\left(1,000^{\frac{1}{3}}\right)^{-2} = 1,000^n = \frac{1}{100}$

9. $(16^n)^2 = 16^{\frac{1}{2}} = 4$

Model Paper IV

I. **Add or subtract. Write in simplest form.**

1. $\frac{5}{11}+\frac{9}{11}$ **2.** $\frac{5}{8}-\frac{1}{8}$ **3.** $\frac{7}{10}+\frac{7}{10}$

4. $\frac{9}{12}-\frac{5}{12}$ **5.** $\frac{2}{9}+\frac{1}{9}$ **6.** $\frac{1}{4}+\frac{3}{4}$

7. $\frac{17}{21}+\left(-\frac{13}{21}\right)$ **8.** $-\frac{8}{13}+\left(-\frac{11}{13}\right)$ **9.** $\frac{13}{28}-\frac{9}{28}$

10. $\frac{15}{16}+\frac{13}{16}$ **11.** $-\frac{4}{35}-\left(-\frac{17}{35}\right)$ **12.** $\frac{3}{8}+\left(-\frac{5}{8}\right)$

13. $\frac{8}{15}-\frac{2}{15}$ **14.** $-\frac{3}{10}+\frac{7}{10}$ **15.** $\frac{5}{6}-\frac{7}{6}$

16. $\frac{7}{24}+\frac{7}{24}$ **17.** $-\frac{29}{9}-\left(-\frac{26}{9}\right)$ **18.** $\frac{3}{7}-\frac{4}{7}$

19. $\left(\frac{1}{67}+\frac{1}{67}+\frac{1}{67}+\ \ldots\ldots 12{,}000\ times\right) X \left(1-\frac{1}{12{,}001}\right) X \frac{1}{6{,}000}\ X\left(1+\frac{1}{66}\right) =$ ....

20. (1 + 2 + ... 12,000) X $\left(1-\frac{1}{12{,}001}\right) X\ 6{,}000$ = ...

II. **Add or subtract. Write in simplest form.**

1. $\frac{1}{4}-\frac{3}{12}$ **2.** $\frac{3}{7}+\frac{6}{14}$ **3.** $\frac{1}{4}+\frac{3}{5}$

4. $\frac{4}{9}+\frac{1}{2}$ **5.** $\frac{5}{7}-\frac{4}{6}$ **6.** $\frac{3}{4}-\frac{1}{6}$

7. $\frac{3}{5}+\frac{3}{4}$ **8.** $\frac{2}{3}-\frac{1}{8}$ **9.** $\frac{9}{10}+\frac{1}{3}$

10. $-\frac{3}{4}+\frac{7}{8}$ **11.** $\frac{3}{8}+\frac{7}{12}$ **12.** $\frac{3}{5}-\frac{2}{3}$

13. $\frac{2}{5}+\left(-\frac{2}{7}\right)$ **14.** $-\frac{3}{5}-\left(-\frac{5}{6}\right)$ **15.** $-\frac{7}{12}-\frac{3}{4}$

Evaluate each expression if $a=\frac{2}{3}$ and $b=\frac{7}{12}$.

16. $\frac{1}{5}+a$ **17.** $a-\frac{1}{2}$ **18.** $b+\frac{7}{8}$

19. $\frac{7}{8}-a$ **20.** $a+b$ **21.** $a-b$

22. Product of three consecutive numbers is equal to 210. Find the value of all the numbers.

23. Cistern A fills up an empty water tank in 45 minutes and cistern B fills up half of that water tank in half an hour. If both the cisterns kept open then the empty water tank will be filled up in ...... minutes.

24. Pundalik finishes a project work in 20 days while working 7 hours a day. The same work can be finished in .... days if Pundalik works for 5 hours a day.

***.

Model Paper V

I. **Express each number in standard form.**

1. 4.5×10^3
2. 2×10^4
3. 1.725896×10^6
4. 9.61×10^2
5. 1×10^7
6. 8.256×10^8
7. 3.25×10^2
8. 3.1×10^{-4}
9. 2.51×10^{-2}
10. 6×10^{-1}
11. 2.15×10^{-3}
12. 3.14×10^{-6}

Express each number in scientific notation.

13. 720
14. 7,560
15. 892
16. 1,400
17. 91,256
18. 51,000
19. 0.012
20. 0.0002
21. 0.054
22. 0.231
23. 0.0000056
24. 0.000123

25. Write in standard form: 21 thousandths + 21 hundredths + 21 hundreds

26. $\left(\frac{1}{1001} + \frac{1}{1001} + \ \ldots .1{,}000\ times\right)\ X\ 500 = m^n$; m= ....; n = ...

II. **Solve each equation. Check your solution.**

1. $2m = 18$
2. $-42 = 6n$
3. $72 = 8k$
4. $-20r = 20$
5. $420 = 5s$
6. $325 = 25t$
7. $-14 = -2p$
8. $18q = 36$
9. $40 = 10a$
10. $100 = 20b$
11. $416 = 4c$
12. $45 = 9d$
13. $0.5m = 3.5$
14. $1.8 = 0.6x$
15. $0.4y = 2$
16. $1.86 = 6.2z$
17. $-8x = 24$
18. $8.34 = 2r$
19. $1.67t = 10.02$
20. $243 = 27a$
21. $0.9x = 4.5$
22. $\frac{r}{7} = -8$
23. $\frac{w}{7} = 8$
24. $\frac{y}{12} = -6$
25. $\frac{c}{-4} = 10$
26. $\frac{s}{9} = 8$
27. $\frac{m}{8} = 5$

28. Find square root of the following expression: $(33 + 2\sqrt{110} + 2\sqrt{132} + 2\sqrt{120})$

29. $\frac{\sqrt[3]{1331} + \sqrt[2]{121} + 11}{1 + \frac{1}{10}}\ X \frac{(1+2+3......+10)}{1 - \frac{1}{11}}\ \left(1 + \frac{1}{2}\right)^{-1}$ = ...

30. Spontenian family reduced their monthly family expenditure to by curtailing their consumption of fuel by 25% so as to keep the budget on fuel intact. Find the percentage increase in the price of fuel.

31. Sum total of a number and its reciprocal is 8.125. Find sum total of the square and cube root of that number.

III Find the multiplicative inverse of each number.

1. $\frac{2}{3}$ **2.** $\frac{5}{4}$ **3.** 1 **4.** 10

5. $\frac{1}{7}$ **6.** $\frac{9}{16}$ **7.** $1\frac{1}{3}$ **8.** $3\frac{3}{4}$

9. $7\frac{3}{8}$ **10.** $6\frac{2}{5}$ **11.** $33\frac{1}{3}$ **12.** $66\frac{2}{3}$

IV. Solve each equation. Check your solution.

13. $\frac{a}{13} = 2$ **14.** $\frac{8}{9}x = 24$ **15.** $\frac{3}{8}r = 36$ **16.** $\frac{3}{4}t = \frac{1}{2}$

17. $16 = \frac{h}{4}$ **18.** $\frac{m}{8} = 12$ **19.** $\frac{5}{8}n = 45$ **20.** $10 = \frac{b}{10}$

21. $\frac{1}{7}x = 7$ **22.** $5 = \frac{1}{5}y$ **23.** $\frac{4}{3}m = 28$ **24.** $\frac{2}{3}z = 20$

25. $\frac{c}{9} = 81$ **26.** $\frac{m}{9} = 9$ **27.** $16 = \frac{4}{9}f$ **28.** $\frac{15}{8}x = 225$

29. $\left(x + \frac{1}{x}\right) = 1$; $\frac{x^3 - 1}{(x^2+1)} =$ .... 30. $\frac{1}{x} + \frac{1}{x^2} - \frac{1}{x^3} = \frac{8}{27}$; $x^3 - x^2 - x + 1 =$ ....

31. $\left(\sqrt{8 + \sqrt{8 + \sqrt{8 + \ldots\ldots\infty}}}\right) + 151 =$ ....

V. Solve each equation. Check your solution.

1. $3x + 6 = 6$ **2.** $2r - 7 = -1$ **3.** $-10 + 2d = 8$

4. $2b + 4 = -8$ **5.** $5w - 12 = 3$ **6.** $5t - 4 = 6$

7. $2q - 6 = 4$ **8.** $2g - 3 = -9$ **9.** $15 = 6y + 3$

10. $3s - 4 = 8$ **11.** $18 - 7f = 4$ **12.** $13 + 3p = 7$

13. $7.5r + 2 = -28$ **14.** $4.2 + 7z = 2.8$ **15.** $-9m - 9 = 9$

16. $32 + 0.2c = 1$ **17.** $5t - 14 = -14$ **18.** $-0.25x + 0.5 = 4$

19. $5w - 4 = 8$ **20.** $4d - 3 = 9$ **21.** $2g - 16 = -9$

22. $4k + 13 = 20$ **23.** $7 = 5 - 2x$ **24.** $8z + 15 = -1$

25. $92 - 16b = 12$ **26.** $14e + 14 = 28$ **27.** $1.1j + 2 = 7.5$

28. A shopkeeper gains amount equal to selling price of an apple by selling 6 apples. Find the percentage gain made by the shopkeeper by selling apple.

29. $(a^0 + a^1 + a^2 + \ldots\ldots + a^{1000}) = \left(1 + \frac{1}{1,000}\right) X \frac{1}{2} X\ 10^6$. Find the value of $(a^4 + a^3 + 110a^2 - 111a + 999)$

30. A deep well has steps inside it. A monkey is sitting on the topmost step (i.e., the first step). The water level is at the ninth step. If the monkey jumps 3 steps down and then jumps back 2 steps up, how many jumps does it have to make to reach the water level?

31. In a class test containing 10 questions, 3 marks are awarded for every correct answer and (-1) mark is awarded for every incorrect answer and 0 for the questions not attempted. Srinu gets two correct and six incorrect answers out of eight questions he attempts. What is his total score?

32. A lift descends into an underground floor at the rate of 6 metres per minute. If the descent starts from 10 metres above the ground level, how much time will it take to descend 350 metres?

33. Indian cricket team won 4 more matches than it lost with New Zealand. If it won 3/5 of its matches, how many matches did India play?

VI. The average weight of a sample of 10 apples is 52 g and average weight of 12 bananas is 144 g. Later it was found that the weighing machine had shown the weight of each item was 10% less. What is the correct average weight of an apple and 2 bananas?

VII. **Solve each inequality. Graph the solution set on a number line.**

1. $y + 3 > 7$
2. $c - 9 < 5$
3. $x + 4 \geq 9$
4. $y - 3 < 15$
5. $t - 13 \geq 5$
6. $x + 3 < 10$
7. $y - 6 \geq 2$
8. $x - 3 \geq -6$
9. $a + 3 \leq 5$
10. $c - 2 \leq 11$
11. $a + 15 \geq 6$
12. $y + 3 \geq 18$
13. $y + 16 \geq -22$
14. $x - 3 \geq 17$
15. $y - 6 > -17$
16. $y - 11 < 7$
17. $a + 5 \geq 21$
18. $c + 3 > -16$
19. $x - 12 \geq 12$
20. $x + 5 \geq 5$
21. $y - 6 > 31$

22. Find square root of the following: $\frac{(12 - 2\sqrt{12} - 2\sqrt{15} + 2\sqrt{20})}{(14 + 2\sqrt{2} + 2\sqrt{6} + 2\sqrt{3})}$

23. What least number should be subtracted from 12,987 to make this number divisible exactly by 3 and 9?

24. $(1x^0 + 2x^1 + 3^2 + \ldots\ldots\ldots + 10^4 a^{1000}) =$ ....

VIII. **Find each unit rate. Round to the nearest hundredth if necessary.**

1. \$240 for 4 days
2. 250 people in 5 buses
3. 500 miles in 10 hours
4. \$18 for 24 pounds
5. 32 people in 8 cars
6. \$4.50 for 3 dozen
7. 245 tickets in 5 days
8. 12 classes in 4 semesters
9. 60 people in 4 rows
10. 48 ounces in 3 pounds
11. 20 people in 4 groups
12. 1.5 pounds for \$3.00
13. 45 miles in 60 minutes
14. \$5.50 for 10 disks
15. 360 miles on 12 gallons
16. \$8.50 for 5 yards
17. 24 cups for \$1.20
18. 160 words in 4 minutes
19. \$60 for 5 books
20. \$24 for 6 hours

IX: What percentage of all the natural numbers from 1 to 20,000 are multiples of 125? How many of such multiples are also multiples of 250?

X. Find the value of x in each pair of similar figures.

1.

A B
8 cm
E F
4 cm
D 5 cm C H x cm G

2.

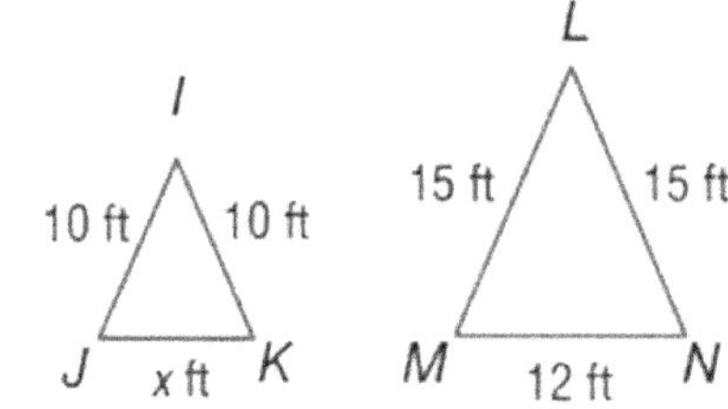

3.

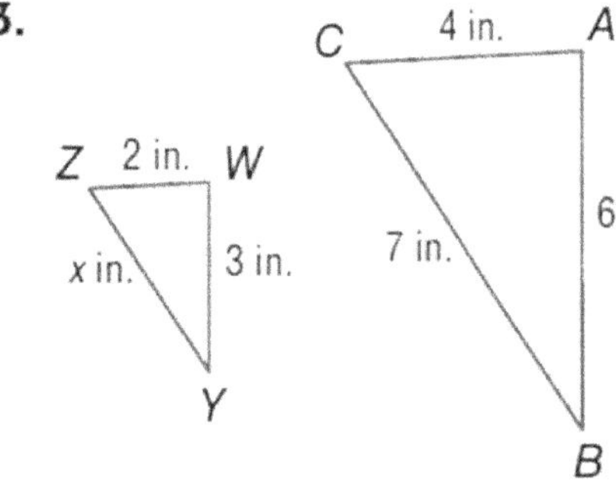

4.

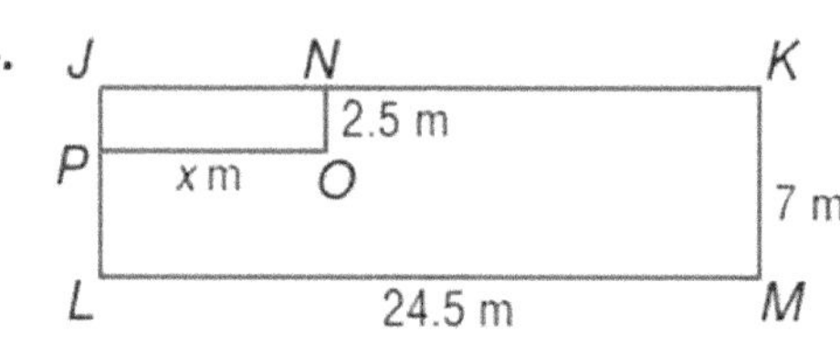

XI. For each pair of similar figures, find the perimeter of the second figure.

1. $P = 15$ mm $P = ?$ mm

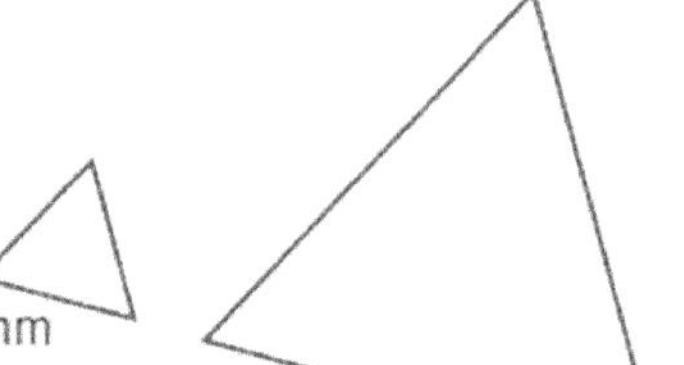

2.  $P = 24$ cm $P = ?$ cm

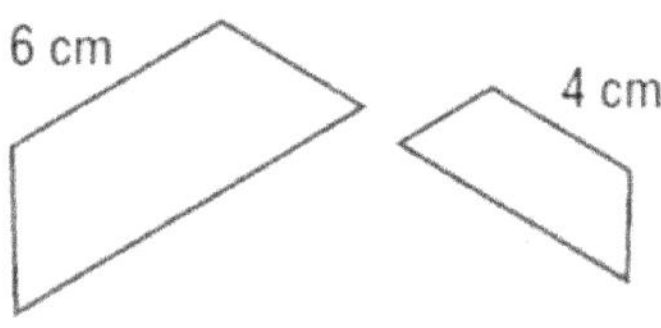

3. $P = 42$ in. $P = ?$ in.

4. $P = 20$ in. $P = ?$ in.

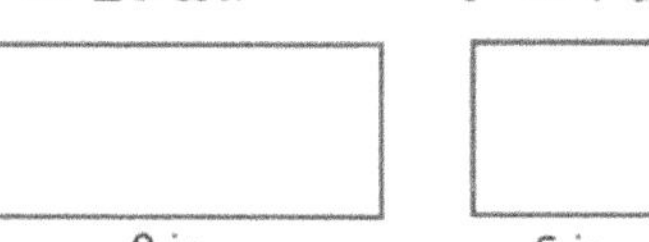

XII. Estimate ....

1. 28% of 48
2. 99% of 65
3. 445% of 20
4. 9% of 81
5. 73% of 240
6. 65.5% of 75
7. 48.2% of 93
8. 39.45% of 51
9. 287% of 122
10. 53% of 80
11. 414% of 72
12. 59% of 105
13. 50% of 37
14. 18% of 90
15. 300% of 245
16. 1% of 48
17. 70% of 300
18. 35% of 35
19. 60.5% of 60
20. $5\frac{1}{2}$% of 100
21. 40.01% of 16
22. 80% of 62
23. 45% of 119
24. 14.81% of 986
25. 20% of 60% of 2,008 + 30% of 70% of 1,004 = ...
26. 50% of (1 + 2 + 3 + ... + 1,000) X $\frac{1}{1001}$= ....
27. 2% of $\sqrt{10 + 2\sqrt{3} + 2\sqrt{18} + 2\sqrt{6}}$ + 3% of 0.4 = ...
28. Sum total of a number and its reciprocal is 4.25. Find 20% of that number.
29. Half of a quarter of a number exceeds three digit smallest number by 16. Find the number.

XIII. **Find each number. Round to the nearest tenth if necessary.**

1. What number is 25% of 280?
2. 38 is what percent of 50?
3. 54 is 25% of what number?
4. 24.5% of what number is 15?
5. What number is 80% of 500?
6. 12% of 120 is what number?
7. Find 68% of 50.
8. What percent of 240 is 32?
9. 99 is what percent of 150?
10. Find 75% of 1.
11. What number is $33\frac{1}{3}$% of 66?
12. 50% of 350 is what number?
13. What percent of 450 is 50?
14. What number is $37\frac{1}{2}$% of 32?
15. 95% of 40 is what number?
16. Find 30% of 26.
17. 9 is what percent of 30?
18. 52% of what number is 109.2?
19. What number is 65% of 200?
20. What number is 15.5% of 45?
21. 10% of a = 20% of b = 30% of c; find the value of $\left(\frac{a}{b} + \frac{b}{c} + \frac{c}{a}\right)(a + b + c)$
22. ab + bc + ac = 121 and a + b + c = 12. Find the value of $a^2 + b^2 + c^2$
23. $\left(\frac{1}{\sqrt{3}} + \frac{2}{\sqrt{3}} + \frac{3}{\sqrt{3}} + \cdots \ldots + \frac{1000}{\sqrt{3}}\right) X \left(1 - \frac{1}{1001}\right) X \left(1 - \frac{1}{5}\right) =$ ....
24. By selling 11 fruit basket a shopkeeper gains an amount equal to the selling price of a fruit basket. Find percentage gain of shopkeeper.

Model Paper V

I: Simplify ...

1. -8×0.25
2. $-12.2 \div 5$
3. $-3 \times \left(-4\frac{1}{2}\right)$
4. $2\frac{1}{2} \times \left(-\frac{3}{4}\right) \times \left(-\frac{1}{5}\right)$
5. $-28.5 \div 4$
6. $-\frac{7}{8} \times \frac{1}{2} \div \frac{1}{4}$
7. $12.5 \div (-5)$
8. $\frac{3}{5} \div \frac{1}{2} \div \left(-\frac{1}{8}\right)$
9. $7 \div \left(-\frac{1}{2}\right)$
10. $\frac{5}{9} \times \frac{1}{5} \times 9$
11. $-12 \times \left(-\frac{7}{8}\right)$
12. $-121 \div 11$
13. $-4.2 \times (-3.8)$

II: Repeated decimal ...

$n = 0.86$	Start with the number.
$100n = 86.\overline{86}$	Multiply by 100.
$-n = -0.\overline{86}$	Subtract original number.
$99n = 86$	Find the difference.
$n = \frac{86}{99}$	Divide both sides by 99.

1. $\frac{2}{9}$
2. $-0.\overline{6}$
3. $0.\overline{14}$
4. $\frac{2}{13}$
5. $-\frac{1}{6}$
6. $\frac{6}{7}$
7. $-0.\overline{09}$
8. $0.\overline{4}$
9. $-0.\overline{72}$
10. $-\frac{5}{6}$
11. $-\frac{2}{7}$
12. $0.\overline{8}$
13. 1.33333.......... + 2.5555555555555...... + 3.444444444..... = ...
14. 1.111... + 2.2222....... + 3.3333 .... - 6 = ...
15. Divide 7 by 9 and identify the type of decimal duly obtained.

16. Francesca typed 496 words in 8 minutes. Which of the following is a correct understanding of this rate?

17. At 8 a.m., the temperature was 13 ^{0}F below zero. The temperature rose 22 ^{0}F by 1 p.m. and dropped 14^0 F by 8 p.m. What was the temperature at 8 p.m.?

18. 40% of 60% of 70% of 100,100,100 = ...

19. Three flash lights blink repeatedly at a uniform interval of 20 s, 30 s and 50 s respectively. Find the time interval after which all the three lights blink together.

20. What fraction of all the days starting from April to August are Sunday?

21. Rahim sold a book to Kareem at a profit of 10%. Kareem sold that book to Muller at a gain of 10%. What percent of extra price will be paid by Muller for that book?

22. Somanthika painted half of a poster in 4 days. Rithika painted quarter of the same type of poster in 3 days. Both of them continued working together to finish their works of painting eight similar kinds of posters. In how many days do they finish their works?

23. (1.001 + 1.001 + ...1,000 times)X$\left(1 - \frac{1}{1001}\right) X$ 64 = 2^p X 10^q ; p =..........; q = ...;

Model Paper VI

Directions: Determine if the sum or product in each problem is rational or irrational. Circle the letter of each answer and write the letters of the sums or products that are rational numbers. Rearrange the letters to spell a word related to the definition of "rational."

1. $0.1\overline{6}+0.\overline{3}$ (I. Rational R. Irrational)
2. $0.1\overline{6}\times 0.\overline{3}$ (C. Rational N. Irrational)
3. $1\frac{1}{2}+\sqrt{2}$ (E. Rational B. Irrational)
4. $\sqrt{3}+3$ (U. Rational Z. Irrational)
5. $\sqrt{1}\times\sqrt{4}$ (O. Rational T. Irrational)
6. $\sqrt{1}+(-1)$ (L. Rational U. Irrational)
7. $\sqrt{1}+\sqrt{5}$ (D. Rational K. Irrational)
8. $3\times\pi$ (F. Rational R. Irrational)
9. $3\times\sqrt{3}$ (R. Rational N. Irrational)
10. $7.5+8\frac{1}{3}$ (L. Rational M. Irrational)
11. $5\times\sqrt{25}$ (A. Rational W. Irrational)
12. $7.5\times 8\frac{1}{3}$ (G. Rational E. Irrational)

The letters ________________ can be unscrambled to spell ______________.

13. What fraction of following shapes have curved faces?

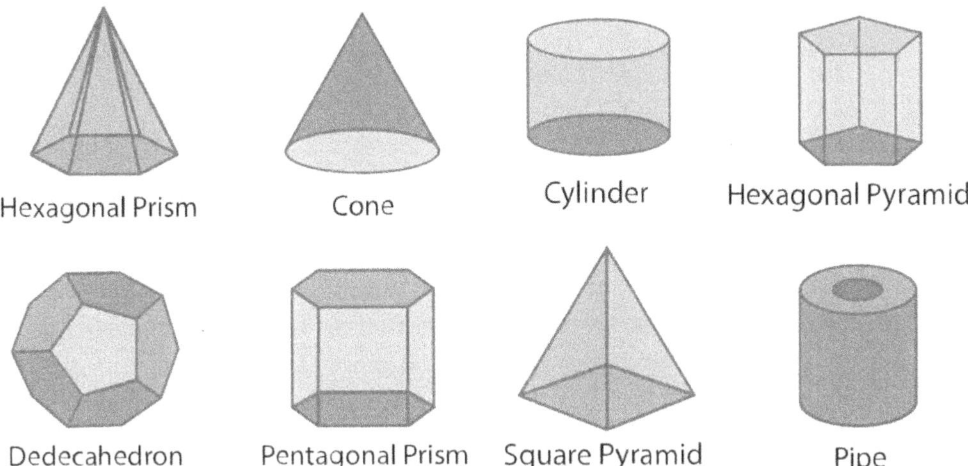

14. Find magnitude of the interior angles of a regular hexagon.

15. How many non-overlapping triangles can be accommodated in a heptagon?

16. Is there any solid shape having six faces, ten edges and eight vertices?

Model Paper VII

Choose the term that *best* completes each statement.

1. The equation $-3.21 \times 0 = 0$ is an example of the ___?___.
2. The equation $29.2 \times 42.3 = 42.3 \times 29.2$ is an example of the ___?___.
3. The equation $64.5 \times 1 = 64.5$ is an example of the ___?___.
4. Numbers multiplied by each other are ___?___.

Multiply.

5. 5.6×7.8
6. $0.423 \times (-56)$
7. 30.5×6.78

Simplify each expression. Give a reason for each step.

8. $(p \times 6.2) \times 1.3$
9. $(u \times 2.3) \times 4.6$
10. $6.6(a + 7.1)$
11. $15.1(0.7 + x)$

Divide.

12. $580.5 \div 64.5$
13. $22.638 \div 3.2$
14. $5.01 \div 1.67$

Round each quotient to the nearest hundredth.

15. $24.6 \div 10.7 = 2.299$
16. $58 \div 12.4 = 4.677$
17. $57.7 \div 0.49 = 117.755$
18. $0.35 \div 1.69 = 0.207$

19. Find out outer boundary of the following shape having combination of square units.

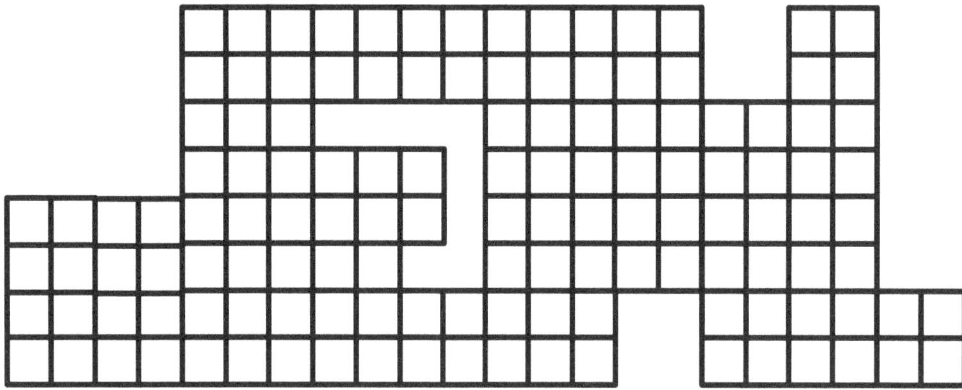

20. How many cubes each of volume 64 sq.cm. is needed to construct a rectangular base of length 40 cm, breadth 36 cm and height 16 cm?

21.

Model Paper VIII

1. P = 515.15 –15.51–1.51–5.11– 1.11.
   Find the value of 2P + 1

2. If a = (7.5 × 7.5 + 37.5 + 2.5 × 2.5), then find the value of
   $$\frac{a^2+1}{a^2-1} - \frac{a^2-1}{a^2+1}$$

3. A began a business with Rs 45000 and B joined after wards with Rs 30000. At the end of a year, the profit is divided in the ratio 2:1. When did B join ?

4. An employer reduces the number of his employees in the ratio 7: 5 and increases their wages in the ratio 15 : 28. State whether his bill of total wages increase or decrease and in what ratio.

5. In three vessels, the ratio of water and milk is 6 : 7, 5 : 9 and 8 : 7 respectively. If the mixtures of the three vessels are mixed together, then what will be the ratio of water and milk ?

6. A drum contains 20 litres of a paint. From this, 2 litres of paint is taken out and replaced by 2 litres of oil. Again 2 litres of this mixture is taken out and replaced by 2 litres of oil. If this operation is performed once again, then what would be the final ratio of paint and oil in the drum ?

7. If a : (b + c) = 1 : 3 and c : (a + b) = 5 : 7, then b : (a + c) = ___.

8. 15 men, 18 women and 12 boys working together earned Rs 2070. If the daily wages of a man, a woman and a boy are in the ratio 4 : 3 : 2, the daily wages (in Rs) of 1 man, 2 women and 3 boys are ________________.

9. Ratio of the incomes of A, B and C last year was 3 : 4 : 5. The ratio of their individual incomes during the last year and this year are 4 : 5, 2 : 3 and 3 : 4 respectively. If the sum of their present incomes is Rs 78800, then find the present individual income of A, B and C.

10. 10% of A = 20% of B = 30% of C. Find the value $\frac{AB+BC+AC}{ABC}$.

11. $\frac{1}{10}$ of a number x exceeds $\frac{1}{15}$ of another number y by 5. Find the value of P.

$$P = \frac{3x-2y}{3x+2y} + \frac{3x+2y}{3x-2y}.$$

12. Tap A can fill a tank in 30 minutes and tap B can fill the same tank in 40 minutes. Both the tap can fill the tank jointly in ____ mins.

13. In two alloys, copper and zinc are related in the ratio of 4 : 1 and 1 : 3. 10 kg of 1st alloy, 16 kg of 2nd alloy and some of pure copper are melted together. An alloy was obtained in which the ratio of copper to zinc was 3 : 2. Find the weight of the new alloy ?

14. Railway fares of 1st, 2nd and 3rd classes between two stations were in the ratio 8 : 6 : 3. The fares of 1st and 2nd class were subsequently reduced by $\frac{1}{6}$ and $\frac{1}{12}$ respectively. If during a year, the ratio between the passengers of 1st, 2nd and 3rd classes was 9 : 12 : 26 and the total amount collected by the sale of tickets was Rs 1088, the collection from the passengers of 1st class was ____________.

15. Salary of Mark is increased by 16%. His previous salary was ____ % less than that of the increased salary.

16. Solve the following equation :

$$\frac{11}{144} X \frac{12}{169} X \frac{13}{121} X \frac{132}{341} X \frac{682}{1001} X \frac{13}{19} =$$

17. What least number must added to the smallest six digit number and must be subtracted from the largest five digit number to make both of them a multiple of 11?

18. What least number must be added to 121.098 to make it a multiple of 1.001?

19. First tap can fill a water tank in 30 minutes and second tap can empty the half filled tank in 1.5 hours. By what time the empty tank will be filled up if both the tap kept open?

20. Half of a cake is given to all friends, half of the remaining portion of the cake retained by parents, one third of what remaining was distributed amongst John's classmates. Finally John received only 200 g of the cake. Find the quantity of that cake.

Model Paper IX

1. How many different possible solutions can satisfy the following equation?

$$(x^2 - 5x + 5)^{(x^2-12x+45)} = 1$$

2. A three digit number is such that the number N = 100a + 10b + c. Again the number is a product of two factors b and 10c + b. Find the number.

3. An integer is a palindrome when the same number is obtained when digits are reversed. 121,253, 132 etc. are all palindromes. Find a number n such that n^2 will be a palindrome with 6 digits.

4. Sum of the digits of a smallest possible number N is 18. Sum total of all the digits of 2N is 27. Find out the value of N.

5. What least number must be added to a six digit smallest number to make the number 1210214 divisible by 74.

6. Evaluate the following.

$$(\sqrt{2} + \sqrt{11} + \sqrt{13})(\sqrt{2} + \sqrt{11} - \sqrt{13})(\sqrt{2} - \sqrt{11} + \sqrt{13})$$
$$(-\sqrt{2} + \sqrt{11} - \sqrt{13})$$

7. Each interior angles of a heptagon is obtuse. Angles are multiples of 9. Find the degrees of sums of the two largest angles.

8. A three digit number is multiplied by 3 and 1 added to it then the result is a reverse of the original number. Find the original number.

   [Hints:
   (100 a+ 10b + c)X3 +1 = 100c + 10b + a .

   100 a+ 10b + c = ?]

9. If $ab = a^b$ and $\frac{a}{b} = a^{3b}$, find b^{-a}

10. $0.33 < \frac{m}{n} < \frac{1}{3}$. Find the smallest possible value of n to satisfy the above mentioned relationship.

11. Find the smallest seven digit number which is divisible by 11. What are the two digits will be there in tens and ones place of that number?

12. Mark deposited \$ 23,500 in his savings bank account which was offering 4% simple interest per year. Find the amount that Mark will obtain after a tenure of 4 years and 5 months.

13. -4.5 + 5.64 + ______ = 0. Make this equation true.

14. Solve the following

    a. $7 \times 20 - 2 \times 4 + 3^2 + 12 \div 4$

b. $\frac{\left(\sqrt[3]{0.125}+\sqrt[2]{.0064}\right)}{\sqrt[3]{1.331}-\sqrt[2]{0.0081}}$

c. If $x+\frac{1}{x}=9$ then find the value of

$$(2x-9)^2$$

15. A shopkeeper purchased 16 dozen bananas at the rate of Rs 24 per dozen and found that 5% of his stock became non sellable. Rest of his stock was sold at the rate of Rs 30 per dozen. Find out the rate percent of his gain or loss incurred in this business.

16. Simplify the following:

$7[120-2(4+3)^2+12]\div 2$

17. X = 0.3333... + 0.4444 + 0.9999.. Find the value of $\frac{x+1}{x-1}+\frac{x-1}{x+1}$

18. Shweta joined a Yoga Centre and her body weight was reduced from 76 kg to 65.6 kg. Find the percentage weight loss that she made during the tenure of her exercises.

19. Base of a triangle is reduced by 5% and its height is increased by 5%. Find the total percentage increase or decrease in the area of the triangle.

20. All the five sides of a regular pentagon is 12 cm each and apothem is 8 cm. find the area of this pentagon.

    [Hints: The apothem of a regular polygon is a line segment from the center of the polygon perpendicular to a side.]

21. A __________ angle is an angle with its vertex at the center of a circle whose sides are radii.

22. Calculate the total surface area of a cuboidal room of dimension 8mX6mX5m.

23. Arrange the following values in ascending and descending order:

24. What is the next number in the following sequence: 2, 4, 8, 16, _____, ______ ?

25. Write 3/7 and 5/9 in their corresponding decimal form. What are the common things in both the decimal form?

26. The cost of a camera is reduced by 10% to make it equivalent to another camera having a selling price calculated on the basis of 10% profit on the cost price of 21,850. Find the original cost price of the first camera.

27. 3% of 600 is ________ less than 5% of 500.

28. A college offers 25% of all seats of the Graduate programme to local candidates. Last year 125 local candidates got admission in that college. Find the total seat capacity available in that college for Graduate programmes.

29. A shopkeeper offers two discounts of value 5% and 8% on an item. Calculate the equivalent discount of two such consecutive discounts.

30. Population of a city increases at the rate of 10% of previous year's population. Calculate the population of a city in which population before two years was 125,000. Also calculate the population of that city after two year.

31. Parking lot of a school is represented by an expression:

$$\frac{3}{4}\left(2(2+4k)+2\left(3+\frac{5}{6}k\right)\right)$$

Convert this expression in simplest form.

32. 30% of a number is equal to 40% of another number. Calculate the ratio of both the number.

33. $P = \sqrt{20} - \sqrt{20} + \sqrt{20} - \sqrt{20} \ldots\ldots\ldots \infty$. Find the value of $P^2 + 3P - 20$.

34. $\sqrt{15} = 3.88$. Find the value of $\sqrt{\frac{5}{3}}$.

35. A person moved on towards countryside at 6 O'Clock. He travelled certain distance at an average speed of 4 km/h, and then another distance at 3 km/h and again a distance at an average speed of 6 km/h. After reaching he turned back and reached the place from where he had started. That time it was 12 noon in his wrist watch. Find the distance travelled by him.

[Ans: 24 km]

36. A 500 m long train crosses a telephone post in 20 seconds. The same train crosses a platform in 90 seconds. Find the length of that platform.

[Ans: 1 km 750 m]

37. Two trains of length 200 m and 400 m respectively. They cross each other in 15 seconds while moving in opposite direction and 75 seconds while moving in the same direction. Find speed of both the train.

[Ans: 24 m/sec. and 16m/sec]

38. Normally Nikita performs her morning walk at an average speed of 12 km/h. Today her speed was $5/6^{th}$ of the average. Because of this reason she was late by 10 minutes. Find the normal time that she spends daily for morning walk.

[Ans: 50 minutes]

39. Speed of a train was reduced from 65 km/h to 50 km/h. Earlier this train was taking 1.5 hours to cover certain distance. Now it will take ________ minutes more to cover the same distance.

[Ans : 27]

40. In a kilometer race A beats B by 100 meters, B beats C by 100 meters. A beats C by ____ meters.

[Ans : 190 meters]

41. A bus moves a distance without stoppage at an average speed of 420 km/h. With stoppages the same distance is covered by that bus at an average speed of 28 km/h. find the hourly stoppage time of that bus.

[Ans: 20 minutes]

42. A 300 m long car is running at an average speed of 90 km/h. another car of length 200 m is running in the same direction at an average speed of 60 km/h. Find the time taken by the first car to overtake the second one.

[Ans: 50 seconds]

43. Length of a train is half that of a km long bridge. A train clears this bridge in 2 minutes. Find the speed of that train.

[Ans: 45 km/h]

44. A train of length 110 m passes a man, who is walking against it at an average speed of 6 km/h, in 6 seconds. The speed of this train is ____________. [Ans: 60 km/h]

45. A boat running upstream takes hours 48 minutes to cover certain distance. It takes 4 hours to cover the same distance running downstream. Find the ratio between the speed of the boat and speed of the stream.

[Ans: 8:3]

46. What fraction of numbers in between 1 and 50 are prime numbers?

47. What least number must be added to 1029.1016 to make it exactly divisible by 1029?

48. Third multiple of a prime number which is greater than 90 and less than 100 = _____.

49. Complete the following:

a. $a^3b^4c^5 \; X \; a^3b^7 = $ ____

b. $a^5b^8c^5 \div a^3b^7 = $ ____

c. $\frac{1}{\frac{1-\frac{1}{1-x}}{x-1}} + \frac{1}{\frac{1-\frac{1}{x^2-1}}{x+1}} = $ ________.

d. $\left(1-\frac{9}{10}\right)\left(1-\frac{99}{100}\right)\left(1-\frac{999}{1000}\right) = 10 ----$

50. Find the value of $\frac{m^2+1}{m^2-1} - \frac{m^2-1}{m^2+1}$,

if $\sqrt[3]{m} = \left(1-\frac{1}{2}\right)\left(1-\frac{1}{3}\right)\ldots\left(1-\frac{1}{1000}\right)$

51. If $\frac{2}{1+\frac{1}{1+\frac{x}{1-x}}} = 1$, then find the value

of $\left(\frac{x+1}{x-1}\right)^2 + \left(\frac{x-1}{x+1}\right)^2$.

52. Reciprocal of x^8 = __________.

53. A boat covers 30 km in 3 hours in the direction of a stream. It covers the same distance in opposite direction of the stream. Find speed of the boat in still water.

[Ans: 8 km/h]

54. Find the least number located in between 454003 and 354302 which is a multiple of 209. Also find other two factors.

Model Paper X

1. Capacity of three cans is in the ratio of 1:2:3. Smallest can holds 200 ml less than a liter of any liquid. Find capacity of all the cans.
2. Find the value of x if $x^2 + x + 1 = 0$. Consider value of x as positive.
   [hints: $(x^3 - 1) = (x-1)(x^2 + x + 1)$;
3. Find the two largest numbers of four digits having 531 as their HCF.
4. Find the value of q.
5. Calculate value of n.

$$\sqrt[2]{2^n} = 16, \ then\ n = \_\_\_\_ \qquad\qquad 64X\,56 - \sqrt[3]{q} = 128X\,24$$

6. 15 men, 18 women and 12 boys working together earned Rs 2070. If the daily wages of a man, a woman and a boy are in the ratio 4 : 3 : 2, the daily wages (in Rs) of 1 man, 2 women and 3 boys are __________.
7. Bolton started business investing Rs 8000. Three months later John joined him investing Rs 6000. If they make a profit of Rs 5100 at the end of the year, how much should be John's share ?
8. The employer reduces the number of employees in the ratio 9 : 8 and increases their wages in the ratio 14 : 15. If the previous wage bill was Rs 189000, what is the amount by which the new wage bill will increase or decrease ?
9. Rs 2010 are to be divided among A, B and C in such a way that if A gets Rs 5, than B must get Rs 12 and if B gets Rs 4, then C must get Rs 5.50. The share of C will exceed that of B by _________.
10. Find the ratio of 12% Of 12 and 15% of 15.
11. What least number must be added to 1968 to make it divisible by 11?
12. A bottle is full of spirit. One-third of it is taken out and then an equal amount of water is poured into the bottle to fill it. This operation is done four times. Find the final ratio of spirit and water in the bottle.
13. The students in three classes are in the ratio 2 : 3 : 5. If 40 students are increased in each class, the ratio changes to 4 : 5 : 7. Originally the total number of students was ___________.
14. Find the least number which when divided by 12, 24, 36 and 40 leaves a remainder 1, but when divided by 7 leaves no remainder.

15. A drum contains 20 l of a paint. From this, 2 l of paint is taken out and replaced by 2 l of oil. Again 2 l of this mixture is taken out and replaced by 2 l of oil. If this operation is performed once again, then what would be the final ratio of paint and oil in the drum ?

16. 100 ml 80% alcohol and 150 ml 90% alcohol mixed up properly to make a new combination having strength ______ %.

17. Concentrations of three solutions A, B and C are 20%, 30% and 40% respectively. They are mixed in the ratio 3 : 5 : x resulting in a solution of 30% concentration. Find x.

18. Ratio of incomes of A, B and C last year was 3 : 4 : 5. The ratios of their individual incomes of last year and this year are 4 : 5, 2 : 3 and 3 : 4 respectively. If the sum of their present incomes is Rs 78800. Find the present individual income of B.

19. Ravi earns 25% more than Nisha, gut his earning is 18% less than that of Faquir. Find the ratio of their earnings.

20. The cost of manufacturing a TV set is made up of material costs, labour costs and overhead costs. These costs are in the ratio 4 : 3 : 2. If materials costs and labour costs rise by 10% and 8% respectively, while the overhead costs reduce by 5%, what is the percentage increase in the total cost of the TV set ?

21. A number is increased by 20% and then again by 20%. By what per cent should the increased number be reduced so as to get back the original number ?

22. The number of employees working in a farm is increased by 25% and the wages per head are decreased by 25%. If it results in x% decrease in total wages, then the value of x is __________.

23. A candidate who gets 20% marks in an examination fails by 30 marks but another candidate who gets 32%, gets 42 marks more than the pass marks. The percentage of pass marks is _________.

24. In the expression xy2 , the values of both variables x and y are decreased by 20%. By this the value of the expression will be decreased by ______________________.

25. In an examination Nancy obtained 20% more marks than Hary but are 10% less than Della. If the marks obtained by Hary are 1080, find the percentage of marks obtained by Nancy, if the full marks are 2000.

26. A student took five papers in an examination, where the full marks were the same for each papers, this marks in these papers were in the proportion 6 : 7 : 8 : 9 : 10. In all the papers together, the candidate obtained 60% of the total marks. Then, the number of papers in which he got more than 50% marks is equal to ____________________.

27. A tax payer is exempted of income tax for the first Rs 100000 of his annual income but for the rest of the income, he has to pay a tax at the rate of 20%. If he paid Rs 3160 as income tax for a year, his monthly income is ________________

28. A house-owner was having his house painted. He was advised that he would require 25 kg of paint. Allowing for 15% wastage and assuming that the paint is available in 2 kg cans, what would be the cost of paint purchased, if one can costs $ 2 ?

29. By receiving 5% less vote than the winner of a by-election a candidate received only 12% of the total vote. Find the ration of votes received by both the candidate.

30. In an election, 10% of the people in the voter's list did not participate. 60 votes were declared invalid. There are only two candidates A and B. A defeated B by 308 votes. It has found that 47% of the people listed in the voters' list voted for A. Find the total number of votes polled.

31. Prices register an increase of 10% on food grains and 15% on other items of expenditure. If the ratio of an employee's expenditure on food grains and other items be 2 : 5, by how much should his salary be increased in order that he may maintain the same level of consumption as before, his present salary being Rs 2590.

32. What is the least number which when divided by the numbers 3, 5, 6, 8, 10 and 12 leaves in each case a remainder 2, but when divided by 13 leaves no remainder.

33. Find the value of p. $144X\ 36 - \sqrt[3]{p} = 72X\ 48$

34. What fraction of a fortnight is an hour?

35. Half a cup sugar measures 130 g. There are __________ cups of sugar in 5.2 kg pack of sugar.

36. Here m = ____

$$\sqrt[4]{\sqrt[5]{\sqrt[6]{p^8}}} = p^m$$

37. Prices register an increase of 10% on food grains and 15% on other items of expenditure. If the ratio of an employee's expenditure on food grains and other items be 2 : 5, by how much should his salary be increased in order that he may maintain the same level of consumption as before, his present salary being Rs 2590.

38. 10% of 29 is ______ less than 5% of 300.

39. A sold a watch to B at 20% gain and B sold it to C at a loss of 10%. If C bought the watch for Rs 216, at what price did A purchase it ?

40. A man sold two steel chairs for Rs 500 each. On one, he gains 20% and on the other he loss 12%. How much does he gain or loss in the whole transaction ?

41. Three items are purchased at $ 450 each. One of them is sold at a loss of 10%. At what price should the other two be sold so as to gain 20% on the whole transaction? What is the gain% on these two items?

42. Three bells toll at an interval of 12 seconds, 36 seconds and 45 seconds. After what time interval do they toll together? How many times do they toll together in a gap of three hours?

43. A train moving with a uniform speed of 72 km/h took 2.5 minutes to cross a light post. Find the time taken by it to cross a 1.8 km long platform.

44. Find the value of $\sqrt{272^2 - 128^2}$

45. The square root of 0.4444.... is __________.

46. 4320 X p is a perfect cube value. Find the value of $p^2 + 3p + 9$

47. $\sqrt[3]{4\frac{12}{125}} = x$. Find the value of $3x^2 + 4x + 5$

48. $x^3 - 2mx\ 2 + 16$ is divisible by $x + 2$. Find the value of m.

49. $2x^4 - px^3 + 3x^2 + 3x - 2$ is exactly divisible by $x^2 - 3x + 2$. Find the value of $p^2 + 3p + 17$.

50. Find the following:

$$64^a = \frac{1}{256^b},$$

$$i)\ 3a + 4b = \_\_\_\_\_\_\_\_$$

$$ii)\ \frac{(a+b)}{ab} = \_\_\_\_\_\_\_\_$$

51. Complete the following:

$$6^x - 6^{x-3} = 7740;\ x^x$$

52. Find the value of $p^2 + 8p + 21$

$$p = \left(2^{\frac{1}{4}} - 1\right)\left(2^{\frac{3}{4}} + 2^{\frac{1}{2}} + 2^{\frac{1}{4}} + 1\right) = \_\_\_\_\_\_\_\_$$

53. Find the value of p.

$$a = (\sqrt{3} + \sqrt{2})^{-3}, \quad b = (\sqrt{3} - \sqrt{2})^{-3},$$
$$\text{p} = [(a+1)^{-1} + (b+1)^{-1}]$$

54. Half a dozen banana costs $ 12. Find the cost of 20 bananas.

55. Arrange in ascending order.

$$16^{\frac{1}{2}}, \sqrt[4]{16}, \sqrt[2]{81}, \sqrt[3]{125}$$

56. Some bananas are to be shared among a number of children. To give each child 9 bananas would require 15 more bananas. But if the share of each is 8 there are 10 bananas left over. How many bananas are there?

57. In a number of three digits the units digit is double the tens' digit. The sum of the number and the number formed by reversing the digits is 1191 and the average of three digits is 5. What is the number ?

58. $(x - 3)(x + 3)(x^2 + 9)(x^{12} + 81x + 81^2) = 0$; find value of $(x^6 + x^3 x^2 + x + 9)$

59. Find the value of k, if x = 2, y = 1 is a solution of the equation 2x + 3y = k.

60. Give the equations of two lines passing through (3, 16). How many more such lines are there, and why?

61. A plastic box 2.5 m long, 3.25 m wide and 75 cm deep is to be made. It is opened at the top. Ignoring the thickness of the plastic sheet, determine
(i) The area of the metal sheet required for making the box.
(ii) The cost of sheet for constructing this box, if a sheet measuring $1m^2$ costs ₹200.

62. The floor of a rectangular hall has a perimeter 2500 m. If the cost of painting the four walls at the rate of ₹10 per m^2 is ₹150,000, find the height of the hall.
[Hint: Area of the four walls of the hall = Lateral surface area]

63. A small indoor greenhouse (herbarium) is made entirely of glass panes (including base) held together with adhesive tape. It is 3 m long, 75 cm wide and .3 m high.

(i) What is the area of the glass?

(ii) How much of tape is needed for all the 12 edges?

Mental Mathematics

I: Solve the following..

Compare ...

1. $\frac{7}{8} \underline{\ ?\ } \frac{5}{8}$

2. $\frac{9}{20} \underline{\ ?\ } \frac{9}{20}$

3. $\frac{14}{30} \underline{\ ?\ } \frac{26}{30}$

4. $\frac{17}{21} \underline{\ ?\ } \frac{10}{21}$

5. $\frac{12}{7} \underline{\ ?\ } \frac{16}{7}$

6. $\frac{9}{8} \underline{\ ?\ } \frac{8}{8}$

7. $\frac{22}{6} \underline{\ ?\ } \frac{32}{6}$

8. $\frac{19}{19} \underline{\ ?\ } \frac{20}{19}$

Rename each pair of fractions using the LCD as their denominator.

9. $\frac{3}{5}$ and $\frac{1}{4}$

10. $\frac{3}{4}$ and $\frac{1}{10}$

11. $\frac{7}{8}$ and $\frac{5}{6}$

12. $\frac{1}{2}$ and $\frac{2}{3}$

13. $\frac{1}{12}$ and $\frac{3}{24}$

14. $\frac{1}{3}$ and $\frac{4}{9}$

15. $\frac{5}{7}$ and $\frac{12}{49}$

16. $\frac{2}{5}$ and $\frac{4}{7}$

Compare. Write <, =, or >. You can use a number line to help.

17. $\frac{1}{4} \underline{\ ?\ } \frac{7}{16}$

18. $\frac{7}{10} \underline{\ ?\ } \frac{3}{5}$

19. $\frac{4}{21} \underline{\ ?\ } \frac{1}{7}$

20. $\frac{6}{14} \underline{\ ?\ } \frac{2}{7}$

21. $\frac{3}{5} \underline{\ ?\ } \frac{5}{8}$

22. $\frac{4}{7} \underline{\ ?\ } \frac{6}{9}$

23. $\frac{7}{12} \underline{\ ?\ } \frac{9}{15}$

24. $\frac{10}{25} \underline{\ ?\ } \frac{7}{10}$

II: Evaluate.

1. Jaime is covering the decorative wall art shown below in felt, including the back and bottom.

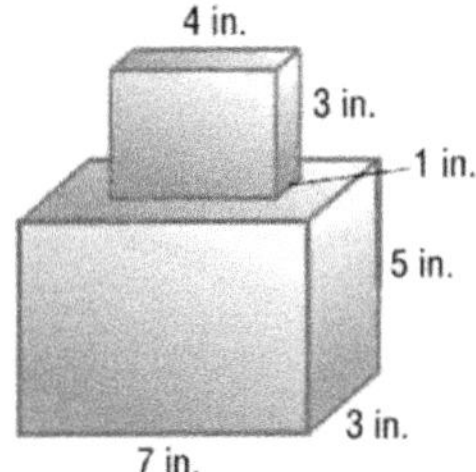

What is the total area to be covered with felt?

A. 23 in^2

B. 117 in^2

C. 172 in^2

D. 1,260 in^2

2. Which of the following formulas cannot be used to find the volume of the composite figure?

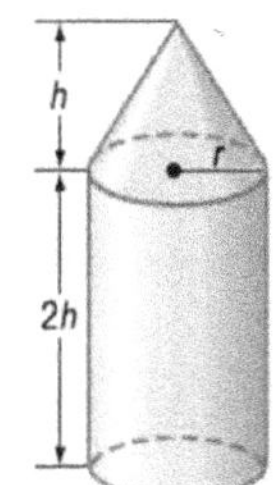

F. $V = 2\pi r^2 h + \frac{1}{3}\pi r^2 h$

G. $V = \frac{7}{3}\pi r^2 h$

H. $V = \pi r^2(2h) + \frac{1}{3}\pi r^2 h$

I. $V = \frac{2}{3}\pi r^2 h$

III: Simplify

Rewrite each repeating decimal with a bar over the part that repeats.

1. 0.66666 . . . **2.** 0.11111 . . . **3.** 0.45454 . . . **4.** 0.09090 . .

5. 0.83333 . . . **6.** 0.26666 . . . **7.** 2.384848 . . . **8.** 5.13232 . .

Write each repeating decimal showing eight decimal places.

9. $0.\overline{1}$ **10.** $0.\overline{12}$ **11.** $0.1\overline{4}$ **12.** $0.2\overline{8}$

13. $5.\overline{3}$ **14.** $12.\overline{06}$ **15.** $7.2\overline{7}$ **16.** $13.2\overline{17}$

Rename each fraction as a terminating or repeating decimal.

17. $\frac{1}{8}$ **18.** $\frac{13}{20}$ **19.** $\frac{5}{11}$ **20.** $\frac{1}{3}$ **21.** $\frac{3}{4}$

22. $\frac{2}{9}$ **23.** $\frac{7}{16}$ **24.** $\frac{5}{12}$ **25.** $\frac{11}{18}$ **26.** $\frac{1}{16}$

IV: Compare:

Compare. Write < , = , or >. Use the number line.

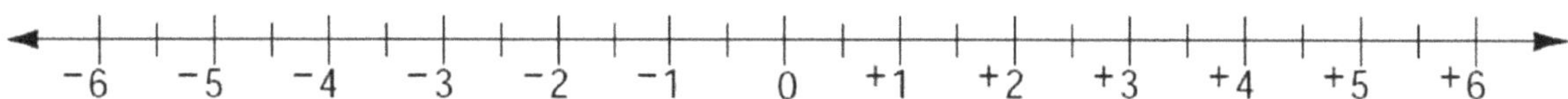

1. $^{-}\frac{1}{2}$ _?_ $^{-}\frac{3}{4}$ **2.** $^{-}0.5$ _?_ $^{+}0.75$ **3.** $^{-}3.5$ _?_ $^{-}4.25$ **4.** $^{+}3\frac{1}{4}$ _?_ $^{+}3\frac{1}{8}$

5. $^{-}4$ _?_ $^{-}\frac{6}{3}$ **6.** $^{+}2.5$ _?_ $^{-}3\frac{1}{2}$ **7.** $^{-}5\frac{1}{8}$ _?_ $^{+}4$ **8.** $^{-}6$ _?_ $^{-}5.75$

9. 0 _?_ $^{-}3.25$ **10.** $^{+}\frac{3}{4}$ _?_ 0 **11.** $^{-}\frac{8}{2}$ _?_ $^{-}4$ **12.** $^{-}\frac{1}{8}$ _?_ $^{-}0.125$

Write in order from least to greatest. Use the number line above to help.

13. $^{-}3, {}^{-}4\frac{1}{2}, 2$ **14.** $0, {}^{-}\frac{1}{2}, 2\frac{1}{4}$ **15.** $5, 0, \frac{2}{1}$ **16.** $^{-}4, 3\frac{1}{4}, {}^{-}1.5$

17. $^{-}2.25, {}^{+}0.25, {}^{-}1.5$ **18.** $^{-}2\frac{1}{2}, 2.5, {}^{-}1\frac{1}{4}$ **19.** $\frac{1}{4}, {}^{-}\frac{1}{4}, 0$ **20.** $5\frac{1}{4}, {}^{-}1, {}^{-}2\frac{3}{4}$

Test Paper

Set 1

1: The ratio of the number of boys to the number of girls in a school of 1638 is 5: 2. If the number of girls increased by 60, then what must be the decrease in the number of boys to make the new ratio of boys to girls as 4 : 3?

2: If y varies inversely as x, and y = 3 when x ⍰ 2, then find x when y ⍰ 21.

3: If 45% of a certain number is 990, then find the value of 54% of that number.

4: There are three numbers. The first and the second numbers are 50% less and 60% less respectively than the third. What percentage of the first number is the second?

5: Ram got 30% in a test and failed by 10 marks .If the pass marks in the test was 70, find the maximum marks in it.

6. The price of an article is decreased by 20%. By what percentage must the consumption of it be increased in order to retain the expenditure on it?

7. The length of a rectangle increases by 14% and the breadth by 8%. What is the consequent percentage increase in area?

8. A trader defrauds the seller by 10% when he purchases goods from him, and while selling the same to a customer, he defrauds once again by 10%. Find the net gain made by the trader.

9. A merchant purchases an item for Rs. 500. He marks the item at a price of Rs. 700 but allows a discount of 10% on cash payment. What is the total profit in terms of amount and percentage made by the merchant?

10. A milkman defrauds by means of a false measure to the tune of 20% in buying and also defrauds to the tune of 25% in selling. Find his overall % gain.

11. The cost price of 20 pens is equal to the selling price of 25 pens. What is the net loss percentage?

12. A milkman claims to sell milk at the cost price but uses a measure of 800 ml instead of a litre. Find the net profit made by him.

13. Bhuvan, a fruit seller bought bananas at the rate of Rs. 5 a dozen. He sold 2 bananas for Rs.1. Find his net profit percentage?

14. A, B and C enter into a partnership. A contributes Rs. 320 for 4 months, B contributes Rs. 510 for 3 months and C contributes Rs. 270 for 5 months. If the total profit is Rs. 208, then find the profit share of each of the partners.

15. A and B together invested Rs. 12000 in a business. At the end of the year, out of a total profit of Rs. 1800, A's share was Rs. 750. What was the investment of A?

16. If Rs. 650 amounts to Rs. 790 in 4 years, then what sum of money will it amount to in 7 years at the same rate of interest?

17. What annual installment will be required to repay a borrowed amount of Rs.1,32,400 in 3 years at 10% per annum compounded annually?

18. A certain sum of money at C.I. amounts to Rs. 811.25 in 2 years and to Rs. 843.65 in 3 years. Find the sum of money.

19. In what ratio should two different types of mixtures containing milk and water in the ratio of 5:1 and 2:1 respectively be mixed to obtain a final mixture containing milk and water in the ratio 3:1?

20. A tea merchant buys two kinds of tea, the price of the first kind being twice that of the second. He sells the mixture at Rs.14/kg there by making a profit of 40%. If the ratio of the first to second kind of tea in the mixture is 2:3, then find the cost price of each kind of tea.

21. A group of soldiers can completely destroy an enemy bunker in 7 days. However 12 soldiers fell ill. The remaining now can do the job in 10 days. Find the original group strength.

22. If an inlet pipe can fill a tank in 4 hours and an outlet pipe empties the full tank in 5 hours, then what is the net part filled in 1 hour when both the pipes are opened?

23.

www.ingramcontent.com/pod-product-compliance
Ingram Content Group UK Ltd.
Pitfield, Milton Keynes, MK11 3LW, UK
UKHW061134310726
14090UKWH00038B/1445

9 798887 176772